BEGAT

BEGAT

THE KING JAMES BIBLE AND THE ENGLISH LANGUAGE

David Crystal

OXFORD

UNIVERSITY PRESS

OXFORD

UNIVERSITY PRESS

Great Clarendon Street, Oxford ox2 6dp
Oxford University Press is a department of the University of Oxford.
It furthers the University's objective of excellence in research, scholarship,
and education by publishing worldwide in

Oxford New York

Auckland Cape Town Dar es Salaam Hong Kong Karachi
Kuala Lumpur Madrid Melbourne Mexico City Nairobi
New Delhi Shanghai Taipei Toronto

With offices in

Argentina Austria Brazil Chile Czech Republic France Greece
Guatemala Hungary Italy Japan Poland Portugal Singapore
South Korea Switzerland Thailand Turkey Ukraine Vietnam

Oxford is a registered trade mark of Oxford University Press
in the UK and in certain other countries

Published in the United States
by Oxford University Press Inc., New York

British Library Cataloguing in Publication Data
Data available

Library of Congress Cataloging in Publication Data
Data available

Typeset by SPI Publisher Services, Pondicherry, India
Printed in Great Britain
on acid-free paper by
Clays Ltd., St Ives plc

ISBN 978-0-19-958585-4

4

Contents

Contents

Contents

Prologue 1

'No book has had greater influence on the English language.'

That's the sort of thing people always say about the translation of the Bible known as the King James or Authorized Version—the King James Bible, as I'll refer to it. This particular comment was made by Alan G. Thomas, in his *Great Books and Book Collectors*. Is it true? Or is it one of those notions that people would like to believe is true?

A lot of famous people seem to agree. Winston Churchill called it a 'masterpiece', uniting English-speaking peoples everywhere. Samuel Taylor Coleridge claimed its study would 'keep any writer from being *vulgar*, in point of style.' And Charlton Heston thought it was 'an enormous force in shaping the development of the English language.' Why Heston, out of a thousand film stars? He was reading it while preparing to play Moses in *The Ten Commandments*.

Lady Holland visited Lord Macaulay one day in May 1831, and they had a genteel discussion about words in English that she found distasteful, such as *influential*, *gentlemanly*, and *talented*. Macaulay picked her up on *talented*. Didn't Lady Holland know that it came from the parable of talents in the Bible? 'She seemed surprised by this theory,' he later remarked in a letter to Hannah More, 'never having, so far as I could judge, heard of the parable of the talents.' And he adds: 'I did not tell her, though I might have done so, that a person who professes to be a critic in the delicacies of the English language ought to have the Bible at his fingers' ends.'

Prologue 1

So there we are. It all seems very cut and dried. And when linguists concur, what more is there to be said? Here is one, expressing no doubt about the matter: 'The King James Bible—either directly, from its own translators, or indirectly, as a glass through which we can see its predecessors—has contributed far more to English in the way of idiomatic or quasi-proverbial expressions than any other literary source.' I have to agree with that, seeing as it appears in Chapter 11 of my own *The Stories of English* (2004).

But actually there's a great deal more to be said. Someone having read my book and searching for precision might well ask: 'How many expressions, exactly?' And in 2004, I would have had to admit, in some discomfiture, that I did not know. I could illustrate my contention by citing examples—I listed forty or so from St Matthew's Gospel in *The Stories of English*—but if you pressed me on the point, and insisted on knowing how many there were in the King James Bible as a whole, I would not have been able to tell you.

Nor, it seems, would anyone else. Several writers have explored the King James Bible—Old Testament, New Testament, and Apocrypha—to identify expressions which have had a permanent influence on the development of the English language. Many websites will give you lists. No two lists are the same and nowhere can I find a definite total. Nor is it a question that has a ready, intuitive answer. Stop and think now: how many such expressions might there be? Expressions like *salt of the earth* and *whited sepulchre*—100? 500? 1,000? You will not be able to answer this question confidently. No more could I, when I asked it of myself in 2009.

I know the answer now, having made the journey, and will reveal it in my Epilogue. But it turned out to be a much harder question than I thought. It emerges that it isn't always easy to decide whether an expression comes from the King James Bible or not. And evaluating the notion of 'influence' proves to be remarkably difficult.

Prologue 2

Before starting on my journey, it's worth reflecting on why there is a problem. It's easy enough to say that the King James Bible has influenced or shaped the English language, but what do such words as 'influence' and 'shaping' really mean? This is where commentators can become rather vague, talking about such difficult-to-define properties as the 'cadence' or 'character' of the language.

Let's be more precise. Which aspects of English have been shaped, *exactly*? There are only so many possibilities: if there is an influence on our present-day written language, it has to appear in grammar, vocabulary, spelling, punctuation, or the broader patterns of usage that we impressionistically refer to as matters of 'idiom' or 'style'. Not all of these are relevant.

English hasn't changed that much over the past 400 years, but Modern English is obviously different in certain respects from the kind of Early Modern English represented in the King James Bible. We notice the changes straight away: old spellings such as *asswaged* and *pluckt*; old punctuation such as *their's* and *our's*; old vocabulary such as *peradventure, tarry, wot*, and *damsel*; old grammar such as verb endings (*moveth, creepeth*), past tenses (*builded, digged*), and word orders (*in the likeness of God made he him; I laughed not*). When we read such a sentence as *in the day that thou eatest thereof thou shalt surely die*, there's only a limited sense of continuity with today's English. Nobody says that sort of thing now. A modern colloquial equivalent would be something like: *the day you eat it you'll certainly die*. There's little shaping influence here.

On the other hand, there are many cases where expressions have become so thoroughly assimilated into the language that any sense of a biblical origin is quite lost. Not many know, and only etymologists care, that *a fly in the ointment* comes from Ecclesiastes. Foreign learners of English would simply pick it up as an idiom, along with *kick the bucket* and all the other expressions that have nothing to do with the Bible at all. Their religious beliefs are neither here nor there. Indeed, they may have no religious belief of any kind. Yet the biblical expression will be part of their English language ability. These are the clearest cases where we could assert with confidence that the King James Bible has helped to shape the modern English language—if it turns out that they are unique to that translation. How many such cases are there?

Also important are those powerful and memorable sentences which have entered the stylistic consciousness of English speakers all over the world. Sentences such as these from Ecclesiastes are well known and, with sometimes minor adjustments, are often used today: *there is no new thing under the sun*; *much study is a weariness of the flesh*; *the race is not to the swift, nor the battle to the strong*; *to every thing there is a season*. People who use these are often well aware of their biblical origin. Again, how many are there? And are they unique to the King James?

We find expressions like these in a wide variety of circumstances. Sometimes they appear as exact quotations, with the biblical reference clearly in mind. But often they're used in relation to nonbiblical situations. I found an article on an Arsenal football website which had the headline: *The race is not to the swift*. What's it got to do with football? The writer was making the point that, in aiming for championship victory, 'the most important lesson must be that the race is not to the swift but to those who endure.' I found the same expression on several internet horse-racing blogs, too, but with the language altered to make a similar point: *The race is not always to the swift.*

It's these adaptations which provide the best evidence of lasting linguistic influence. The most interesting cases of the Bible shaping our language are when we find expressions in daily use, where people take a piece of biblical language and use it in a totally nonbiblical context, knowing that the allusion will be recognized. Even clearer are the cases where a biblical expression is linguistically manipulated to make people sit up and take notice—as in *The race is not always to the swift.* The writers aren't expecting us to know which bit of the Bible the allusion refers to, only that they've done something clever with the English language. And we enjoy the joke—as long as we recognize it.

That's the point. We have to recognize the allusion to appreciate the stylistic effect. When someone begins a website on healthy eating habits with the headline *Be fruitful*, the writer is assuming we'll get the joke. The unusual construction would puzzle any English-language learner who wasn't familiar with the biblical phrase *Be fruitful and multiply*. Learners have quite a task ahead of them, in this respect. When studying the English language, they have to assimilate English historical literary culture too. They have to realize that this is a special case. They mustn't go round saying *Be fruitful* to everyone.

Who knows who first thought of extending the meaning of these expressions to nonbiblical situations? When did the first adaptation of *the race is not to the swift* take place? Or the first time someone said *Be fruitful* as a joke? It probably happened several times in different kinds of setting, and quite quickly.

It only takes a phrase to enter public consciousness, and immediately people adapt it to suit themselves. When Barack Obama used *Yes we can* in his victory speech in 2008, I heard it soon after in an extraordinary range of circumstances—some serious, some comic—coming from individuals who each felt they were doing something original with it. A hitherto unknown saying can achieve worldwide fame when used by a prominent person. Thanks to television, the *Yes we can* adaptations were heard around the globe within hours. How long would it have taken in the seventeenth century for a phrase to enter public consciousness? Although the King James Bible was being routinely read at church services, an encounter with a particular expression would not have been frequent—a couple of times a year, perhaps. The influence must therefore have been indirect, through the weekly recitation of the psalms, through sermons, and through other writings. Is there evidence of this happening? We will see.

Some caveats, before I start my journey. When people talk about English being shaped by the King James Bible, they have to be careful—and so do I. The historical context is excellently summarized in Gordon Campbell's *Bible: The Story of the King James Version, 1611–2011*. As is well known, the team of translators didn't start from scratch. Rather, as they say in their Preface, their aim was not to make a new translation, 'but to make a good one better, or out of many good ones, one principall good one.' They had little choice in the matter, as the guidelines for their work, which had been approved by the King, required them to use the Bishops' Bible of 1568 (in its 1602 edition) as their first model, making as few alterations as possible; and when this was found wanting they could refer to earlier versions, including Tyndale. Much of the memorable linguistic distinctiveness of the King James Bible in fact originated in Tyndale, whose translation of the New Testament and the first six books of the Old appeared nearly a century before—between 1526 and 1530. But Tyndale's work, considered heretical at the time, had limited impact. It was the King James Bible that made most of this language known. 'Most' is important: a major exception—the Psalter—is discussed in Chapter 16. When the Book of Common Prayer was first introduced (1549), it used the text of the Great Bible, published a decade earlier, and the version of the Psalms it contained was the work of Miles Coverdale.

We also have to be aware of the likelihood that other important translations of the time contributed to the shaping of modern English. It is a fact, as we will see, that several biblical idioms used today can't be found in King James, but seem to originate in one of the other early translations. A full-scale study of the language of all the available translations would require a book many sizes larger than this one. To put King James in perspective, I have therefore limited the comparisons to just six: the later (1388) version of Wycliffe's Bible, which was the first full translation into English; Tyndale, as above; Coverdale's Psalter (1535), as above; the Geneva Bible (first edition in 1560), widely used in its day and a popular quotation source for Elizabethan authors, including Shakespeare; the Bishops' Bible (first edition in 1568); and the Roman Catholic translation of the New Testament at Douai then Rheims (1582) and Old Testament at Douai (1609–10), known collectively as Douai-Rheims. We will see that a surprising number of the expressions we associate with King James also appear in these other versions. A complete listing is in Appendix A. And when the versions differ, as they often do, the comparison can be linguistically illuminating. The only way to appreciate the distinctive stylistic features of a text is to compare it with others.

So, when people talk about the King James Bible introducing various expressions into English, it doesn't mean that it always originated them. Rather, it gave them a widespread public presence through the work being 'appointed to be read in Churches'. Despite its popular name being the 'authorized version', the work was never authorized in any legal sense. But no other translation reached so many people over so long a period as King James. And this probably explains why so many of its usages entered public consciousness.

This influence continues today. The Bible always provides several pages of material for a book of English quotations, and it's invariably the King James which is cited, with its numbering of chapters and verses (a practice I follow in this book). Take the opening line: *In the beginning God created the heaven and the earth.* We don't find it quoted as *In the beginning God created heaven and earth*, which is what appears in Tyndale, or *In the beginning God created ye heaven and the earth*, as in Bishops, or *In the beginning God created heaven, and earth*, as in Douai-Rheims. If we go to the section headed 'Bible' in *Chambers' Dictionary of Quotations* we see the point stated plainly: 'All quotations are taken from the King James, or Authorized, translation of the Bible (1611).' The *Oxford* anthology does similarly. So does the *Penguin Thesaurus of Quotations*. Nor is this a peculiarly British thing. Only King James is used by the best-selling *International Thesaurus of Quotations*, published since the 1970s in the USA. (In actual fact, what we see in these anthologies is not the original 1611 text, but a modernized version deriving from F. S. Parris's Cambridge edition of 1743 and Benjamin Blayney's Oxford edition of 1769.)

If someone is looking to the Bible for a catchy title for a book, film, or pop song, or wanting to grab the reader's attention in a headline for a newspaper or website, it is the King James Bible they're most likely to pick up. And it's remarkable just how often biblical phrases come to be used in this way. It's not so much the number of phrases that is impressive, but the range of nonbiblical settings into which they've been introduced, with the writers displaying considerable linguistic ingenuity. We find biblical expressions appearing in such disparate worlds as nuclear physics, court cases, TV sitcoms, recipe books, punk rock lyrics, and video games. Those are the worlds this book will explore.

Chapter 1
In the beginning

'Would you Adam-and-Eve it!'

I was recently walking along London's Fleet Street when I heard that expression, loud and clear, coming from a man standing in a pub doorway talking into his mobile phone. People sometimes say that Cockney rhyming slang is dying out, but that expression, at least, was alive and well. The speaker—a native Eastender, judging by his accent—was using it as a colloquial substitute for *believe*. It's a usage which has been traced back to the early 1900s, and is probably much earlier. In those days it was also being used as a rhyming alternative to *leave*, especially when the speaker meant 'depart in a hurry'. *Time to Adam-and-Eve*, someone might say.

In 2009, a special needs teacher, Keith Park, compiled a short collection of poems called *Bible stories in Cockney rhyming slang*. One of the items goes like this:

'Cos they didn't
Adam and Eve it
When God said
'Oi! Apple—leave it!'

Here the slang usage is pointing us back towards the original biblical setting. The wheel has turned full circle.

Who would ever have predicted that the two characters from the creation story in Genesis would end up as rhyming slang! Or, for that matter, as a slangy way of describing eggs on toast: *Adam and Eve on a raft*. That's British military talk, also from the early twentieth century. The eggs could be fried or poached—but not scrambled. That would be *Adam and Eve wrecked*.

The couple can also be found in regional British dialects as the name of various plants and roots. And in parts of North America a type of perennial orchid (*Aplectrum hyemale*) is commonly called *Adam and Eve*. Why? It's a reference to the plant's unusual growth habits: the leaf and flower (*Eve*) grow while the previous year's bulb (*Adam*) is still present. The botanical link is also found in pagan magic, where the name is used for a pair of love talismans. The Eve root is carried by a woman, the Adam root by a man. The practice is supposed to promote fidelity, closeness, and mutual attraction.

Adam, unlike *Eve*, sometimes turns up alone in modern idioms. If you *don't know him from Adam*, then you don't recognize him. Gender is irrelevant here. You can just as appropriately say *I don't know her from Adam*. And likewise, either a he or a she can be *as old as Adam*—that is, extremely old. Water is sometimes humorously described as *Adam's ale* or (especially in Scotland) *Adam's wine*. Men and women also both have *Adam's apples*, though the front of the thyroid cartilage is prominent only in the male throat. Why the name? The legend goes that a piece of the biblical apple lodged in Adam's throat, causing the bulge. If Eve had performed a Heimlich manoeuvre, men might have looked very different.

Adam and Eve presents us with an interesting test case in any discussion of biblical influence on English. Without the Bible, there would have been no Adam and Eve. But *Adam and Eve*, as a linguistic expression, comes from no bible translation. The names *Adam* and *Eve* appear at different points in the Genesis story, and are never linked together. It is later story-telling tradition which has done that, along with *forbidden fruit, David and Goliath, doubting Thomas, the wisdom of Solomon,* and several other familiar expressions. King James has no direct linguistic influence here.

Chapter 2
Let there be light

Adam and Eve have left their linguistic mark outside the original biblical setting, but their impact is tiny compared with the way some of the other expressions in Genesis have come to be used. We don't have to read very far in the creation story before we find a sentence that has been so thoroughly assimilated that we encounter it in all kinds of present-day situations, none of which have anything directly to do with the biblical account. In 1:3 we read:

Let there be light; and light was made.

The translation as *Let there be light* is not unique to King James. It was in Tyndale and Bishops, and many others. The Douai-Rheims translators opted for *Be light made*, but that never stood much chance of competing in the popular mind with *Let there be light*, whose Beethovenesque 'te-te-te-tum' stress pattern reflected more naturally the language's rhythmical norms. Once King James became the standard for public performance, *Let there be light* ruled.

Type the expression into a search engine and you'll find over a million hits, with only a small minority (one in ten, in a sample I collected) relating literally and directly to the Genesis story.

It has been put to use in all sorts of nonbiblical settings. We find it in the arts, as the title of exhibitions (or headlining articles about exhibitions) on photography, sculpture, painting, and architecture. We find it in the movies: it's the title of a John Huston 1946 documentary film on the treatment of wartime trauma. We find it in pop music: Mike Oldfield is one of several musicians who have used it as the name of a song. We find it in the world of fashion: Balenciaga used it to label one of his 2008 collections. And we find it on television: an edition of the BBC series *Imagine* in 2008 used it—the theme was the way light was used in art. It even turned up as the title of an episode of the series *Sex and the City* (No 87). The story involved one of the characters learning how to cope with blindness.

The optical theme has generated a huge amount of usage: several internet and press reports on eye surgery are headed *Let there be light*, as are descriptions of light therapy for medical conditions, such as cancer. The energy theme offers lots of scope: articles on energy efficiency lead with it, or extend it in ingenious ways. A piece on an oil find in Israel was headed: *Let there be light crude*. One on maintaining power supplies in Ghana began: *Let there be light off the grid*. And we mustn't forget the metaphorical use. The light bulb is often used as a symbol of intellectual illumination. So it's perhaps not surprising to find that a university (California) has *Let there be light* as its motto.

Spelling variations provide a further playful dimension. *Lite* has some presence in American English as an informal alternative to *light*, much as *nite* has developed alongside *night*. *Let there be lite* has been used a few times in pop song lyrics, for instance. It's also used, with this spelling, as the title of a satirical novel by Rupert Morgan, as well as the title of a low-fat recipe book by Jay Disney. (*Light* meaning 'not heavy' has a different linguistic history from *light* meaning 'not dark', but that sort of distinction never bothers modern writers searching for an allusion.) There's no copyright on titles, so we find it from time to time in other guides to fat-free cooking. The *lite* spelling reminds one of earlier periods of English, so it commends itself to fantasy authors who want to introduce a medieval flavour into their writing. And it's a favourite of those who invent names for lamps, spotlights, and light-reflecting material (such as *Scotchlite*). The *Oxford English Dictionary* records such usages as *strobe lite* and *lite-lift*, which became quite common in the second half of the twentieth century. *Let there be lite* was quickly picked up by the admen as a way of drawing attention to such devices.

The best evidence that an expression has been fully assimilated into a language is when it generates creative, playful alternatives. The availability in English of many words rhyming with *light* has made this an enormously productive area. Several blog reports on airline delays are headed *Let there be flight*. An astronomy site mourning the loss of dark skies in cities begins *Let there be night*. Boxing and wrestling sites go for *Let there be fight*. And what do you make of the following: *Let there be height*? An article on new architectural styles. *Let there be blight*? A report on agricultural diseases. *Let there be Knight*? A piece about fashion photographer Nick Knight. Google was often bemused when I searched for such strings. *Did you mean to search for 'Let there be light'?*, it asked me wistfully.

I found my favourite playful variation on this expression when I discovered the Saturday afternoon television programme on Channel 17 in Philadelphia during the 1970s. Magician Joe Zawislak used to dress up as a human-cum-vampire to host a horror show called *Mad Theatre*. He signed off each week with the words *Let there be fright.*

But I leave the last word on *Let there be light* to journalist and broadcaster Alistair Cooke, who won an award for 'Best Speaker of English' in 1998. In his acceptance speech, he satirized the wordiness and jargon of US politicians, suggesting that they could learn something from the clarity and succinctness of the King James Bible. To illustrate, he gave a hypothetical version of Genesis 1:3 as it might emanate from the White House: 'The Supreme Being mandated the illumination of the Universe and this directive was enforced forthwith.'

Chapter 3
Be fruitful and multiply

As the creation story unfolds, we encounter many memorable expressions, of the kind which fill books of quotations, but only a few have achieved the same sort of widespread adaptation that we see with *Let there be light*. Anyone familiar with the King James Bible or its sources will recognize the following examples straight away, but when we look for their use in everyday linguistic life today we find that they are generally found only in biblical contexts:

fowl of the air	beast of the earth
after his kind	lights in the firmament
every creeping thing	he rested on the seventh day
evening and morning came	tree of knowledge of good and evil

We do find the occasional use in nonbiblical settings. I have come across a book on natural history called *Every creeping thing*. Educational courses sometimes make use of a *tree of knowledge* as part of their narrative. And a Flickr item in November 2008 showed a picture of a bright blue sky and a shining sun along with the heading *New light in the firmament*. It celebrated the election of Barack Obama. But these are very rare uses. The vast majority of cases where we find phrases from the opening chapters of Genesis remain resolutely religious. There are just a few exceptional phrases that achieve wider currency. One occurs in 1:16:

And God made two great lights; the greater light to rule the day, and the lesser light to rule the night

Lesser light, found also in Geneva and Douai-Rheims (other versions have *less light*) has come down to us with a figurative meaning, referring to someone considered to be less important than others. Shakespeare was an early user of the phrase: in *Pericles* (II.iii.41), the hero reflects on the glory of the king: 'None that beheld him, but like lesser lights/Did vail their crowns to his supremacy.' Shakespeare probably got the phrase from the Geneva translation, which scholars think was his primary source for biblical references in his later plays. Today, the expression is widespread. For some reason it has especially appealed to sports writers. In Australian football, the *Brisbane Times* in 2009 reported how one of the less well-known players made all the difference in a game: *Lions lesser light gets special thanks.* A UK report in the *Independent*, also in 2009, told how some of Manchester United's stars were going to miss a game through injury, thus giving an opportunity to other players: *Lesser light Fletcher's chance to shine.*

Another expression which has developed a limited present-day currency outside the religious setting derives from Genesis 1:26:

And God said, Let us make man in our image

The phrasing isn't unique to King James: it's also in Bishops and Geneva, and Wycliffe and Douai-Rheims have *to our image* (Tyndale is the odd one out, opting for *likeness*). In the following verse, we find *in his own image*. Both versions, with and without *own*, have come down to us. The phrasing has been seized upon by artists of all kinds to name projects or exhibitions, especially in such areas as photography, painting, and drawing. It's a perfectly standard metaphor now for those who create something to reflect their own personalities or behaviour. Employers are often accused of missing out on new ideas by appointing staff 'in their own image'. *New CEO to remake Yahoo in her own image* headed a report about the appointment of a new female manager in 2009. A *Newsweek* piece in 2008 began: *Upstart designers make fashion in their own image.*

A Genesis expression which has had considerable present-day influence is *Be fruitful and multiply*. It is used twice in the creation story (Genesis 1:22, 28)—and again later to Noah and Jacob—when God addresses his newly created creatures and newly created mankind:

And God blessed them, saying, Be fruitful, and multiply, and fill the waters in the seas, and let fowl multiply in the earth.

The King James translators followed Bishops in choosing this phrasing. As with *Let there be light*, it's probably the rhythm of the expression, with its prosodic symmetry, which made it appeal to them: 'te tum-te-te tum-te-te'. Certainly this is a marked improvement over the rhythmically unbalanced *Grow and multiply* of Tyndale or Geneva's ponderous *Bring forth fruit and multiply*. Douai-Rheims has *Increase and multiply*, which is a promising alternative, but its rhythm is problematic, as people have long been divided over how to stress the first verb: is it *increase* or *increase*?

It's the ambiguity inherent in the words *fruitful* and *multiply* which has led to the massive exploitation. *Fruitful* isn't being used literally in the biblical quotations: it doesn't mean 'productive of fruit' but 'productive of offspring'. As a consequence, it offers playful possibilities to those who want to use the expression to talk about activities in which fruit literally does play an important part. *Be fruitful* is the heading of an online report from the National Gardening Association which urges its readers to eat more fruit each day. A dieting site sends the same message: *Be fruitful and flourish*. And an article in the *New York Times* (2008) asks: *Consumers urged to be fruitful, but can sales multiply?* This headline needs some context to be understood. It transpired that a company which sells gift arrangements of freshly cut fruit, styled to resemble floral arrangements, was launching its first national television advertising campaign.

Multiply is ambiguous too. The word arrived in English from French in the twelfth century with its basic sense of 'increase in number', and this is the sense found throughout the Bible, where it's used nearly a hundred times. The mathematical sense of 'multiplication' developed a century or so later. Today, its two senses inhabit largely separate semantic domains; but the opportunity for interaction is always there. So it's not surprising to find the biblical expression transferred to contexts dealing with various mathematical issues. I've seen a website which uses it to introduce a page explaining the importance of exponential functions.

In maths, *multiply* is part of a system which includes *add*, *subtract*, and *divide*, and this immediately offers a new set of playful substitutes. Interestingly, the mathematical sense of these words disappears when they're used as part of the biblical expression. There's an article headed *Be fruitful and divide* but it's nothing to do with maths: it's on evolution. Nor is *Be fruitful and subtract* on maths: it's an argument for single-child families.

These days the commonest nonbiblical use of *Be fruitful and multiply* is in relation to articles on contraception, fertility treatment, and population growth. *Be fruitful and multiply with the Ovy fertility tracker* is an illustration. The expression is also the title of a 2005 film about childbearing in a group of Jewish women. Occasionally we find it being used in other domains. It heads one online piece discussing ways in which more people can be persuaded to go to church and another about how new pop groups can increase the numbers listening to their music: *Be fruitful and multiply (your fanbase).*

The possibilities are endless. *Be fruitful and replenish the earth* heads an article on biodiversity. *Be fruitful and replicate* introduces one on plant physiology. They form a fairly predictable pattern. But every now and then a new adaptation emerges. In 2008, Robert E. Wilson published a novel about a New York pastor who is hiding a deep, dark secret. He called it: *Be fruitful and multi-lie.*

Chapter 4
My brother's keeper

As the Genesis narrative unfolds, there are long passages where linguistically influential phrases are conspicuous by their absence, then a familiar usage suddenly jumps out at you. Here's an example, in Chapter 4, where we find the story of Cain and Abel.

4:1 And Adam knew Eve his wife; and she conceived, and bare Cain, and said, I have gotten a man from the LORD. 4:2 And she again bare his brother Abel. And Abel was a keeper of sheep, but Cain was a tiller of the ground. 4:3 And in process of time it came to pass, that Cain brought of the fruit of the ground an offering unto the LORD. 4:4 And Abel, he also brought of the firstlings of his flock and of the fat thereof. And the LORD had respect unto Abel and to his offering: 4:5 But unto Cain and to his offering he had not respect. And Cain was very wroth, and his countenance fell. 4:6 And the LORD said unto Cain, Why art thou wroth? and why is thy countenance fallen? 4:7 If thou doest well, shalt thou not be accepted? and if thou doest not well, sin lieth at the door. And unto thee shall be his desire, and thou shalt rule over him. 4:8 And Cain talked with Abel his brother: and it came to pass, when they were in the field, that Cain rose up against Abel his brother, and slew him. 4:9 And the LORD said unto Cain, Where is Abel thy brother? And he said, I know not: Am I my brother's keeper?

There it is. One of those rare phrasings which is so appealing that it is found in virtually every translation (only Wycliffe differs:

whether I am the keeper of my brother). It's succinct, direct, and rhythmically neat, using the 'te-tum' iambic beat which was the metrical driving force of so much of the dramatic poetry of the early 1600s. The rhythm is far superior to what we find in the occasional alternative version, such as Wycliffe's *whether I am the keeper of my brother?* And as its meaning readily relates to a host of everyday domestic circumstances, it probably transferred into daily use very quickly.

Today it has come to be used, either with those exact words or with some playful manipulation, extraordinarily often. *Brother's keeper*, with or without the *my*, has named over a dozen episodes in television series, such as *Knight Rider* (No 203), *Law and Order* (No 250), *ER* (No 85), and *Tales from the Crypt* (No 23). It was actually chosen as the first (pilot) episode of *Miami Vice*. A whole US sitcom with this name was aired in 1998–9 on ABC: the storyline was a single father who had to raise his son at the same time as keeping his brother out of trouble.

(My) brother's keeper has been used in this way for decades. We find it in an episode of *The Brady Bunch* (No 103); that was back in 1973. Even further back, it was the title of a 1948 film starring Jack Warner. At least another three films have been called *My Brother's Keeper*, not counting a documentary about a controversial death which took place in a family of four elderly brothers. The phrase doesn't seem to lose its freshness, as the years go by. I expect it will be used again next year—and the year after.

Moving on from films, it's the title of two songs, and two record albums (one by singer and songwriter Rich Mullins; the other by US R&B group the Neville Brothers). It's the name of a popular piece of software for organizing information about your family history. It's the title of several books, including two novels, a *Star Trek* spin-off, and a few nonfictional accounts of family relationships—one of which was Dakin Williams' biography of his famous brother called *His Brother's Keeper: the life and murder of Tennessee Williams*. Perhaps as far as you can get from traditional biblical connotations, an American hardcore punk rock band called itself *Brother's Keeper*. And an Afro-German anti-racism group bringing together hip-hop, reggae, and soul musicians was called the *Brothers Keepers*. They were all men. A female version of the group called itself the *Sisters Keepers*.

In these last examples, we can see the way the expression has begun to be modified. The pronoun change from *my* to *his* is a natural kind of extension, so it's not surprising to find writers exploiting all the other pronoun options available in English. There's a Walt Disney cartoon called *Her brother's keeper*. An organization which offers support to persons with HIV/AIDS is called *Our Brothers' Keepers Foundation*. An article on traffic congestion in a US city is headed *Their Brother's Keeper*. Many websites take up the implied challenge, asking their readers to be *Your brother's keeper*. Even an old pronoun can be resuscitated: an article on mutual aid for low-cost health insurance in the USA is headed *Thy brother's keeper*. It's one of around 800 instances of this variant found on Google in 2009. I never expected the figure to be so high.

The gender change is frequently implemented. Several books and films are called *My sister's keeper*. Quite a few websites go out of their way to avoid any hint of sexism. *Am I my brother and sister's keeper?* asks one. And a report in the New York *Daily News* of Barack Obama's Christmas Day message in 2008 was headed *Be your brother's keeper, President-elect Obama urges*. In fact his urging was not so restricted. What he actually said was: 'Now, more than ever, we must rededicate ourselves to the notion that we share a common destiny as Americans—that I am my brother's keeper, I am my sister's keeper.'

If *brother* can become *sister*, then we might expect to see the expression being used for other relatives. And so it proves to be. Any story of someone who has had to look after an ageing mother or father can motivate such usages as *My parents' keeper*. The nuance is especially poignant if one or both of them is suffering from a disease such as Alzheimer's. Sometimes the title makes the nature of the problem explicit: one website begins: *Am I my Asperger brother's keeper?* Often it provides a note of intrigue: a book appeared in 1985 called *My mother's keeper*. Its author, B. D. Hyman, was the daughter of film-star Bette Davis.

The original expression is often used when the press talks about institutions which look after people: the common denominator is *how* one can best be a brother's keeper under such circumstances. It is likely to turn up, accordingly, when reporting on events in prisons, borstals, hospitals, mental health institutions, nursing homes, philanthropic foundations, and other places which guard people or care for them. In a nice twist, an article on professional nursing reverses the word order: *I am my brother's keeper*. But the use of the phrase in this way extends well beyond the media. An official report by PricewaterhouseCoopers on new hospital strategies in the USA was called *My brother's keeper*. As is the often the case with biblical allusions, an explanatory subtitle immediately followed: *Growing expectations confront hospitals on community benefits and charity care*.

Playfulness is never far away. One stylistic trick is to increase the number of possessives before the final noun. In 2008, a Wisconsin court ruled that a homeowner looking after someone else's dog is liable for any personal injury caused if the dog runs out of the house and attacks a passer-by. The report began: *Am I my brother's dog's keeper?* The grammar was taken a step further by a blogger who gave an account of how he was reluctantly persuaded to go to the aid of a relative in computational trouble. The blog began: *Am I my brother's sister-in-law's computer's keeper?* I've not yet come across anyone using a fourfold iteration, but it's only a matter of time…

Another ploy is to give *brother* an attribute of some kind. The economic downturn of 2008 raised many questions about the ownership and management of major financial institutions. *Am I my Lehman Brothers' keeper?* asked one report wryly. And in a law report the same year, a California court decided that the warnings used by a prescription drug manufacturer relating to its own name-branded product applied even when a prescription had been filled with a generic version of the drug. This led to the unusual headline: *Am I My (Generic) Brother's Keeper? In California, Yes.*

More daring is to tweak one or other of the salient words. Sometimes it is *keeper* which provides the focus. *Am I my brother's goalkeeper?* headed an article on a soccer transfer deal. *Am I my brother's gatekeeper?* began an article on healthcare. And a different sense of *gatekeeper* turned up in an article on the semantic web: *Am I my brother's Web 2.0 gatekeeper?* There's plenty of expressive potential here, given the many compound nouns in English which end in *keeper—housekeeper, gamekeeper,* and so on. And if the word is completely replaced, the options are legion. An article on how to deal with colleagues perceived to be incompetent began: *Am I my brother's warden?*

It's less easy to play with the word *brother,* though I would recommend a linguistic medal for the editor who created the headline for an article by a former sex worker about legalizing prostitution: *Am I my brothel's keeper?* More usually the whole word is replaced. *Am I my senator's keeper?* headed a political comment. *Am I my water's keeper?* headed a piece on the environment. More cleverly, an article about a US church minister who discovered an accounting error made by a colleague began: *Am I my bookkeeper's keeper?* But cleverest of all, to my mind, was the first person to tell the joke about the ape in the zoo caught reading Darwin and asking *Am I my Keeper's brother?* I emphasize 'first'. It ceases to be funny after you've seen a hundred online retellings.

Chapter 5
Two by two

People with a Judaeo-Christian background learn the big stories of Genesis at an early age—Noah and the Flood, Joseph and his brothers... But people without this background learn some of them too. You don't have to be Jewish or Christian to know that Noah had an ark or that Joseph had an 'amazing technicolour dreamcoat' (with music by Andrew Lloyd Webber). You may not know exactly what the ark was, but at least you've heard that *the animals went in two by two*—and probably, if you remember your kindergarten days, *for to get out of the rain*. As for Joseph, you'll certainly know that he had *a coat of many colours*.

These are just two of the many expressions from the early books of the Bible that have become widely known; but I link them in this chapter because they display the two extremes of influence that biblical phrases can have on the English language. *Two by two* illustrates a type of case where there has been negligible influence. *A coat of many colours* illustrates one which has been hugely influential. I'll look at that in the next chapter.

Two by two is actually a modern phrasing. What we find in King James is different (7:9):

There went in two and two unto Noah into the ark, the male and the female, as God had commanded.

Two and two is the form we find in most of the translations of the period—though not Tyndale, who opted for *by cooples* (i.e. *couples*), and Wycliffe, who had *by twain and by twain*. But it isn't a specifically biblical expression. It was in widespread secular use long before English translations of the Bible arrived. We find it in Anglo-Saxon texts, 600 years before the King James Bible was thought of.

The same applies to the modern usage. Around the turn of the eighteenth century people began to say *by two and two*, but this phrasing was soon replaced by the more succinct *two by two*. Again, there's nothing especially biblical about it. Apart from the occasional explicit nod in the direction of the Noah story (such as the Richard Rogers 1970 musical, *Two by Two*), the modern use of the expression doesn't rely at all on biblical awareness for its effect.

The same sort of point applies to the description of Judah as a *lion's whelp* (49:9). *Whelp*, meaning 'the young of a wild animal' isn't biblical. It dates from the early ninth century, and was in widespread use in relation to dogs, as well as to all kinds of wild animals, not just lions. *Lion's whelp* turns up half a dozen times in Shakespeare (three of the instances are in *Cymbeline*). 'I fear thee as I fear the roaring of the lion's whelp', says Falstaff to Prince Hal (in *Henry IV Part 1*). It's tempting to think that when the navy built a fleet of auxiliary war vessels in the 1620s, calling the series the *Lion's Whelp*, they were thinking of the King James Bible a decade before. Not so. They were designed to attend upon HMS *Lion*, and took their name from that.

Just because a notable phrase is in King James doesn't mean that it's guaranteed an influential role, and several other familiar

Genesis expressions have had little permanent impact on English outside their originally biblical context. For instance, hardly any general use has been made of the phrase which describes the baby Esau as being red all over, like a *hairy garment* (25:25), nor of the phrase which Jacob uses when he tells his household that God has answered him *in the day of my distress* (35:3).

Or take the story of the Flood, which we are told was caused by rain which lasted *forty days and forty nights* (7:4). That's a phrase which is used several more times in the Bible, in relation to Moses and Jesus. Tyndale, Bishops, Geneva, Douai-Rheims… they all use it. But today, it's rarely encountered outside those original biblical settings. I've found it in a blues song by Muddy Waters, and also in a travel brochure advertising a cruise, and hardly anywhere else. No real influence here.

The same applies to the phrase describing what happened to Lot's wife, who looked back at the destruction of Sodom and Gomorrah, after being advised not to do so, and as a result became *a pillar of salt* (19:26). This is the expression which has come down to us, as opposed to such other translations as *image of salt* (Wycliffe) and *statue of salt* (in Douai-Rheims). It's the sort of vivid description that we might think would be picked up and widely used, but in fact it isn't. A US pop group, The Thermals, used it once to name a song; and I've seen it as the title of a book by Janice Haaken on women's recovered memories, which uses the 'think about the past' sense of *look back* to produce the intriguing subtitle: *Gender, memory, and the perils of looking back.*

I was beginning to despair of finding anything else to say about *pillar of salt* when I came across a tall, white, lighthouse-shaped road sign on Angel Hill in Bury St Edmunds, in Suffolk, next to the cathedral of St Edmundsbury. Erected in 1935, it is thought to be the first internally illuminated street sign in Britain, which had to be granted special approval as it didn't conform to regulations. It is now a recognized heritage site, listed Grade 2—quite an accolade for a street sign. And it is called *Pillar of Salt*.

Still, two or three allusive references to a biblical expression do not amount to very much by way of linguistic influence. And several of the most familiar words and phrases in Genesis fall into this category. Take the two examples people immediately recognize in verse 4:16:

And Cain went out from the presence of the Lord, and dwelt in the land of Nod, on the east of Eden.

For most of us, each of these phrases has just one nonbiblical resonance.

Land of Nod. Every child knows what this means: bedtime. At least, every child since the early 1700s, for the first known use of the phrase in the sense of 'sleep', according to the *Oxford English Dictionary*, is in 1738. There we find a reference to the dialogue piece by Jonathan Swift, widely known as 'Swift's Polite Conversation'. In full its title reads: *A compleat collection of genteel and Ingenious Conversation according to the most polite Mode and Method, now used at Court, and in the best Companies of England*. On the very last page, the party is breaking up. 'Time for all honest Folks to go to bed', says Lady Answerall. And Colonel Atwit responds, 'I'm going to the Land of Nod.'

How did the semantic shift arise? The *Nod* of the Bible is a Hebrew word which means 'wandering' (Wycliffe expresses this sense by having Cain *fleeing about*). It has nothing to do with the English word *nod*, meaning 'make a brief inclination of the head', which is Germanic in origin. But in the popular mind, there was an identity. And it was a short step from here to the use of *nod* meaning 'nod off', where drowsiness makes the head fall forward in a short, involuntary motion. Both of these senses are known from around 1400. Also ancient is the use of *land* to mean 'realm' or 'domain', as in *land of the living*. That's known from Anglo-Saxon times, when it was often used with poetic connotations of a distant or mysterious place. Once the English translations of the Bible became widely used, it would have been another short step to make a pun, and give *Land of Nod* a new meaning. It must have been very common in the seventeenth century, for Swift was satirizing well-established patterns of discourse in his 'Polite Conversation'.

The semantic journey of the phrase isn't over yet, so maybe there'll be more to say about this expression one day. Drug users, for instance, sometimes describe their initial state of intoxication as entering 'the land of Nod'. And it has been used a few times in pop songs, either as a title or as a passing reference. *The Brotherhood of Nod* appears in a video game, *Command and Conquer*. But at present the nonbiblical applications of the phrase are very limited.

Similarly, little has happened to the related phrase in 4:16: *east of Eden*. For most people, this is simply the title of John Steinbeck's novel (1952) or the subsequent film by Elia Kazan (1955). Pop music aficionados know it as the name of a British band from the late 1960s. And a similar literary/musical pairing turns up in the one instance I've found of a derived name: *West of Eden*. This is the title of a science-fiction novel by Harry Harrison, as well as the name of a Swedish band that specializes in Irish music.

So we have to be careful, when exploring the influence of the language of the Bible. Simply recognizing a phrase as coming from King James, or one of the other translations, tells us very little about the extent to which that phrase has become part of our linguistic consciousness. If we know the stories, then we will know the language, but more by way of quotation than linguistic assimilation. The creation story is a good example, but an even better one is the listing of the Ten Commandments in the second book of the Bible, Exodus (see Chapter 9). Innumerable people have been taught these by heart; but the language in which they are formulated stands alone, proud and self-contained.

Chapter 6
A coat of many colours

Genesis 37:3 contains this well-known expression:

> Now Israel loved Joseph more than all his children, because he was
> the son of his old age: and he made him a coat of many colours.

With this phrase we see the opposite extreme, as far as linguistic influence is concerned. *Coat of many colours* has generated thousands of nonbiblical applications.

It certainly has an appealing ring. Wycliffe, Tyndale, Geneva, and Bishops all use it before King James does. (Not Douai-Rheims, which has *divers colours*.) Probably it's the concept rather than the language which has attracted people to it—notwithstanding the controversy over whether this is the best translation of the Hebrew (other proposals suggest that it was a coat with long stripes or a coat with sleeves). It's a nice idea, a multi-coloured coat. Whatever the reason, few biblical phrases have generated such a wide range of fresh associations and creative manipulations.

The *Joseph* musical is probably the most famous adaptation of the story, but it isn't the only musical use of the phrase. Dolly Parton used *Coat of Many Colours* as the name of a catchy

A coat of many colours

biographical folksong, telling us how her mother made her such
a coat out of rags:

> Although we had no money
> I was rich as I could be
> In my coat of many colors
> My momma made for me.

It was a popular piece. It even motivated a parody by another
singer about a group of brawny men on a carnival parade plat-
form: he called it *Float of many bubbas*.

The main areas of application for the phrase have nothing to
do with music at all, but tap into its underlying notion of diversity. For instance, if you're writing a piece on the way different
nations or cultures have come together to celebrate something,
or drawing together several different points of view, then a *coat
of many colours* headline would work very well. I've seen it heading reports on international meetings, party political statements,
and reports on a country's multi-ethnic population. When talking about people, the metaphor isn't far away from South Africa's
self-description of 'rainbow nation'.

The most obvious application, I suppose, is within the clothing industry—and, sure enough, in one fashion publication a
journalist writes about 'the bold and the beautiful in winter
coats'. Her headline: *Winter coats of many colours*. Another article, for a different firm, begins: *When looking for outerwear this
cold-weather season, think coats of many colours*. There are several websites which say the same sort of thing.

We might expect the phrase to appear as a headline for virtually anything in which colour plays an important part. I've found
it at the top of an article about a fine display of autumnal leaves,
about a trend in watercolour painting (with a pun on coats of

36

paint), and about carnival decorations in Cameroon. It's the name of a blog for bi-colour, tri-colour, and solid-coated cats, and it turns up as the heading for reports on colourful varieties of several other species, such as dogs, monkeys, deer, and fish. It was, I thought, an apt description of an Irish politician who at various times had been a member of the socialist (red), conservative (blue), and ecology (green) parties. And it was a perfect way of describing the contents of a tube of Smarties.

Modern writers love to play with this expression. Some play games with *colours*; some with *coat*. Either way, the phrase remains recognizable. Here's a selection of headlines which replaced *colours*: in biochemistry: *A coat of many proteins*; in clothing: *A coat of many pockets*; in publishing: *A coat of many authors*; in sociology: *A coat of many cultures*.

My vote for the most intriguing manipulation goes to *A coat of many corpses*. This was an article about the West African assassin bug, which evidently has a unique fashion instinct. In its nymph stage, it covers itself with a dust coat adorned with dead ants, termites, and flies whose bodies it has sucked dry. A close competitor was *A coat of many chinchillas*. Apparently pop-star Madonna once outraged animal rights groups by wearing a fur coat made from the skins of forty chinchillas.

Replacing the word *coat* is often not so stylistically effective, because sentences like *we have trousers of many colours* are so frequent in everyday speech that they are hardly likely to remind us of anything biblical. There has to be something else in place for us to make the link, and this is usually provided by a phonetic cue—another word which contains some of the sounds of *coat*. The two consonants are enough to do it when we see a quilt shop called *A quilt of many colours*. And there's a classic story of Italy by Nannine Meiklejohn called *The Cart of Many Colors*.

37

Rather clever was the heading of a report on a new kind of computer program which brought together features from several sources: *A code of many colours*. *A book of many colours* might one day make a good title for a work devoted to lexical diversity in the Bible, if the Americans and British could agree on the spelling.

But the best pieces of linguistic playfulness use rhyme. Quite a few words rhyme with *coat*, and they're fully exploited. *A quote of many colours* was one which caught my eye: a marketing report about an online financial quotations service. A story about a versatile singer was headed *A throat of many colours*. A report in the *Guardian* in 1999 about the impending elections in South Africa focused on the yellow, green, and black of the African National Congress flags dominating an election rally for Thabo Mbeki, under the headline: *Thabo's vote of many colours*. The most unexpected rhyme I found was *The Goat of Many Colours*—an extra-large pub sign from the Pub World Memorabilia collection. But undoubtedly the most groanworthy variant came from the journalist responsible for headlining a *Guardian* piece on holiday travel to Zagreb in Croatia: *Croat of many colours*.

Chapter 7
Fire and brimstone

etween the negligible influence of *two by two* and the substantial influence of *coat of many colours* there remain a number of expressions in Genesis which we might refer to as of minimal or moderate influence. This is because their meaning is so specific, in the biblical setting, that writers have only a limited opportunity to apply them to fresh contexts.

There's relatively little we can do with *for dust thou art, and unto dust shalt thou return* (3:19), for example. The expression is widely known because it's used in several religious events, such as in the Christian ceremony of Ash Wednesday. It is echoed in the burial service: *ashes to ashes, dust to dust...* The tone of the original also militates against flippancy. Having said that, we do occasionally encounter nonbiblical applications. The presence of dust particles everywhere has given it a certain presence in articles about global warming and space exploration.

Similarly limited is *There were giants in the earth in those days* (6:4). This has somewhat more appeal, as it stimulates the creative juices of writers of science fiction and fantasy. It can also turn up in relation to anything large, such as skyscrapers, wind-farm towers, Californian redwood trees, or great men and women of history. It is of course a gift for writers wanting to be clever when they talk about the fortunes of the New York (football) Giants or the San Francisco (baseball) Giants.

The story of *Babel* (11:9), where God *did there confound the language of all the earth*, is also semantically limited. There are really only two directions of influence. One possibility is the theme of confounding, or confusion. The name has been used to identify a situation where there's been considerable misunderstanding, as in the 2006 film *Babel*, which interwove the fortunes of four families from different parts of the world. And we find it used for the opposite effect, to name projects whose aim is to remove misunderstanding or achieve simplification. An example is the system of computer software conversion called *Babel*.

The other possibility is the language theme. The name has a natural appeal for anyone working in translation, interpreting, multilingualism, jargon explanation, and suchlike. The *Babel fish* of Douglas Adams' *The Hitch-hiker's Guide to the Galaxy*, which allows instant person-to-person translation (when plugged into the ear) has been supplemented by *Babelfish*, a Yahoo! translation service. Doubtless one or other of these facilities would have been a boon to the crew of the Starship Enterprise during the first season of *Star Trek: Deep Space Nine*, when a virus disrupts the audio and visual processes of the people, so that nobody understands each other. They called the episode *Babel*.

Fire and brimstone (i.e. sulphur) has just one function: to destroy things, as it did in 19:24, when *the Lord rained upon Sodom and upon Gomorrah brimstone and fire*. We can disregard the word order here, even though it was used by Tyndale and several other sixteenth-century bibles. The popular preference was the reverse order, recorded from around 1300, and found later in King James, appearing in Psalms (11:6), Luke

(17:29), and John the Divine (Revelation: 14:10, 20:10, 21:8). This would have been reinforced by the translation in Coverdale's Psalms, where we find the same order. No wonder, then, that Sir Toby Belch explodes with 'Fire and brimstone!' in *Twelfth Night* (II.v.56). The even sequence of stressed and unstressed syllables ('tum-te-tum-te') seems to have appealed more to the English ear than one where two stressed syllables are separated by two unstressed ('tum-te-te-tum'). Certainly there is no doubt about the preference today: a Google search in 2009 yielded 30,000 instances of *brimstone and fire*, and half a million of the reverse.

Perhaps it's the vivid description, in tune with the religious temperament of the times, which led to *fire and brimstone* being soon attested in the seventeenth century. In 1670, we find it as the title of a book written by the Puritan preacher Thomas Vincent: *Fire and brimstone in hell, to burn the wicked*. And during the Great Awakening, half a century later, preachers such as Jonathan Edwards and George Whitefield were called 'fire and brimstone preachers'. Modern usages that move away from the original religious context also reflect this ominous history: *Hold your fire and brimstone*, said a headline in the *Washington Post*, the writer defending a politician from supposedly unfair criticism. *Gaffes and brimstone* was another headline, reporting a political debate about Israel—again, nothing light-hearted here.

So it was a relief to find a usage with a positive and celebratory note—in St Paul, Minnesota, where they have been celebrating a Winter Carnival since 1886. A Fire King and his associates, called the Vulcan Krewe, fight against Boreas, the king of the winds, and his royal family, chasing him out of town. The organization is known as *The Imperial Order of Fire and Brimstone*.

Chapter 8
Begat

G enesis holds a special place in any study of the linguistic influence of the Bible because it contains so many instances of expressions which have carried through into modern English. Several of the other books, as we'll see, contain far fewer such expressions—and some have none at all.

Why is Genesis so fruitful? Probably because it has been so widely read. As the first book of the Bible, dealing with dramatic events of the greatest import, it has attracted all kinds of readers, not just those from a Jewish or Christian background. By contrast, there are some books of the Bible which are typically read in their entirety only by people with a special religious or historical motivation—those which have long passages detailing ancient Jewish ritual practices, census numbers, genealogical lists, law codes, and battle plans, or the building specifications for the ark of the covenant and the temple in Jerusalem.

Most of these have made no linguistic impact on English. There is nothing likely to emerge from sequences of sentences such as Exodus 25:10:

And they shall make an ark of shittim wood: two cubits and a half shall be the length thereof, and a cubit and a half the breadth thereof, and a cubit and a half the height thereof.

But the lists in Genesis yield an important exception. There is one word that jumps out at us from these verses:

5.6 And Seth lived an hundred and five years, and begat Enos:
5.7 And Seth lived after he begat Enos eight hundred and seven years, and begat sons and daughters.

Begat—used well over 200 times in King James, as well as in most other translations of the period (Wycliffe has *gendred*; Douai-Rheims has *begot*). Further genealogical lists appear in the first book of Chronicles and, most famously, in the opening sixteen verses of Matthew, where the listing runs from Abraham to Jesus. This archaic past-tense form of *beget* carries a phonetic punch which has made it a popular stylistic choice among present-day writers commenting on how one thing has led to another. It has even become a book title.

In the modern world, it is not only humans who beget, as the headlines illustrate. Films do it: *Jaws 2 begat Jaws the Revenge.* Cars do it: *Mini begat Mini, begat new Mini...*Even institutions such as banks do it: *Commerce begat Chase, who begat...*The ellipsis dots show that the writers are well aware of the way the Bible's genealogies go on and on. They are a regular feature of such headlines. This one introduced a family tree of programming languages: *And Lisp begat Smalltalk, and Smalltalk begat...*

People are still allowed to beget, however, especially in politics. The *Washington Post* ran a piece in early 2008 headed *How Bush begat McCain.* And the *New York Times* at the end of the year had an article arguing that the positive presentation of a black family in the Cosby show had actually laid the foundations for Obama's presidency. The headline was *Did Bill Cosby beget Obama?* More to the present point, a follow-up piece argued that the influence affected the women too: *And Clare begat Michelle.*

However, not everyone who uses the word seems to understand its grammatical status. Some writers take it as a brand-new verb in its own right. *Will the wave begat the tsunami?*, says one. *T4 shall begat T5* says another—the reference being to the fifth film in the *Terminator* (T) series. And indeed, when you see the way the verb is sometimes used, you could be forgiven for taking it either as a present or a past tense. It's even a noun, in the musical *Finian's Rainbow*. Bill, who has had the colour of his skin magically changed from white to black (don't ask!), becomes a new member of a singing group called the Passion Pilgrim Gospeleers. They rehearse the song they are planning to sing at a wedding. 'We take our text from Genesis', says one of the singers (in the 1968 film version). 'What do I sing in that?' he asks them. 'You stress the word *begat* and keep stressing it', they tell him. And that's what he does. The word has never had such prominence in modern times, turning up 38 times in the lyrics (by E. Y. Harburg). 'The time has come', says Adam to Eve, 'to begin the begat.' And they do a roll call of the begetting nations of the world:

> The white begat, the red begat,
> The folks who shoulda stood in bed begat.
> The Greeks begat, the Swedes begat,
> Why, even Britishers in tweeds begat.

The song, appropriately enough, is called 'The Begat'.

Chapter 9
Thou shalt not

Exodus is very much like Genesis, in that the familiarity of the stories—Moses, Pharaoh and the plagues of Egypt, the parting of the Red Sea—has led to certain phrases becoming well known outside the Judaeo-Christian tradition. And there are set pieces, notably the formulation of the Ten Commandments (20:1), whose words have been part of Jewish and Christian children's rote learning for generations.

The phrase *ten commandments* (34:28) has itself been hugely influential through the compilation of innumerable lists. A few minutes search on Google brought to light:

Ten commandments for computer ethics

The ten commandments of distance learning

Ten commandments for good teaching

Ten blogging commandments

The Mafia's ten commandments

The Pope's ten motoring commandments

There are hundreds more. Nor is the influence restricted to the number ten. Many lists use adjacent numbers. *The nine commandments of travel writing. The eleven commandments for controlling your e-mail.* Pamela Boucher Gilberd wrote *The eleven commandments of wildly successful women* in 1998. It was so successful she wrote a sequel a year later: *The twelfth commandment of wildly successful women*. In fact virtually any number can be found, though they are pretty rare after twenty. *The fourteen commandments for tractor operators. The seventeen commandments for dogs.* I guess there are only so many commandments that people or animals can take.

Some of the individual commandments contain phrases that resonate in nonbiblical contexts. The repeated *Thou shalt not* is widely used, sometimes alone (as in the name of a pop group and a 2001 musical), but more usually followed by a modern take on the tradition. The rhetorical contrast works best when the archaic opening is followed by an up-to-the-minute extension, such as *Thou shalt not upload* (on a website about vitriolic blog posts) or *Thou shalt not kill, except in a popular video game.* When in March 2009 the Italian bishops came up with some modern ideas about what to give up for Lent, several reports began with headlines like this one from the *Independent on Sunday*: *Thou shalt not text nor listen to thy iPod.*

The principle of lexical incongruity—what in traditional rhetoric would be called *bathos*—explains many of the other extensions of individual commandments. *Covet* is quite a rare word (in 20:17: *Thou shalt not covet thy neighbour's house, thou shalt not covet thy neighbour's wife*), so the contrast is striking when it is used in headings like these, all found on internet sites:

Thou shalt not covet thy neighbor's Triumph Bonneville
Thou shalt not covet thy neighbor's WiFi
Thou shalt not covet thy neighbor's Uzi

Similarly, the imperative *honour* (in 20:12: *Honour thy father and thy mother*) is not a very common usage, so we see such bathetic examples as:

Honour thy mother and anyone living with her

Honour thy father—and employer

False witness is another instance (in 20:16: *Thou shalt not bear false witness against thy neighbour*):

Thou shalt not bear false witness against thy therapist

Thou shalt not bear false witness (or thou shalt be fined by the Council)

Thou shalt not bear false witness against thy object browser

Thou shalt not bear false witness against thy true clothing size

This last was one of the 'Ten Commandments of Retail Apparel Shopping'.

A rather different use is made of the locution in 20:7: *Thou shalt not take the name of the Lord thy God in vain*. The idiom is found in biblical contexts from the 1300s, and it appears in Tyndale, Coverdale (Psalm 139), and (with a change in word order) Wycliffe; but its use outside a strictly religious setting is not recorded by the *Oxford English Dictionary* until Swift's 'Polite Conversation' (1738): 'Who's that takes my Name in vain?' asks Miss Notable—anticipating the commonest modern usage, when someone overhears their name being used. Also common today is the replacement of *Lord thy God* by another name, as in this heading about Che Guevara: *Don't take Che's name in vain*. And there are some clever variants too, such as the heading of an article on identity theft (*Taking your name in vain*) or one about the care some organizations take to name their projects appropriately (*US military don't take names in vain*).

The other distinctive phrases in the ten commandments don't seem to have been taken up so widely. Doubtless the narrow semantic range of *graven image* (20:4: *Thou shalt not make unto thee any graven image*) has restricted its modern use to such areas as tattooing and piercing, engraving, carving, and graphic design, though it's sometimes encountered in book titles on other topics. And probably it is the twentieth-century sado-masochistic sense of *bondage* which has restricted the present-day take-up of *house of bondage* (20:2). Apart from in sexual contexts, I've found it only in works to do with slavery and in relation to astrology (where it is one of the names for the twelfth astrological house).

Finally, in relation to the ten commandments, we mustn't forget the phrase *tables of stone*, used in 31:18 when Moses is given *two tables of testimony, tables of stone, written with the finger of God*. The rhythm of King James, also found in Bishops, would have made this much more appealing than Tyndale's *which were of stone*, and that is how the phrase is most often used today. *It's not written in* (*tables of*) *stone*, someone might say, advocating a flexible way of behaving.

Surprisingly, the phrase doesn't appear in a very wide range of figurative contexts. It's used in more literal settings, such as the name of a firm specializing in stone table countertops or in the name of a book about rock formations. Perhaps this is because usage is split, with an alternative expression, *tablets of stone*, competing for public attention. That's the phrasing found in the Geneva Bible. It isn't as common as *tables of stone* today, but it does seem to have attracted rather more creative usage. One headline reads: *Should drug testing in sport be set out in tablets of stone?* Another reads: *New jobs created—in tablets of stone—*the wordplay making sense only when we read that the jobs have been created by the Scottish firm, Stone Engineering. A third reads: *Taxman reviews its tablets of stone.* (I wasn't expecting the pronoun *its*, but it feels appropriate somehow.)

Chapter 10
Manna, milk, and honey

For many people, the phrase from Exodus which best captures its theme, and which is in all the main translations, is *Let my people go* (5:1). It has been repeatedly used in recent times when a repressed minority group is struggling to obtain freedom. It achieved modern fame as the title of a William Faulkner novel and as the refrain of the Negro Spiritual 'Go Down Moses', sung by Paul Robeson and later also by Louis Armstrong. The underlying message is very serious, so it tends to be adapted only when issues of freedom, rights, access, and suchlike arise. *Let my software go* was one such appeal. *Let my children go* was another. In 2008, slogans supporting a movement to free an Egyptian blogger jailed for voicing dissent included *Let my blogger go*.

The meaning of *go* is played with too—but again, usually with serious intent. An argument about access in social networking sites is headed *Let my people go social*. Yvon Chouinard's book about the role of flexibility in business success is called *Let my people go surfing*. An article on famine in Africa is headed *Let my people go hungry*. The only jocular tone I've encountered was in an article about the huge effort involved when Jewish families are preparing for Passover. It was headed *Let my people go... to bed!*

In the journey of the Israelites out of Egypt, two expressions captured the later popular imagination—both of them to do with food. One is the unusual word *manna*, found in 16:15 but explained earlier:

16:4 Then said the Lord unto Moses, Behold, I will rain bread from heaven for you;

16:15 And when the children of Israel saw it, they said one to another, It is manna: for they wist not what it was.

Manna is also found in other early translations, but not in Tyndale, who uses *bread* in both verses. It is used repeatedly, and occurs in later books, notably John (in Chapter 6), where Jesus focuses on it (in the 'bread of life' passage). It's a word of uncertain etymology, traditionally thought to be a noun derived from the (probably Aramaic) question *man hu*, and glossed 'What is this?' in the marginal note to the passage in King James. This is linguistically plausible as an explanation, for there are several recorded instances of people interpreting an utterance wrongly in a language they do not know. An explorer might ask a speaker: 'What's the name of your language?' The speaker replies by saying 'this' or 'don't know' in his language. The explorer then assumes that what he has heard is the language's name. But, whatever the etymology, *manna* has retained its appeal in English, usually as part of the phrase *manna from heaven*—a phrase that doesn't actually appear in King James, which uses *bread from heaven*. Both expressions are found. I've lost track of the number of restaurants which are called *Bread from Heaven*.

The meaning, of course, has become generalized. *Manna from heaven* today refers to any unexpected gift or source of benefit—hence its use in a 2008 online article about the way Tiger Woods' golfing successes improved television ratings: *Tiger is TV's manna from heaven*. It's a popular title, used for a wide range of books, both fiction and nonfiction, as well as naming a 2002 film about a supposed gift that turns out to be a loan. It's a tempting name for any food shop that sells something really tasty, such as organic food or ice cream. And the word on its own, in the sense of 'nourishment', is used in both religious and nonreligious settings. A site providing daily Bible readings is called *Daily Manna from the Net*. *Manna from Hell* heads a story about how poisoned bread caused a kidney disease. Rhyme is exploited neatly in a report on West Country cooking recipes using local produce: *Manna from Devon*. A proposal by Yale University in 2004 to open new schools in New Haven, Connecticut is headed: *Manna from Haven*. And one of the most ingenious pieces of wordplay I've seen is the cheeky multiple pun in the title of an article about Cuban ballet star Carlos Acosta: *Manna from Havana*.

The collocation with *rain* is strong too. *Cash is raining down like manna from heaven* is a typical example, referring to a group of people who made a wise financial investment. And the link with *rain* allows *manna* to be replaced by all kinds of other nouns. Best known is *pennies from heaven*, as in the 1936 film title and the associated Bing Crosby song. The title was reprised in a 1981 film (starring Steve Martin) and became well known in the UK as the name of a 1978 BBC television series written by Dennis Potter. But it isn't just pennies that rain down from heaven: *blessings, candy, waffles, fire, photos, babies*, and *acid rain* have all come down into a website at some time or other.

The other food-related expression from Exodus, far outranking the others in modern popularity, appears in 3:8:

And I am come down to deliver them out of the hand of the Egyptians, and to bring them up out of that land unto a good land and a large, unto a land flowing with milk and honey

What is it that made *milk and honey* so attractive? Perhaps it was the frequency with which it is used—over 20 times in King James, and similarly in the other early translations—or the unusual nature of the collocation to Western eyes. It is found in virtually all the early biblical translations, beginning in Anglo-Saxon times, with just the occasional variation—such as the fourteenth-century *Cursor Mundi*, which has *honi and milk*. The earliest nonbiblical example in the *Oxford English Dictionary* is from 1648, and its popularity grew enormously during the following century. Today it is everywhere.

A country only has to have some concerns regarding immigration or diet and the phrase appears in the headline. A 2007 web report about the problems of immigrants in Australia is headed *No milk and honey*, and begins:

Australia has always traded off its image as a land of milk and honey.

Because of its welcoming immigration history, the USA is often called a land of milk and honey, though the message is different in this *Independent* headline from 2000: *The US, a land of milk and honey and mass obesity*. In Tanzania, an article about the role of goats in providing new food sources for children was headed: *Moses Leads the Children to a Land of Goat's Milk and Honey*. (Moses? The name of one of the goats.)

Nor is Israel itself exempt. *Israel no longer land of milk and honey* said a headline in the *Telegraph* in 2008. It went on:

The land of milk and honey is in danger of becoming just the land of milk after a 60 per cent fall in local honey production because of poor rainfall.

And there are no prizes for guessing how several editors handled an archaeological report on the lack of a balanced diet among the people living in ancient Israel. There was a notable shortage of meat and vegetables, it seems, as well as a lack of vitamins and minerals. *Land of milk and honey... but not a good diet* was one banner headline. By contrast, during the same period it appears the Scots were having a great time. *Bronze Age land of milk and honey*, said the headline. An analysis of a 2500-year-old cooking pot found in the Outer Hebrides had found evidence of meat and dairy products, including actual milk and honey. The report (in the journal *Nature*) by Dr Oliver Craig of the University of Newcastle-upon-Tyne commented: 'Barley porridge made with milk and water and perhaps sweetened with honey and garnished with berries may have been a popular dish.'

Actually, any location or event which offers a pleasant visitor experience is likely to employ the phrase. I've found it used for tourist destinations as far apart as Cornwall and Indonesia. Sometimes it's the *land flowing* part of the expression which provides the stimulus. An Israel tourism brochure describes *a land flowing with babes and beaches*. An Atlanta, Georgia guide refers to *a land flowing with peaches and honey* (because of the many streets in the city which have *peach* as part of their name). Sometimes, it's the *milk and honey* part. That's the name of a private members' bar in Soho, London and one on New York's Lower East Side. A kosher restaurant in Golders Green, London is named *Milk 'n' Honey*. And a day spa in London takes the phrase literally:

our experience begins with the Savana Milk and Honey Body Experience, which is a gentle body brush followed by a warm oil and honey massage

The name has appealed to artists too. Several pop music groups have called themselves *Milk and Honey*, and it's the name of an album by John Lennon and Yoko Ono. It's even been the name of a 1961 Broadway musical. The storyline? A busload of lonely

American widows hope to catch husbands while touring Israel. Nor is the pleasant experience restricted to humans. In *The New Adventures of Winnie the Pooh*, Rabbit and Tigger travel with Piglet to the *Land of Milk and Hunny* to get a friendship present for Pooh. And we mustn't forget hamsters, according to the manufacturers of Vitakraft:

Milk and Honey drops that have been specially formulated for Hamsters and are prepared with milk, honey and lecithin to please your favourite pet.

With such a popular phrase, adaptations are very common. Each of the words attracts substitutions. A report on Israel as a technology development area (Silicon Wadi) is headed *Land of Milk and Start-ups*. An article about the plans of a Phoenix-based company to build a combined dairy and biorefinery is headed *Land of Milk and Biofuel*. Then, in the other direction, a British lingerie and swimwear company calls itself *Bras and Honey*. An American handyman company is called *Work and Honey*.

The rhyming properties of the word *honey* make it especially attractive to wordplay. Susan Yankowitz wrote a screenplay in 1976 called *Milk and Funny*. A comedy about suburban USA in 2004 was called *In the Land of Milk and Money*. A 2005 article about a new ad campaign for a US company, Purity Dairies, refers to a *land of milk and yummy*. An article about the huge business opportunities arising from the global branding of Peter Rabbit, one of Beatrix Potter's characters, is given the headline *The Land of Milk and Bunny*. And an episode of the UK's Channel 4 show *Big Brother* about a hole in a milk tank is called *The Land of Milk and Runny*. I can't think of anything more linguistically demotic than to find a biblical phrase appearing on *Big Brother*.

Chapter 11
Eyes, teeth, and loins

There's very little else in Exodus. Lengthy sections of the book, such as those describing in minute detail the building of the tabernacle, yield us nothing by way of modern usage.

26:17 Two tenons shall there be in one board, set in order one against another: thus shalt thou make for all the boards of the tabernacle.

26:18 And thou shalt make the boards for the tabernacle, twenty boards on the south side southward.

26:19 And thou shalt make forty sockets of silver under the twenty boards; two sockets under one board for his two tenons, and two sockets under another board for his two tenons.

Also, there are several passages which present a kind of lexical repetition that is out of fashion today, as in these two examples:

32:35 And the Lord plagued the people, because they made the calf, which Aaron made.

35:22 And they came, both men and women, as many as were willing hearted, and brought bracelets, and earrings, and rings, and tablets, all jewels of gold: and every man that offered offered an offering of gold unto the Lord.

These are examples where the writing has definitely not influenced present-day practice. I can't imagine a modern copy-editor letting such passages through. And it's important to remember that these less palatable stylistic traits exist, when making a judgement about the linguistic influence of the King James Bible.

A few expressions have had a limited take-up outside their use as a biblical quotation. God's self-definition to Moses, *I am that I am* (3:14) is one, adopted by groups and individuals as an affirmation of the importance of identity or individuality. Several singers have used it, such as reggae singer Peter Tosh, and it has come to name the occasional school or training centre. But it hasn't been taken up as a source of wordplay. We don't find playful extensions such as *You are that you are*. Perhaps people have unconsciously responded to the gravitas of the utterance.

Fleshpots is quite interesting because of the way its meaning has changed. It is found in 16:3:

Would to God we had died by the hand of the Lord in the land of Egypt, when we sat by the flesh pots, when we did eat bread to the full

It originally meant, literally, a pot in which flesh was boiled. All the early translations have it, apart from Wycliffe, who has *pots of flesh*. But, as *flesh* in English developed alternative meanings, *fleshpots* kept pace, so that by the sixteenth century it was already being used figuratively to refer to all sorts of envied luxury, and especially those which offered an opportunity to indulge in 'the sins of the flesh'. Today, the locational sense is paramount: people talk about the fleshpots of a city or a street.

Some modern expressions derive from Exodus but their exact phrasing doesn't appear in King James at all (or, for that matter, in any of the other translations), as we saw in Chapter 1. *Golden calf* is an example. We talk about people *worshipping the golden calf*, meaning wealth or some other worldly thing. *The stock market has become America's golden calf* said one report, and people *worship it daily.* A few stores use it as their name, especially if they sell luxury goods. The phrase was used in English long before the major Bible translations, which don't actually use this formulation at all, but (32:4) talk about *molten calf, calf of molten metal*, and such like. There are however two instances of *golden calves* later in King James (in 1 Kings 10:29 and 2 Chronicles 13:8), and these probably explain the other usage.

Burning bush is another example. Moses actually encounters God in a bush that *burned with fire* (3:2). The vivid image has nonetheless come down to us as a more compact adjective and noun combination, and its appeal has led to its use as the popular name of a number of plants with bright red foliage, such as *Euonymous alatus*. It's the name of a group that plays traditional Jewish music. It proved an attractive newspaper headline when wildfires ravaged the wooded countryside of Australia in the 2000s. And the coincidence of surname made it an obvious choice whenever George W. Bush got angry about something.

I had to search quite hard for these examples. And that is the story of the second half of Exodus (Chapters 21 to 40) where, apart from the references to the ten commandments, I've found very few really productive expressions. One of them continues the food theme, in 23:16:

And the feast of harvest, the firstfruits of thy labours, which thou hast sown in the field

Firstfruits, meaning 'the first products of the soil', today hyphenated or spelled as two words, is frequently used in King James (over 30 times), though it wasn't an original expression there, being found in Tyndale and several other sources. By 1600 it had already come to be used in the more general sense of 'the earliest products or results of an endeavour', with no reference to fruit or food, and this is the sense in which it is most often used today. We find such expressions as *the first fruits of the Spitzer space telescope* and *the first fruits of civil disobedience*. And a number of enterprises capitalize on the positive connotations of the phrase, adding it to their name: *The First Fruits Education Centre*, *First Fruits Investments*, *First Fruits Price Comparison*.

Stiff-necked appears in 32:9 and several times thereafter:

And the Lord said unto Moses, I have seen this people, and, behold, it is a stiffnecked people.

All the early translations use it, apart from Wycliffe (who has *hard nol*, a word for the head or neck, still heard in regional dialects). It meant 'obstinate, stubborn' then, and it continues to have that meaning today. The only development is that it is used now in a wide range of collocations: people talk about *stiff-necked attitudes*, *theatre-goers*, *fools* (an association made famous by Bob Marley in a 1983 recording), *parents*, *unions*, *employers*, and so on.

A very productive Exodus expression is in 21:24:

Eye for eye, tooth for tooth, hand for hand, foot for foot,
21:25 Burning for burning, wound for wound, stripe for stripe.

In fact, it is a later version in Matthew 5:38 which has had more influence:

Ye have heard that it hath been said, An eye for an eye, and a tooth for a tooth

As with *firstfruits*, the phrasing is found in several earlier translations, all displaying the same syntactic difference. It's presumably Jesus's focus on the first two expressions in Exodus which explains why the others haven't achieved any modern linguistic presence. But the eye and tooth motifs have attracted a huge following, not only in the titles of books and films, but also in pacifist thinking. As Gandhi famously said: *An eye for an eye makes the whole world blind.*

Adaptations abound. The literal meaning of the phrases is taken in a fresh direction in this 2008 report from the Irish *Independent*, where a father's sight was saved, following an accident, when a canine tooth from one of his sons was fitted with an optical cylinder and inserted into his eye cavity. *For one father and son,* the report began, *the Biblical exhortation of 'an eye for an eye and a tooth for a tooth' has acquired a unique new meaning.* In fact, there have been several other accounts of new eye treatments, such as using stem cells, which have attracted the *eye for an eye* rhetoric.

You never know where a phrase of such wide applicability is going to end up. Among the more remarkable adaptations is an article on detective fiction called *A tooth for a private eye* and a piece on the one-sidedness of a massacre in Gaza headed *An eye for an eyelash*. A Melbourne pop group, Ground Components, called a 2006 album *An Eye For A Brow, A Tooth For A Pick*. Then there is this extraordinary story, from Bangalore, which begins:

The police are looking for a dentist who allegedly lopped off her doctor friend's private parts after he recently married another girl.

The article, in *The Hindu* newspaper, is headed: *Dentist extracts more than a tooth for a tooth*. After this, it was something of a relief to find *Tooth for tooth* heading an article on precise gear-cutting.

There's no shortage of vivid expressions in Exodus, but most have achieved no currency outside their original biblical context.

We don't find people routinely talking about a *pillar of fire* (13:21), *my strength and song* (15:2), *a peculiar treasure* (19:5), or *the gift blindeth the wise* (23:8), for example, though these are all vivid expressions (and the first of them was used by science-fiction writer Ray Bradbury). It's possible that some phrases had greater usage in the past. *As still as a stone* (15:16), for instance, is recorded hundreds of times in the Middle Ages, and is found in Tyndale and Coverdale, as well as in later translations. But the *Oxford English Dictionary* has no examples after the sixteenth century. Later usages there certainly are, but they are all very literary. Tom sits *as still as a stone* (*The Adventures of Tom Sawyer*, Chapter 14). Ginger stands *as still as a stone* (*Black Beauty*, Chapter 26). The *Oxford English Dictionary* may be right to call it '?obsolete', as far as everyday use is concerned.

Harden your heart is certainly used today, but it too has a literary ring to it. It's used repeatedly with reference to Pharaoh, as in 4:21:

I will harden his heart, that he shall not let the people go.

The hardening of hearts (and sometimes necks) is a regular observation in describing the sometimes tense relations between God and his chosen people in the Old Testament. The usage well precedes the King James period: it can be found, in various senses of *harden*, as far back as around 1200 (for example, in the writing of Orm). Tyndale uses it (though not Wycliffe, who has *make hard his heart*, nor Bishops, which has *hold his heart*). It's also in the Psalms (95: *harden not your hearts*), and it is probably this, along with its New Testament use (John 12:40 *He hath blinded their eyes, and hardened their heart*) that gave the expression real popularity. Today, outside the religious setting, it's mainly heard in romantic popular ballads. Lyrical lovers are always being asked not to harden their hearts. I'm not sure it's much used in normal everyday life.

Is *girded loins* (12:11) really alive today? The usage which has come down to us derives from the imperative, *gird up thy loins*, used in the second book of Kings (4:29) and a few other places, both in King James and in earlier translations. *Girded loins* appears nowhere. It quickly developed the sense of 'be prepared for action'—'roll up your sleeves', I suppose, comes close. Indeed, a figurative sense is already in the Bible, when Peter advises his readers to *gird up the loins of your mind* (1 Peter 1:13). Today we find the expression used in the media chiefly in relation to an impending drama or crisis. *Gird up your loins to hit 8% growth* said *The Hindu* newspaper's *Business Line* in 2002. And we find *gird your loins*, which is actually about three times more frequent in the search engines. Neither has been very common, but *gird your loins* achieved a new lease of life in 2008, when US politician Joe Biden encouraged a crowd of supporters to be ready for action with those words. As a result, it turns up regularly on pages commenting on Obama's presidency. A year later, and we read headlines like these: *Obama's 'gird your loins' moment has arrived*; *Obama's choices: gird your loins*; *Obama's Supreme Court choices: gird your loins*. The phrase needed something like this to lift it. It was beginning to feel artificial and self-conscious. Still, it will take a lot more than a Joe Biden to keep it alive in popular English usage around the world.

The two examples from *The Hindu* illustrate an important point. I don't know how many readers of that newspaper would have recognized the biblical origins of the expressions—more than we might think, perhaps, given the central role of British literature in traditional Indian education—but the fact that they were being used at all is itself worthy of comment. These were headlines in a national newspaper belonging to a country where most people have religious beliefs that are very different from Judaism and Christianity. They illustrate the great cultural distance biblical expressions can travel, once they become incorporated within the English language.

Chapter 12
What hath been wrought

aving found so many expressions of English linguistic interest in Genesis and Exodus, we might think things are going to carry on like that. But it isn't so. The first five books of the King James Bible, known as the Torah in Hebrew tradition, are given special significance, with authorship traditionally ascribed to Moses. But Leviticus, Numbers, and Deuteronomy provide us with relatively little by way of influential phrasing. Leviticus has long and repetitive sequences expounding the detail of ancient Jewish laws and ritual. Numbers has similar sequences detailing the census numbering of the Israelites and their historical movements in the wilderness. Deuteronomy goes into a law code in great detail. Such culturally and historically specific information is unlikely to yield many expressions of general appeal. As with Exodus, we find long sequences like this in Leviticus:

11:13 And these are they which ye shall have in abomination among the fowls; they shall not be eaten, they are an abomination: the eagle, and the ossifrage, and the ospray,

11:14 And the vulture, and the kite after his kind;

11:15 Every raven after his kind;

11:16 And the owl, and the night hawk, and the cuckow, and the hawk after his kind,

11:17 And the little owl, and the cormorant, and the great owl,

11:18 And the swan, and the pelican, and the gier eagle,

11:19 And the stork, the heron after her kind, and the lapwing, and the bat.

And there are further examples of stylistic traits which are far from being attractive to modern eyes and ears, like this from Leviticus:

1:8 And the priests, Aaron's sons, shall lay the parts, the head, and the fat, in order upon the wood that is on the fire which is upon the altar:

However, the few examples of real influence that do emerge are certainly dramatic—such as this one, from Leviticus 13:45:

And the leper in whom the plague is, his clothes shall be rent, and his head bare, and he shall put a covering upon his upper lip, and shall cry, Unclean, unclean.

The drama of this expression, which is also found in Bishops, can be sensed when we contrast it with the way Tyndale, Douai-Rheims, and Geneva translate it: *and shall be called unclean* says the first; *he shall cry out that he is defiled and unclean* says the second; *and shall cry, I am unclean, I am unclean* says the third. It is the directness and colloquial character of *Unclean, unclean* that has made it appeal to modern eyes and ears. Invariably, it has a jocular force. I think most people will have visited a mildly sick person, or, mildly sick themselves, received such a visit, and heard these words resound. And they do resound. People do not say them softly: they're meant to be heard! But the operative word is 'mildly'. I doubt they would be spoken when visiting someone suffering from cancer.

Written English seems to be more tolerant of its use in serious as well as jocular settings, as these next examples illustrate. The words have been used as headlines for reports on:

derelict buildings in New Orleans after Hurricane Katrina
a mumps alert
the arrival in port of a cruise ship with norovirus
a blight on tomato plants
a bad review of a guest house

And there are literally hundreds of blog pages reporting the sickness of the writer, or the writer's family, which have been given this heading.

Leviticus is also interesting because it introduced us to one of the few genuinely biblical words that have entered the language. We see it here (16:8):

And Aaron shall cast lots upon the two goats; one lot for the Lord, and the other lot for the scapegoat.

Tyndale used it first, and it became the norm for translating that passage. By the mid-eighteenth century it was so familiar a word that writers were beginning to play with it, coining such words as *scape-horse* and *scape-rat*. In 1765, Walpole described Lord Halifax as a *scape-goose*. We continue to play with it today: *scape-goatism* in politics is first recorded in 1961.

The most dramatic moment in Numbers, from the viewpoint of present-day English, is in 23:23:

Surely there is no enchantment against Jacob, neither is there any divination against Israel: according to this time it shall be said of Jacob and of Israel, What hath God wrought!

As with *Unclean, unclean*, King James opts for the more dramatic expression. Tyndale and Douai-Rheims have a somewhat bland statement: *what God hath wrought*. Bishops, Geneva, and King James turn it into a direct question: *What hath God wrought?*

I can find no examples of the expression being extended beyond its religious context until quite recently. It was probably Samuel Morse who started the trend, using this expression for his first telegraphic message in 1844. Today, it is one of the most commonly adapted biblical expressions. Anyone or anything can replace the word *God*. All the technological innovations are there: innumerable articles are headed *What the Internet/the Wii/Google/the iPhone/Open Source/Twitter...hath wrought*, with the occasional extension: *What Sun hath wrought for MySQL*. So are institutions and governments. *What hath Moscow wrought* was about Russian monetary policy. *What the Fed hath wrought (so far)* was a commentary on the current economic situation.

Note that in these articles, the originally positive connotation of *wrought* (a variant of the verb *work*, meaning 'created') has usually been replaced by a negative one—probably because of a popular association with the verb *wreak* (which strongly collocates with *havoc*, *anger*, and other negative experiences). And this is invariably the case when a person is named: in mid-2008, for example, the *Boston Globe* had an article headed *What Bush hath wrought*. It was not especially sympathetic. I wasn't expecting the article *What hath fifty years of Barbie wrought?* to be very positive, for the same reason. I was right.

We have to be careful with this next familiar phrase, which we encounter first in Numbers (12:10):

Miriam became leprous, white as snow

As white as snow is often cited as a biblical expression, but in fact it had been in the language, as a rather obvious simile, since Anglo-Saxon times. What is interesting is that its usage ameliorated, as we move through the Bible. The original association was with the appearance of leprosy, but Isaiah (1:18) uses it more positively:

though your sins be as scarlet, they shall be as white as snow

And the positive connotations carry through into the Psalms (68:14) and into the New Testament, where at one point Jesus's garments shine *white as snow* (Mark 9:3) and the one speaking to John has hair *as white as snow* (John the Divine 1:14). The Bible, then, may well have kept the simile in the front of people's minds, but it did not source it.

Two other expressions in Numbers have done well in modern English. In 22:31, Balaam sees the angel of the Lord:

he bowed down his head, and fell flat on his face.

The expression is shared by Tyndale, Bishops, and Geneva; Wycliffe has *lowly in to earth* and Douai-Rheims *flat on the ground*. The literal meaning is of course still possible today, but it is the more recent figurative sense, of 'dramatically failing to achieve something', which appears in a wide range of contexts. It's a popular idiom for any individual, group, or enterprise that hasn't fulfilled expectations. One report begins: *Car sales fall flat on their face*. A poor performance in the 2006 soccer World Cup elicited the headline: *Why America fell flat on its face*. The tone is always negative—though James Thurber did try to give it a different spin, when he wrote in the *New Yorker* (for 29 April 1939): *You might as well fall flat on your face as lean over too far backward*.

Then in 33:55, we find this:

But if ye will not drive out the inhabitants of the land from before you; then it shall come to pass, that those which ye let remain of them shall be pricks in your eyes, and thorns in your sides, and shall vex you in the land wherein ye dwell.

Pricks in your eyes hasn't caught on, doubtless because of the risqué associations of *prick*; but the associated expression has, in its singular form and with a variable pronoun: *thorn in my/your side*. The use of *thorn* has been strongly reinforced by the very similar expression in 2 Corinthians, where Paul says (12:7):

And lest I should be exalted above measure through the abundance of the revelations, there was given to me a thorn in the flesh, the messenger of Satan to buffet me, lest I should be exalted above measure.

It must have been the repeated use of *thorn* that has given the King James expression an edge over the other translations, any of which might have been influential, for they are all concretely vivid:

Tyndale: thorns in your eyes and darts in your sides
Douai-Rheims: nails in your eyes, and spears in your sides
Bishops: pricks in your eyes, and darts in your sides.

Geneva is the same as King James, but differs in Corinthians, as do the others:

Tyndale: unquietness of the flesh
Douai-Rheims: a sting of my flesh
Bishops: a prick to the flesh
Geneva: a prick in the flesh

Both *thorn in the/my (etc.) side* and *thorn in the/my (etc.) flesh* are widespread today in nonbiblical contexts. Dozens of book titles use them. A 2008 short documentary film was called *Thorn in your side*, described on one site as 'a gender-bending view of the world from the San Francisco Trans March'. And expect to encounter quite a lot of bending if you go to any site called *Thorn in her flesh*.

For some reason these expressions have proved attractive to pop groups. *Thorn in my side* was recorded by the Eurythmics, Quicksand, and others, *Thorn in her side* by the Subdudes, and *Thorn in your flesh* by Omen. The Smiths recorded *The boy with the thorn in his side*—and when problems arose within the group over take-over bids and personal matters, it was only a question of time before someone wrote an article headed *The band with a thorn in its side.*

The expressions appear in many media contexts, in the sense of 'someone or something that is causing a real problem', as these headings illustrates:

ZanuPF is a thorn in the flesh

Myanmar: ASEAN's thorn in the flesh

Usually, the owner of the side/flesh is made explicit:

Turkey is a thorn in the side of a cosy western consensus

Huckabee still a creationist thorn in McCain's side

Second Division: McManus a thorn in Alloa's side again

HMCS Winnipeg constant thorn in the side of the Somali pirates

Select committees: a thorn in the side of government?

MAC codes still a thorn in the side for switchers

After all these figurative usages, it's nice to find the occasional literal application, in an article about plants not behaving as they should: *Are your unruly rose bushes a thorn in your side?*

I've found very few examples of these expressions manipulated as wordplay, and most of them are somewhat forced. I don't think much of *China calls Tibet a thorn in its EU ties*. Rather better is *Not a Thorn in our side*—a 2007 travel article about the pleasant character of countryside walks between the North Yorkshire villages of Thornton-le-Moor and Thornton-le-Street.

I like the capitalized *Thorn*. But first prize (in a very poor field) has to go to the name of episode 115 (segment 1) of the US television animated series *WordGirl*, which aims to foster interest in the English language among children aged 6 and over. It was called *Thorn in the sidekick*. (WordGirl, incidentally, was born on the planet Lexicon, and arrived on Earth as an infant when her spaceship crashed. She was adopted by human parents and now, known as Becky Botsford, uses her great vocabulary to defeat villains. It's important to know about these things.)

Chapter 13
Bread alone

From Deuteronomy to Ruth we enter the first of several linguistic wildernesses, as far as biblical influence on modern English is concerned. Deuteronomy presents a detailed code of laws. Joshua is preoccupied with the detailed allotment of land. Judges is a history of early Israelite rulers. Ruth is a short story. These are not the kinds of situation likely to yield many long-lasting everyday expressions. And so it proves to be.

One modern linguistic oasis is found in the Deuteronomy wilderness—a usage which has come down to us through being reinforced in the New Testament. The original appears in 8:3:

And he humbled thee, and suffered thee to hunger, and fed thee with manna, which thou knewest not, neither did thy fathers know; that he might make thee know that man doth not live by bread only, but by every word that proceedeth out of the mouth of the Lord doth man live.

It is taken up by both Luke (4:4):

And Jesus answered him, saying, It is written, That man shall not live by bread alone, but by every word of God.

and Matthew (4:4):

But he answered and said, It is written, Man shall not live by bread alone, but by every word that proceedeth out of the mouth of God.

As with *an eye for an eye*, it's the New Testament version which has had the greater influence. *Bread alone* was more likely to be remembered because, as with several other biblical expressions, its iambic rhythm (**bread alone**) is more appealing than a pair of adjacent strong syllables: *by* **bread only**. The translations are split. Tyndale, Bishops, and Geneva opt for *bread only*; Douai-Rheims and King James opt for *bread alone*.

Today both versions are used, but in the search engines *bread alone* is encountered 30 times more frequently than *bread only*. The most popular modern application of the phrase moves away from the figurative force of the biblical expression, where the needs of the body are opposed to the needs of the soul. Rather, modern writers like to extend the bodily theme, especially in articles about malnutrition, where the emphasis is on a varied diet. The contrast is usually on bread vs other types of food. A dairy company, for example, talks about how people *can't live by bread alone*—they need cheese as well. Interestingly, at least one bakery has denied the claim. The headline advertising one London firm ran: *Man can't live by bread alone? We bake to differ.*

Apart from this, Deuteronomy yields little of note. It probably helped to spread the occasional vivid expression, such as *a dreamer of dreams* (13:1), to *heap mischiefs* on someone (32:23), or *apple of his eye* (32:10). All had been in the language for some time before King James. The *apple* metaphor is known both literally (meaning the pupil of the eye) and figuratively from Old English times, and appears in all the other early biblical translations. It would especially have been heard through its occurrence in the Psalter: Coverdale's translation of Psalms 17:8 is *Keep me as the apple of an eye*. But very likely King James popularized its use, for it is the phrasing with a personal pronoun which has come down to us.

Joshua yields one example which is particularly intriguing because it is so 'ordinary'. Most biblical expressions that have achieved wider currency have something striking about their phrasing—a vivid metaphor, a memorable comparison. But in 23:13 we have this unremarkable construction:

Know for a certainty that the Lord your God will no more drive out any of these nations from before you

Know for a certainty is a somewhat cumbersome construction, but it is quite widely used today, providing a more emphatic alternative to *know for certain*. The latter also appears in King James. In 1 Kings 2:37 we read:

thou shalt know for certain that thou shalt surely die.

Certain and *certainty* both arrived in English from French in the early Middle Ages, and soon lent themselves to phrases expressing the notion of 'beyond doubt': *in certain, of certain, of a certain, for certain, for a certain; in certainty, of certainty, for certainty.* As these examples show, there has long been uncertainty about which preposition to use: *at* and *to* also appear in later centuries. King James itself is variable: apart from the above two examples, we find *know for a certain* (in 1 Kings 2:42) and *know of certainty* (in Daniel 2:8). Other translations also vacillate: for the Joshua example, Geneva has *know ye for certain* and Douai-Rheims has *know ye for a certainty*. (Bishops opts for the more down-to-earth *be ye sure*, and Wycliffe *wit ye right now*.) The *for* constructions eventually dominated, as we now know.

Judges gives us two examples: a phrase and a spelling. The phrase is here, in the story of Gideon (6:15):

behold, my family is poor in Manasseh, and I am the least in my father's house.

To be 'the least in a house' has achieved some currency as a jocular self-abasement in everyday informal speech. I recall once hearing a somewhat harassed father complaining that he was 'the least in this house'—the point being that he felt his priorities were rated well below those of the children and the hamsters. But it's unusual to see any use of the phrase in writing, outside its religious setting. It's surprising, really, as the expression was much reinforced by Jesus' sayings, found in Matthew 5:19 and 11:11 (and also Luke 7:28):

5:19 Whosoever therefore shall break one of these least commandments, and shall teach men so, he shall be called the least in the kingdom of heaven

For some reason the locution hasn't received the same level of literary exploitation as most other biblical expressions have.

The spelling example appears in a word found in 12:6, where we are told how the regional accent of an unfortunate Ephraimite, fallen into the hands of the Gileadites, reveals his origins:

Then said they unto him, Say now Shibboleth: and he said Sibboleth: for he could not frame to pronounce it right.

All translations from Wycliffe on use the word, but the spelling varies greatly. Wycliffe has *Sebolech*—and gives the Ephraimite a more evident lisp, *Thebolech*. Bishops has *Schibboleth*. Douai-Rheims has *Scibboleth*. Geneva and the King James Bible have *Shibboleth*, and it is this spelling which has prevailed. Spelling is a defining feature of standard written English, and the influences on the present-day system are many and various. It's not often that we can trace a spelling to its origins in a particular text. *Shibboleth* is a rare case in point.

Chapter 14
How are the mighty fallen!

The books of Samuel and Kings, despite their continuing historical emphasis, take us briefly out of the linguistic wilderness. In particular, the second book of Samuel (1:19) gives us one of the most productive expressions of all:

The beauty of Israel is slain upon thy high places: how are the mighty fallen!

Once again, the iambic rhythm gives this phrasing an edge over the Geneva and Bishops versions, which have *overthrown* instead of *fallen*; and the use of *valiant* for *mighty* in Douai-Rheims carries less phonetic impact.

The modern expression appears in a number of forms. Word order varies: *how the mighty are fallen*. And tense varies too: *how have the mighty fallen, how the mighty have fallen*. But, whichever version is used, this seems to be the expression of choice whenever someone wants to describe the decline and fall of a famous person or institution. Government ministers attract the headline, especially in the wake of a political scandal. Countries do, especially if their power is perceived to have diminished: the phrase was used in one report to describe the present state of the Russian army; in another, to the way a fall in global oil prices was causing unaccustomed privation in some countries of the

How are the mighty fallen!

Middle East. The collapse of major financial institutions in the 2008–9 recession led to it being used so much that it became a temporary cliché.

There's often a strong element of irony present. It only takes a top football team to suffer a major defeat, or a celebrity chef to lose a Michelin star, and a headline beckons. Nor is there anything especially modern about this trend. A letter writer to the *New York Times* wrote:

But how are the mighty fallen? What demon possesses us? What blight is there settling on this rich and great country?

That appeared on 10 December 1898. The *Pennsylvania Gazette* contained a similar complaint:

America held a most elevated rank among the powers of the earth; but how are the mighty fallen!

That was on 17 October 1787.

The expression is a popular source of wordplay. All the meanings of *mighty* (physical strength, political power, social pre-eminence, etc.) have been exploited. The commonest application, as in the above examples, is in relation to human success or failure in a political, financial, or social context. It's therefore quite effective when we see the expression used in relation to physical strength, such as the defeat of a wrestler or boxer, or in relation to an article discussing reasons for the extinction of the dinosaurs. The word *mighty* is not often replaced, though I've occasionally seen such headlines as *How have the heroes fallen*. And I liked the heading of an online article about an ordinary MP (i.e. not a government minister) who was facing charges: *How have the unmighty fallen*.

Much more common is to see the sentence with its main verb replaced. Variations such as *How have the mighty disappeared* or…*slipped* are unremarkable. An effect is more likely when there is a stylistic switch from the high tone of *mighty* to something more colloquial, such as *How have the mighty changed their tune* or…*cracked under pressure*. A good example of a stylistic contrast was the *Observer* headline about British politicians' expenses: *How are the mighty rumbled.*

Fallen itself is a word which doesn't allow many punning opportunities, so examples always seem a bit forced, but they do exist. A romantic novel set in the world of football, in which a famous coach is humbled, is called *How the mighty are ballin'*. A *New York Times* story about the way formerly famous American politicians are now earning a living by writing columns for newspapers was headed *How are the mighty filing*. Rather clever, too, are the instances where *fallen* appears in one of its specialist senses. *How the mighty are fallen* headed one gloomy stock market report, echoing the usual collocation of 'falling stock prices'. *How the mighty are varied* headed another. But the news isn't all bad. Sometimes famous people have their fortunes restored. And sometimes famous people become even more famous. A *Daily Mail* columnist in 2007 couldn't get over the sight of former rebel student leader Jack Straw appearing in ornate clothes as a minister of state, attending the Queen's Speech. His summary: *How are the mighty risen!*

1 Kings 19:12 provides another expression which is definitely King James in origin, though not as widespread as the previous example:

And after the earthquake a fire; but the Lord was not in the fire: and after the fire a still small voice.

It's *a still small voice* that has captured the imagination. The other translations scrabble around for a vivid description.

Wycliffe has *the issuing of thin wind*; Douai-Rheims *a whistling of a gentler air*. Geneva comes closer with *a still and soft voice*; and Bishops is closest of all, with *a small still voice*. But King James, with its gradual lengthening of the vowels (short *i*, longer *a*, diphthong *oi*), is more euphonious. The phrase has been frequently used as a title. It named films in 1918, 2005, and (as a plural: *Still small voices*) 2006. For people of a certain generation, it could only be a song by Perry Como (1958).

Another expression which has proved quite productive, though not unique to King James, is in 1 Samuel 13:14, when Samuel says to Saul:

the Lord hath sought him a man after his own heart

Bishops and Geneva concur (Douai-Rheims has the more cumbersome *according to his own heart*). The meaning of 'kindred spirit' has stayed over the centuries, and is now widely encountered with all pronouns (*my own heart, her own heart*, etc.) and often with *God* interpolated—an example is a 2006 book by Elizabeth George, *A woman after God's own heart*. The first noun is no longer restricted to humans: people talk about *a book/blog/parrot/car after my own heart*. A new kind of triple burger was launched in 2009: the ad ran *A burger after our own heart*. A comedy silent film from 1919 dropped the first noun completely: *After his own heart*. Adaptations are common. The Australian paper, *The Age*, gave praise to an art exhibition with a piece headed *Homage to a man after my own art*.

There's also a linguistic surprise in Samuel—surprising because of its length. A notable feature of biblical expressions that enter the language is that they tend to be short—usually phrases or single clauses, staying easily within the auditory memory. The average length of all the items discussed in this book is 4.3 words. An utterance which consisted of two sentences (or more) would be unlikely to survive, except as a learned quotation, and would usually be reduced to something smaller. An example of this happening is *my father hath chastised you with whips, but I will chastise you with scorpions* (1 Kings 12:11), which is echoed today only in the abbreviated form *whips and scorpions*—a gift phrase for satirists of the British political system, of course, with its party whips. But in 2 Samuel 1:20 something different has happened.

In David's lamentation over the deaths of Saul and Jonathan (immediately after *how are the mighty fallen*) we find this:

Tell it not in Gath, publish it not in the streets of Askelon; lest the daughters of the Philistines rejoice

The first two sentences have appealed greatly to orators and essayists over the centuries. Sometimes the second sentence stands alone. This is how the reverend John Allen uses it in an anti-slavery sermon in 1772, 'An oration on the beauties of liberty':

Publish it not in the streets of Boston!

But usually both sentences are present, with the city names changed—often to the names of towns or villages, which adds a mock-heroic effect. We find Thomas Carlyle using it this way in a letter giving some advice to his friend Robert Mitchell (24 October 1814):

Tell it not in Ruthwell—publish it not in the streets of Kir[k]cudbright

A century later, we find Lord Birkenhead making some daring comments about the link between politics and the military (in one of his last essays, 'The despised politician', 1930):

How are the mighty fallen!

Tell it not in Bath, publish it not in the streets of Cheltenham

And so to the present day, where a blog piece in 2009 on politics begins:

Tell it not in Tatton, and publish it not in the streets of Witney, lest the friends of those smug chaps on the Tory front bench rejoice; but it looks to me as though the Brown Bounce may be over.

(The two towns were, at the time of writing, safe Tory seats. Tory leader David Cameron was MP for Witney; Shadow Chancellor George Osborne was MP for Tatton.) And so I could continue, finding town pairs from every part of the world—Australia (Perth and Canberra), the USA (Tampa and Harrisburg), Africa (Niger and Orlu)...

How did a 14-word sequence come to be so widely adopted? We get a clue if we compare the King James version (also used in Douai-Rheims) with that of Bishops and Geneva, which both have *Tell it not in Gath, nor publish it in the streets of Askalon*. The *nor* construction slows the reading down. The juxtaposition of two clauses without an explicit linking word (technically known as *asyndeton*) increases the pace, emphasizes the rhythm, and highlights the syntactic similarity between the two sentences. The effect is often found in proverbs (*Speech is silver, silence is golden*), and the result is to make a sequence more memorable.

Nothing else in Samuel or Kings quite lives up to the extensive use made of *how are the mighty fallen* and *tell it not*... The four books do contain several other familiar expressions, but they are familiar because they reflect, rather than initiate, popular usage, and several are more likely to be remembered by their use in later books of the Bible. The invocation *God forbid*

(1 Samuel 14:45) is known from the fourteenth century, as are the expressions *God save the king* (1 Samuel 10:24), *laugh someone to scorn* (2 Kings 19:21), *take root* (2 Kings 19:30), and *blood* being *upon* one's *own head* (1 Kings 2:37). Not harming *one hair of* one's *head* (1 Samuel 14:45) is also medieval: *hair* meaning 'the smallest part' actually dates from Anglo-Saxon times. The expressions *play the mad man* (1 Samuel 21:15), *play the fool* (1 Samuel 26:21) and *play the men* (2 Samuel 10:12) were all well known in the sixteenth century. *Put the words in* one's *mouth* (2 Samuel 14:3) is an originally biblical expression, but it is found long before King James, in Wycliffe, where Joab 'puttide the wordis in hir mouth'. Incidentally, the use of *into* with this expression didn't arrive in English until the seventeenth century, but its stronger dynamic force soon made it the preferred form. Today, *into* is twice as frequent as *in*, especially when we are using it as a negative command: *Don't put words into my mouth!*

Doubtless King James played its part in popularizing some of these expressions, especially when the Old Testament phrases recur in the Psalter or the New Testament. *God forbid* was a favourite expression of St Paul; *hair of your head* appears in Luke (21:18). Laughing someone *to scorn* appears many times in both Old and New Testaments, including three times in Psalms. *Thy blood shall be upon thine own head* (1 Kings 2:37) is echoed in Ezekiel (33:4) and Acts (18:6), and has come down to us in altered form as *on one's own head be it*. But whether an expression becomes widely used or not is partly dependent on its content. A good example from these books is *Speak, Lord; for thy servant heareth* (1 Samuel 3:9). This is very well known, but it has had surprisingly little modern use outside the Bible, presumably because the number of contexts where *thy servant heareth* could be used to someone is quite small. No modernization of the grammar has taken place: *your servant hears* just isn't used.

In this respect there's an interesting contrast with *on one's own head be it*, which is widely used today in everyday speech, as well as appearing in a remarkably diverse range of literary contexts. *On your own head be it* has headlined articles about road safety (should cyclists wear helmets?), home improvements (what happens if cowboy builders do ceiling repairs?), and hat design. Any pronoun can be used, including the archaic ones: *On thine own head be it* is still common. *On his own head be it* headed a report in 2009 about someone selling tattoo space on his bald head to advertisers. A more bizarre application of a biblical expression it is difficult to imagine.

This is also a good place to recollect that other bibles had a role to play providing modern English with its idioms. In 1 Kings 2:2 we find David saying, as he approaches death:

I go the way of all the earth.

Wycliffe, Bishops, and Geneva all agree, but none of them was influential. The idiom that has come down to us is *way of all flesh*, found only in Douai-Rheims. Today, the phrase is remembered mainly through its use as the title of a book (by Samuel Butler, 1903), silent film (1927, starring Emil Jannings, who won the first Best Actor Oscar award for his role), or album (by French death metal band Gojira). It is no longer a euphemism for death. Indeed, already in the King James period it was being used as a euphemism for the desires of the flesh, with the sexual connotation of *flesh* (known from the fourteenth century) emerging strongly.

Chapter 15
The skin of one's teeth

A nother linguistic wilderness follows Samuel and Kings. The history of David is repeated in the genealogical lists of Chronicles, and Ezra, Nehemiah, and Esther continue the historical narrative. We look in vain for influences on modern English. And then we encounter Job, who brings some comfort—though not because of one of the modern expressions associated with him: *Job's comforter*.

16:1 Then Job answered and said,

16:2 I have heard many such things: miserable comforters are ye all.

Job's friends had been giving him advice which he found unhelpful, and the translations describe them in various ways: Geneva also has *miserable comforters*; Bishops has *miserable givers of comfort*; Douai-Rheims has *troublesome comforters*; Wycliffe has *heavy comforters*. The message is plain. But the expression *Job's comforter* is not in any of them. Its first recorded use, meaning 'someone who professes to comfort but does the opposite', is not until 1680, and not in a bible at all. These days it tends to be an older person's expression, attracting hardly any wordplay—apart from the serendipitous arrival on the scene of Apple co-founder Steve Jobs, whose surname tends to bring up

83

the pun in the media every time his company is perceived to have a problem.

When we look at the language actually found in Job, we do find a few phrases which have echoes in modern general usage. A good example is in 15:7:

Art thou the first man that was born? or wast thou made before the hills?

The modern simile is *as old as the hills*, and it's possible that this was influenced by the biblical expression. On the other hand, comparisons to express the notion of 'extremely old' can be traced back to the fourteenth century—*old as Methuselah, Adam, the Flood, the ark, the pyramids*. Surprisingly, *old as the hills* has a first recorded use in the *Oxford English Dictionary* as late as 1819. But, whatever the link between the modern locution and Job, it is not of King James origin, as the same phrasing turns up in Bishops, Geneva, and Douai-Rheims.

Nor is this next metaphor, in 19:20, original to King James:

My bone cleaveth to my skin and to my flesh, and I am escaped with the skin of my teeth.

The same words appear in Geneva. (Wycliffe and Douai-Rheims have a different focus: *lips are left about my teeth*.) Coverdale and Bishops are similar, having *the skin about my teeth*, but *of* makes for a better rhythm than *about*, and that is the usage which has come down to us. The other change—the use of *by* instead of *with*—took place in the nineteenth century. Given that teeth do not have skin, the question of what the metaphor originally meant, in English or in Hebrew (from which it is a literal translation) has attracted much debate. The intention seems to be to express the notion of 'a narrow escape', hence the present-day meaning 'with difficulty, narrowly, barely'. But whether the 'skin' element refers to the surface covering of the teeth, or the gums, or some other feature of the anatomy, remains unclear. Surprisingly, despite its frequency in modern English, the expression has generated few adaptations. When we encounter it in titles, it is usually in connection with some sort of escape from disaster, as in the Thornton Wilder play *The Skin of Our Teeth* (1943). It also attracts dentists, for obvious reasons. An article on dental veneers that change the appearance of teeth was headed, appositely, *the skin of your teeth*.

There is another modern echo in 10:19:

I should have been as though I had not been; I should have been carried from the womb to the grave.

Most bibles give this translation (though Wycliffe has *from the womb to the sepulchre*). But a century later, the expression appears with *cradle* instead of *womb*, first recorded in 1709 when Richard Steele used it in an edition of *Tatler* magazine, but with personal pronouns (*A modest Fellow never has a Doubt from his Cradle to his Grave*). By the twentieth century, it was being used as an adjective (e.g. *cradle-to-grave Christianity*) and in its generic sense (*the cradle... the grave*) had become a thoroughly established part of modern idiom.

Why did *cradle* replace *womb*? Probably the alliteration (*cr-...gr-*) and assonance (the repeated [ei] diphthongs) made it more appealing. That we have a penchant for sound effect is evident from many idioms and proverbs (*a stitch in time saves nine*, etc.). Interestingly, the same sort of phonetic effect is seen in the twentieth-century analogous expression *from the womb to the tomb*, as well as in the way that the biblical phrase has been adapted. Rhymes stand out. A music critic who had a baby, and thus found it difficult to maintain a programme of visits, wrote a piece headed *From the cradle to the rave*. A travel company advertised visits to underground sites showing the earliest art of the human race: from the *cradle to the cave*. The title of an article about someone who had been surfing since childhood was *From the cradle to the* ... well, you can guess the rest.

Job several times, depressed, talks about 'giving up the ghost' (3:11, 10:18, 13:19, 14:10). He isn't the first biblical character to use the phrase, but he does use it more than anyone else. In Genesis, Abraham (25:8), Ishmael (25:17), and Isaac (35:29) all 'give up' the ghost, though Jacob 'yields' his up (49:33). The New Testament is mixed: Jesus 'gives up' the ghost in Mark (15:37, 39), Luke (23:46), and John (19:30), but 'yields' it up in Matthew (27:50). In Acts, Ananias 'gives' up the ghost (5:5), but a few lines later his wife 'yields' up hers. The remaining references—Herod (Acts 12:23), Heliodorus (Maccabees 3:31), and Tobit (Tobit 14:11)—all allude to 'giving' up their ghosts. So *give up* is the norm, and this was probably the determining factor in the rise of the modern idiom.

The expression can in fact be traced back to Anglo-Saxon times, in a variety of forms, such as *give the ghost* and *give away the ghost*. *Give up* emerges as the usual form during the eighteenth century. The sense also changes: it no longer refers to death but to a loss of hope or action. *Don't give up the ghost on High Streets*, said one 2009 headline. *Employees giving up the ghost on their company* said another. Extended uses, these days, tend to focus on the modern meaning of *ghost*: for example, it's the title of a 2007 episode (2.9) of the US television series *Ugly Betty*, involving a haunting. Wordplay is rare. I found just one example, in a blog, where someone who had purchased a toaster that suddenly stopped working, for no reason at all, complained that it had 'given up the toast'.

The expression in Job 19:28 seems to be a King James original:

Why persecute we him, seeing the root of the matter is found in me?

The other translations lack the engaging rhythm and the sense of specificity conveyed by the two definite articles. Wycliffe has *find we the root of a word against him*; Bishops and Geneva have *there was a deep matter in me*; Douai-Rheims, *let us find occasion of word against him*. The sense ('the essential or inner part of something') has stayed, especially in construction with *get* (*getting to the root of the matter*), but *root* is not as frequent today as it might be because it is in competition with several other words that have developed to express the same meaning, such as *core, meat, fact, crux, truth*, and (especially) *heart*.

I leave until last what is probably the best-known line from Job: 'I know that my redeemer liveth' (19:25). Thanks to the popularity of Handel's *Messiah*, the solo that opens Part 3 of the oratorio has given these words a special place. Probably for the same reason, it has achieved no general use outside its original biblical setting. It remains a musical quotation.

We have to wait until the New Testament to find the well-known phrase which sums up this Old Testament character. In James, we read (5:11): *Ye have heard of the patience of Job*. We have indeed.

Chapter 16
Out of the mouths of babes

The Book of Psalms presents a problem for anyone wanting to assess the influence of the King James Bible on the English language. As already noted (p. 8), the Book of Common Prayer used Miles Coverdale's version of the Psalms. The Psalter was required by law to be recited once a month in every parish as part of Matins and Evensong. Coverdale's phraseology thus entered sixteenth-century linguistic consciousness long before the King James Bible arrived; and stayed there even after 1611. In the 1662 revision of the Book of Common Prayer, all biblical passages were revised to conform to the King James Bible—apart from the Psalter. Coverdale's version thus continued to be used in the Prayer Book into the twentieth century, and for those who were part of that communion, it is Coverdale's text which is more likely to be remembered, not King James. Even outside Anglicanism, Coverdale is well known through quotation. For example, some of his translations are used in parts of Handel's *Messiah*.

Most of the time the two versions coincide, but there are some notable discrepancies and, accordingly, differing recollections. A good example is Psalms 137:1. Complete the following quotation:

By the rivers of Babylon...

If you say 'we sat down and wept', as until recently most people did, you are remembering Coverdale, for the King James Bible continues:

there we sat down, yea, we wept, when we remembered Zion.

On the other hand, if you are of an age where you loved Boney M's musical rendition of *Rivers of Babylon* (1978), you will recall the King James version exactly, for that is the one they used (admittedly, with a much elongated 'yeah'). Many people, therefore, have divided intuitions about this quotation, with two versions competing—one of them, of course, accompanied by music and a beat. The example also illustrates the way different translations can blend. The Coverdale text actually begins: *By the waters of Babylon.*

Not all of Coverdale's expressions out-influenced King James. We say today *out of the mouth(s) of babes* (Psalms 8:2, Matthew 21:16). This is not Coverdale, who has *out of the mouth of very babes* (see further, p. 94). Similarly, we say today *the apple of his eye* (or with some other possessive pronoun). This is not Coverdale either, who has *the apple of an eye* (see further, p. 72). Also, there are cases where there is more than one Coverdale version: *two-edged swords* (Psalms 149:6), for example, appears as *sharp swords* in his 1535 translation. The amount of ongoing biblical revision in the sixteenth century was truly phenomenal.

By the rivers of Babylon is a quotation. Like so many other parts of the Psalter, it illustrates a sentiment that is remembered and used as occasion suggests. Quotations are not in the same league as the idioms that have become a daily part of the English language (see further, p. 131). Quotations are context-dependent:

we use them when their sense suits the linguistic setting. They're infrequent, compared with idioms. And we're unlikely to adapt them for use in new conversational situations. We don't find *by the rivers of Babylon* used except when someone has in mind the psalm to which it relates. This is a very different linguistic scenario from, say, *the skin of my teeth*, discussed in the previous chapter, which is used by everyone in a wide range of everyday situations.

The point can be illustrated from another famous line (23:4):

though I walk through the valley of the shadow of death

This happens to be an instance where Coverdale and King James coincide, but the point is the same: this extract is only ever used in particular settings, such as situations of extreme danger, memorial services, or funerals. Again, it is a quotation. Most people do not use these words at all in everyday speech, and encounter them only when they find themselves a part of the relevant situation.

Psalms is full of quotations. Here's a small selection (differences between King James and Coverdale are noted):

23.1 The Lord is my shepherd

37:11 But the meek shall inherit the earth (Coverdale: The meek-spirited shall possess the earth)

90:10 The days of our years are threescore years and ten

107:23 They that go down to the sea in ships

130:1 Out of the depths have I cried unto thee (Coverdale: Out of the deep have I called unto thee)

136:1 O give thanks unto the Lord; for he is good: for his mercy endureth for ever.

The same sentiments (sorrow, hope, praise, etc.) recur throughout the book, and it is notable that they are expressed in distinctively poetic ways. A genre characterized by so much poetic imagery is unlikely to be one which produces expressions that will be adapted for general use. Indeed, I'm surprised that Psalms had any general influence on English at all. But a few phrases did nonetheless come to be adopted, such as this one (2:9): *Thou shalt break them with a rod of iron...*

Rod of iron was widely used in the translations of the time: it is in Coverdale, Bishops, and Douai-Rheims (Geneva has *scepter of iron*). There is New Testament reinforcement, for it also occurs in John the Divine (Revelation)—three times, in fact, in 2:27, 12:5, 19:15. Today the phrase has been so frequently used that it has the status of a cliché in some genres, such as football reportage, where it is the routine description for a manager who adopts a hardline approach with his club. When Juande Ramos arrived at Tottenham Hotspur in 2007, the *Daily Mail* reported the event thus: *Ramos will rule with a rod of iron*. In 2009, the *News of the World* summed up Rafael Benitez's control over the future of Liverpool with the words *Rafa's rod of iron*. And a blog had this comment to make about the new Newcastle manager: *Alan Shearer has denied ruling Newcastle with a rod of iron.*

The rod is not always of iron. Sometimes it is of *steel*. But when writers start to play with the phrase, we find virtually any material being allowed. At various times, people have been ruled with a rod of *cardboard*, *rubber*, *carbon fibre*, and *bamboo* (this last in an article about corporal punishment in schools). The expression will even survive when used with other things than materials. Those who want to 'spare the rod' (see Chapter 17) have ruled with a rod of *flowers*, *love*, and *words*. One of the cleverest adaptations headed an article about style in literature: *ruling with a rod of irony*. One might expect no less from a literary journal.

Out of the mouths of babes

Psalms 69:2 gives us a second example:

I sink in deep mire, where there is no standing: I am come into deep waters, where the floods overflow me.

The notion of water(s) being dangerous is ancient, and metaphorical uses of *deep* can be traced back to Anglo-Saxon times. But *deep waters* in its figurative sense of 'great difficulty, danger, or distress' isn't recorded earlier than Coverdale in the *Oxford English Dictionary*. Most of the translations of the time do something different: Bishops and Geneva have *deep mire*; Wycliffe has *slime of the depth*. The use of the phrase with a static meaning soon motivated the preposition *in* alongside the dynamic *into*: today we can be both *in deep water* and get *into deep water*. The singular usage seems to have been established by the eighteenth century.

Today, anyone or any organization can be 'in deep water', and the phrase is repeated without any awareness of its biblical origins. Those who use it in wordplay tend to focus on the contrast between its figurative and literal meaning. Financial problems in a holiday travel firm had the headline: *Alaskan cruises in deep water*. The *Los Angeles Times* in 2009 ran an article on the decline in maritime trade headed *Shipping industry in deep water*. And any article on flooding—as long as the events are not tragic—is likely to attract the phrase.

Psalms 107:27 provides a nice example of an expression which was already in the language, but which was probably given a huge popularity boost by its biblical use:

They reel to and fro, and stagger like a drunken man, and are at their wit's end.

Middle English poets (such as Langland and Lydgate) used the expression, as did Coverdale, and it's surprising that the other biblical versions didn't use it. On the contrary: they seem to be struggling to find an apt translation. Wycliffe has *all the wisdom of them was devoured*; Bishops, *their wisdom faileth them*; Geneva, *all their cunning is gone*; and Douai-Rheims, *all their wisdom was swallowed up.* The modern usage, with *wit's* usually pluralized to *wits'*, meaning 'totally at a loss', is widespread, though it's unusual to see it playfully adapted.

Coverdale and Geneva lie behind the familiar expression in 84:7:

They go from strength to strength.

The punchy monosyllables and iambic rhythm gave this an appeal which the other versions could not match, even though some retained the parallelism—Douai-Rheims *from virtue to virtue*, Bishops *from a stout courage to a stout courage.* Today, virtually anyone or anything can go from strength to strength, 'from one success to an even greater success'. Here too, it has become such an unconscious modern English idiom that people rarely attempt to play with it, and variations tend to be rather literal, such as *go from strength to weakness.*

It's unclear just how much influence the expression in 72:9 has had:

his enemies shall lick the dust.

Coverdale, along with Bishops, Geneva, and Douai-Rheims, all use it. Wycliffe has *her tongue passed in earth*, but in 71:9 he also has *lick the earth*, so he may well have prompted the later extension. From the late seventeenth century, however, an alternative locution developed, using *bite.* Dryden in his *Aeneid* (1697, Books 11 and 12) has several examples, such as *And with his bloody teeth he bites the ground.* A few years later, Pope, in his *Iliad*

(1718, Book 5) describes the fall of Odius, who *bites the bloody sand*. Then, in 1750, we have Smollett's translation of *Gil Blas* (1.3.2) saying this: *We made two of them bite the dust, and the others betake themselves to flight*. Two hundred years later, it was a cliché of Western novels, with *lick the dust* very much in second place. The meaning steadily changed, during this period. In the *lick* era, the expression meant to 'fall prostrate' or 'suffer defeat'. It then developed the sense of 'grovel'. Today, it has extended further to include all kinds of terminal failure. Council services, mortgage companies, and online magazines are just some of the entities which have bitten the dust in recent years.

One other expression from Psalms was widely taken up, in 8:2:

Out of the mouth of babes and sucklings hast thou ordained strength because of thine enemies

Today the expression is usually shorter and in the plural: *out of the mouths of babes...*, though sometimes we find... *babes and children*, or some other variant. It is used when an adult hears a child say something that appears to show an adult understanding of the world, or—rather more commonly—hears a child inadvertently expressing a sentiment which happens to support an adult observation.

What made this particular phrase so appealing? Doubtless its memorability was greatly reinforced through its later use by Jesus (in Matthew 21:16). It's also found in all the translations of the period, but with minor variations: Wycliffe starts with a simple *of*; Geneva begins the Matthew instance with a *by*; Coverdale and Bishops talk about *very babes*; Douai-Rheims has *infants* instead of *babes*; Wycliffe opts for *young children* (in Psalms) and (in Matthew) the rather ponderous *of the mouth of young children, and of sucking children*.

It's a feature of many proverbs that the second part is often dropped, when used in everyday speech. Thus we say *Too many cooks!* rather than *Too many cooks spoil the broth.* We take it for granted that our listeners can read in the missing bit. The same shortening can take place in biblical expressions, and we encounter it here. People will drop the coordinated noun and say simply *Out of the mouths of babes,* or they drop both nouns and say just *Out of the mouths…* There can be no clearer case of linguistic adoption, when people do not bother to say the whole of a phrase because they know they can take it for granted.

As a consequence, playful adaptations abound in the media. Virtually any human noun can complete the phrase, as long as the general sense is preserved. Thus an article on university student complaints was headed *Out of the mouths of undergrads.* And at various times I have seen *Out of the mouths of vicars/ bankers/actors/politicians/terrorists/twitterers,* and many more, the common factor being that someone (or some group) has said something which was revealing, unexpected, or somehow out of character. Rather more literal adaptations include a book of bedtime stories for grandparents published in 2007: it was called *Out of the Mouths of Grandbabes.* Several scientific articles on animal diseases have also taken the phrase literally: one on scabby mouth virus was headed *Out of the mouths of sheep.* And it doesn't take much ingenuity to see its potential relevance for articles in journals of orthodontics.

Chapter 17
Pride goes before a fall

The mention of proverbial expressions leads us neatly into the Book of Proverbs, which is another text where it's extremely difficult to be specific about the influence of the King James Bible—or any of the other translations, for that matter—on the English language. One reason is the restricted range of subject-matter: verses repeatedly express in binary form the difference between the wise man and the fool, the just man and the wicked, and so on. This sequence is illustrative:

10:6 Blessings are upon the head of the just: but violence covereth the mouth of the wicked.

10:7 The memory of the just is blessed: but the name of the wicked shall rot.

10:8 The wise in heart will receive commandments: but a prating fool shall fall.

10:9 He that walketh uprightly walketh surely: but he that perverteth his ways shall be known.

10:10 He that winketh with the eye causeth sorrow: but a prating fool shall fall.

10:11 The mouth of a righteous man is a well of life: but violence covereth the mouth of the wicked.

10:12 Hatred stirreth up strifes: but love covereth all sins.

Dozens of variations on what is essentially the same theme present the popular ear with a problem. Why 'choose' any one rather than any other? Only the most striking of expressions would be candidates for popular adoption; and with so many to choose from, perhaps none would have a mass appeal.

There is a second reason. Proverbs are as old as language. In English several can be traced back to Anglo-Saxon times. There's a didactic poem, written around 1275, called 'The Proverbs of Alfred'. It contains such items as the splendidly alliterative:

Wyth-ute wysdome is weole wel unwurth
(Without wisdom is wealth very lacking in value)

Sentiments such as 'the wise vs the foolish' were well established in English in proverbial form, long before vernacular Bible translations arrived, and this would have greatly reduced the motivation to use biblical formulations. And in many cases, it is likely that the translators simply tapped into this well of traditional expression.

We need to appeal to some such explanations, for the fact of the matter is that Proverbs has had hardly any permanent linguistic influence. And this despite such striking expressions as the following:

4:17 For they eat the bread of wickedness, and drink the wine of violence.

5:15 Drink waters out of thine own cistern, and running waters out of thine own well.

10:26 As vinegar to the teeth, and as smoke to the eyes, so is the sluggard to them that send him.

11:22 As a jewel of gold in a swine's snout, so is a fair woman which is without discretion.

We do not have a contemporary common expression deriving from 'vinegar to the teeth', or any of the others.

In a few cases, it seems likely that the biblical tradition helped to fix an expression in the popular consciousness. A case in point is to 'make a rod for one's own back'. The collocation of *rod* and *back* appears twice in Proverbs:

10:13 In the lips of him that hath understanding wisdom is found: but a rod is for the back of him that is void of understanding.

26:3 A whip for the horse, a bridle for the ass, and a rod for the fool's back.

But the sentiment can be traced back to the early Middle Ages. Thomas Malory in *Morte d'Arthur* (Book 5.2) has one of the Roman senators advising the Emperor that it was unwise to have made Arthur an enemy: *I fear me ye have made a rod for your self.* And an *Oxford English Dictionary* citation from 1546 talks about *a rod made for his own tail.*

The first recorded instance of the modern collocation is in William Hughes' discourse against popery, *The Man of Sin* (1677): *Oh how the good Man smiles to see what a Rod we have made for our own Back.* Given this date, it's highly plausible that the biblical version influenced the outcome. But it would be going too far to say that it was the source of it. And we might argue the same in relation to *spare the rod* in 13:24:

He that spareth his rod hateth his son: but he that loveth him chasteneth him betimes.

Again, the sentiment is ancient, with references dating from Anglo-Saxon times. But the modern expression *spare the rod and spoil the child* is later: it was coined by Samuel Butler in *Hudibras* (1662). The Bible may have influenced him—but if so, it was not the King James version, which says *spareth his rod*, not *spareth the rod* (as in Bishops and Douai-Rheims).

We find the same uncertain history with *pride goes before a fall*. This clearly relates to Proverbs 16:18:

Pride goeth before destruction, and an haughty spirit before a fall.

All the translations of the time have something similar. The usual explanation is that the expression has entered popular idiom as a direct abridgement of the Proverbs text. However, the short form was around long before the era of Bible translations. In 1509, Alexander Barclay translated Sebastian Brant's *The Ship of Fools*, in which we find *foul pride will have a fall*. It seems rather more likely that the modern idiom is a mixture of popular tradition and biblical formulation. And certainly, the amount of variation in the form of the proverb suggests multiple origins. *Pride must have a fall*, says Richard in Shakespeare's *Richard II* (V.v.88). *Pride wou'd have a Fall*, says Mr Neverout in Jonathan Swift's 'Polite Conversation' (1738). *Pride ran before a fall*, says the narrator in Rudyard Kipling's *Captains Courageous* (1897, Chapter 5).

Modern adaptors of the expression of course are unconcerned about etymology. Any disaster in strategy or tactics arising out of someone's hubris is likely to inspire a play on the proverb. Just one example must represent thousands. Too cocky before exams? *Pride goes before a fail.*

Another example of doubtful biblical innovation is in 5:4:

But her end is bitter as wormwood, sharp as a twoedged sword.

The *Oxford English Dictionary* has the earliest recorded usage of *two-edged sword* in Tyndale, where it appears in Hebrews (4:12):

For the word of God is quick and mighty in operation and sharper than any two edged sword.

All the other early translations use the expression (with variable spacing or hyphenation). But it's unlikely to have been a biblical innovation. The *edge of a sword* is found in Anglo-Saxon texts, and *two-handed swords* are recorded in the early 1400s. It's probably fortuitous that *two-edged sword* wasn't recorded before Tyndale.

The expression is still used today, along with *double-edged sword*, which arrived in the seventeenth century. But the sense has changed. In the biblical context, it meant simply a very sharp sword, where both sides were equally dangerous; and this is the way the expression was used when *two-edged* developed figurative senses. In John Fletcher's play, *The Humourous Lieutenant* (1619), Antigonus says of Celia *She has two-edg'd eyes, they kill o' both sides*. (III.iv.32). In modern English, the two sides of the sword perform different roles. When a situation is described in this way, it is being viewed as having favourable as well as unfavourable consequences. A *Guardian* headline in 2009 read: *The double-edged sword of falling debt*, and the accompanying paraphrase explained the dilemma:

The news that people are borrowing less and paying back what they owe has been welcomed—but it could also delay recovery.

Judging by the frequency with which *double-edged sword* is used, virtually everything in modern society seems to have a plus and a minus these days.

Chapter 18
Nothing new under the sun

The Bible glosses Ecclesiastes as 'The Preacher'. Whoever wrote it was—or represented himself as being—a person of importance, as the opening verse states: *son of David* and *king in Jerusalem*. It is traditionally ascribed to King Solomon. We might expect a text coming from such a person, and reflecting aphoristically on the meaning of life and best ways of living, to provide great scope for popular expressions. In fact, there are very few—under a dozen. Many of the preacher's maxims have become well known as biblical quotations, of course, but only a small number of these have become part of everyday English.

The linguistic impact is there from the outset in the keynote phrase: *vanity of vanities* (1:2). This is grammatically striking in English because it reflects a Hebrew way of expressing a superlative—seen also in such phrases as *song of songs*, *king of kings*, and *holy of holies*. We might have expected the phrase to be frequently adopted, therefore, but in fact it's very little used today, noticeable only in the occasional news headline or in the title of an artistic work. I've found a novel, a blog, and an art exhibition all headed *Vanity of vanities*. Probably the negative associations of *vanity* have kept people away from it.

But the opening chapter makes up for that in 1:9:

The thing that hath been, it is that which shall be; and that which is done is that which shall be done: and there is no new thing under the sun.

This expression has been a great source of adaptation, either in its exact King James form or in the more common rephrasing *there's nothing new under the sun* (a version which turns up in several later translations). Wycliffe and Douai-Rheims have the reverse order *nothing under the sun is new*. But this was always less likely to be influential, because the word order goes against the strong tendency in English to place the 'weight' of a clause after the verb.

Presumably it's the way the expression fits so many circumstances which has given it such appeal. It's the perfect headline for an editorial review about politics, for example, where the writer wants to undermine a party claim that a policy is brand new; but it can be found relating to any subject where people see old ideas being recycled. It regularly turns up in the world of the arts, where a play reviewer, for instance, finds a supposedly fresh production to be distinctly old-hat. Rather surprising is to see it used as the headline of a science blog—science always exploring fresh frontiers of knowledge—but it turns out that the writer is paying tribute to new technical ways of doing old things. Even more surprising is to find it in the world of pop music. But in 1999 the US band Coalesce released an album of songs previously recorded by Led Zeppelin: no prizes for guessing what they called it.

The expression has also prompted several variations in news article titles, such as *Is there anything new under the sun?* and *New things under the sun*. The economic downturn in 2008 led to *Nothing new under the depression sun*. And an article on the politics of the *New York Sun* was given the rather clever headline: *Nothing new under 'The Sun'*.

Soon after, in 3:1, we find *to every thing there is a season*. The situations to which this expression applies are even more wide-ranging than in the case of *nothing new under the sun*. It appears in relation to special occasions, anniversaries, feast-days, holidays, economic cycles, gardening, climate change, and any circumstance where people reflect on the way the passing of time affects their lives. It's the title of Jude Daly's children's book on life in South Africa, and of Leo and Diane Dillon's illustrated book on world cultural history. It's the heading of a Web announcement that a wine bar has changed its closing day. And it's the name of an episode of *Baywatch* (1995), whose significance I did not have the energy to research.

People love to play with this phrase. A 2007 food and dining column is headed *To every apple there is a season*. A 2008 article on seasonal beer begins *To every beer there is a season*. A piece on gardening is headed by *For every lawn chore there is a season*. And the sad story of someone deciding to end his blog begins *For every blog there is a season*.

As these examples illustrate, the expression varies a bit. The *to* is often replaced by *for*. *Every thing* can appear as *everything*. And it is often shortened to *there is a season*. As we have seen with proverbs (p. 95), shortenings provide the best evidence that an expression has come to be established in a community's linguistic consciousness.

Something additional takes place in this next example, which I found on the internet. It's a political opinion piece, headed *To every thing there is a season*, but notice how it develops the theme:

Nothing new under the sun

David Horowitz's piece on the home page stomping on the ridiculous, bitter-ender efforts to disqualify Obama from the presidency illustrates what might be an amendment to Ecclesiastes: there is a time to bomb-throw and a time to refrain from bomb-throwing.

The writer dives into the 'a time to' sequence which is one of the most quoted sections of Ecclesiastes (3:1–8):

3:1 To every thing there is a season, and a time to every purpose under the heaven:
3:2 A time to be born, and a time to die; a time to plant, and a time to pluck up that which is planted

Folk singer Pete Seeger was so taken with the words that he used them in a song back in 1950. And others have followed him. It's been recorded by The Byrds, Judy Collins, and Dolly Parton—and renamed in the process, as 'Turn, turn, turn'.

Not surprisingly, then, the 'time' motif has been taken up in its own right. Innumerable headlines begin with it: in a few minutes of internet searching, I found 'a time for' thanks, tears, truth, success, heresy, humility, gratitude, and action. *A time for dancing* is the name of a 2000 film. And in the USA political pundits with long memories still recall a famous speech made during the 1964 presidential election campaign by future president Ronald Reagan on behalf of Republican candidate Barry Goldwater. It was called *A time for choosing*, but after being presented on a number of speaking occasions it came to be dubbed, rather cruelly, as 'The Speech'.

As with the proverbial examples discussed in Chapter 17, the success of the expression probably owes something to the fact that it echoes a long-established proverb *There's a time and a place for everything*. This is recorded in some of the earliest proverb collections, such as *The Ship of Fools* (1509). The rhythm of both the proverb and the biblical expression is a notable feature.

With this next example (9:11), rhythmicality is also an important factor:

I returned, and saw under the sun, that the race is not to the swift, nor the battle to the strong

The galloping rhythm is highly effective, and it isn't surprising to see other versions opting for it (Geneva and Douai-Rheims). The effect is better appreciated if we compare the more cumbersome versions in Wycliffe (*running is not of swift men*) and Bishops (*in running it helpeth not to be swift*).

Writers on any sport involving speed will, sooner or later, be tempted to use or adapt this expression, as I've already mentioned in my Prologue (p. 6). But the contexts range more widely than sport, including any situation where the need to act quickly is critical. I've found it heading an article on parents having to work fast to find the best school for their child. And in this next headline, there is an additional allusion to the following *nor* phrase:

The race is not to the swift. Nor is the lease

The writer tells the story of having to race to beat someone else to rent an apartment in New York. Having viewed the apartment, she was told she had to return to the estate agent's office to complete the deal. Knowing someone else was also in the process of viewing the apartment, she took a taxi back to the office. Caught up in a traffic jam, she left the cab and ran the rest of the way. But when she arrived, she found that the other people had been wily, and phoned in their offer. Despite the fact that phoning went against the agency's procedure, she lost the apartment. Maybe she got some comfort from her use of Ecclesiastes.

As do many authors and academics, I suspect, when they read 12:12:

And further, by these, my son, be admonished: of making many books there is no end; and much study is a weariness of the flesh.

The 'books' part has appealed to writers on the information explosion, especially those speculating on the future of the book in relation to the electronic revolution. *Of making many books there will be an end*, wrote one pundit. And the 'weariness' part has naturally been taken to heart by many writers on education, as well as innumerable students. Writers on medical topics have, just as naturally, focused on the 'flesh' part, where it can be encountered heading articles on all kinds of diseases. The phrase as a whole has had many figurative extensions. One internet writer, evidently exhausted after a long bout of electronic activity, headed his piece with *Much scanning is a weariness of the flesh*. This is definitely a King James influence; Geneva is close with *much reading is a weariness of the flesh*, but the other sources do different things (Bishops, *wearieth the body*; Douai-Rheims, *an affliction of the flesh*; Wycliffe, *torment of flesh*).

The expression in 4:9, *two are better than one*, used also by Bishops and Geneva, was already proverbial in the sixteenth century, also in the form *two heads are better than one*, and it is the latter which dominates today. It's a popular idiom, as shown by its many adaptations, affecting all the content words. The kind of pairs that are 'better than one' include *kittens, browsers, parents, credit cards*, and *tongues* (a plug for bilingualism). *Better* is often replaced by a synonym, such as *cuter* or *cooler*—and even occasionally by an antonym. *Two heads are worse than one*, read the disapproving headline of a 1998 report about the England cricket team when the captains alternated between matches. *One* has been replaced by other numbers, and also by *none*. *Two heads are better than none* was the title of a TV comedy zombie movie (2000) whose content is perhaps best left to the imagination. And *two* can be replaced by virtually any number. *Several thousand heads are better than one*, said an article on cooperative economy. *Six heads are better than one*, said an article reporting a collaboration between a group of school principals.

It's not always clear how a modern expression derives from a biblical source. In 5:15 we read:

As he came forth of his mother's womb, naked shall he return to go as he came, and shall take nothing of his labour, which he may carry away in his hand.

It's probable that the modern expression *You can't take it with you* derives from this verse of Ecclesiastes, along with the similar, shorter verse in 1 Timothy 6:7, but the linguistic 'distance' between the two versions is considerable, so that the modern usage is best viewed as a comment on the biblical text rather than an adaptation of it. The other early translations provide little help. Two of them at least add a *with*: *he shall take away him no thing of his travail* (Wycliffe) and *he shall take nothing away with him of his labour* (Douai-Rheims). Geneva and Bishops take us further from the modern expression by having *bear* and *carry* respectively, instead of *take*. But the generalizing force of the two *you*'s is nowhere to be found. Nor, it seems, did the present-day usage develop quickly: the earliest recorded instance in the *Oxford English Dictionary* is 1841.

I'm also uncertain about this next expression (in 11:1):

Cast thy bread upon the waters: for thou shalt find it after many days.

What is one doing, exactly, when one is *casting bread upon the waters* (sometimes also, these days, *water*)? Geneva uses the same words, but the other translations vary: *lay thy bread upon wet faces*, says Bishops, for example. Its meaning has been variously interpreted, such as 'living generously', taking a chance', 'spreading your knowledge', 'anticipating unexpected returns', and 'seeing what happens'. Having asked several people what it means, and received several different answers, I conclude that it's one of those idioms that is useful (suiting several communicative contexts) yet dangerous (no guarantee that people will understand what you mean). Notwithstanding, it's been used quite a lot over the years. It's been the title of a movie (1913) and various books, and has been frequently adapted. One company was described as *casting its marketing dollars upon the waters*; an online enthusiast described himself as *casting his blog upon the waters*. A fly-fishing forum reverted to the literal meaning with *Cast your flies upon the waters*. And not only on waters: *Cast your bread upon the internet*. The twentieth-century slang use of *bread* to mean 'money' has probably injected some new life into the idiom, which otherwise remains rather literary: *Don't cast your bread upon the stock market*.

With just one important exception, other familiar phrases in Ecclesiastes are more quotations than idioms. *Let thy words be few* (5:2) would probably not have had much general use if it hadn't been adopted by the Quaker movement, being a favourite quotation of founder George Fox. Outside of this context, I noted it appearing, rather neatly, as the title of a collection of epigrams. Bloggers quite like it also, as one of the dangers of that medium is people writing too much—a condition that has been aptly described as *bloggorhoea*. And, with a pronoun change, it appears as the name of several song albums: *Let my words be few, Let your words be few.*

Wine maketh merry (10:19) is very definitely a quotation. Not surprisingly, the words appeal to the modern age. We see it from time to time on T-shirts, shopping bags, and suchlike. I haven't found it being used in contexts other than those referring literally to wine. And the same applies to *money answereth all things* (10:19). It's the heading of several blogs on the economy, for instance, and fund-raising organizations sometimes use it—it's the name of a Nevada Foundation for educational services. The expression was given a boost by being used as the title of an influential eighteenth-century pamphlet by Joseph Vanderlint.

The exception I mentioned above? That deserves a chapter to itself.

Chapter 19
Fly in the ointment

Fly in the ointment has the core meaning of a 'small problem', but it carries a wide range of nuances: a circumstance that interferes with our enjoyment of something—a hitch in one's plans—a trifling impediment—a major obstacle—an irritating flaw—a computer glitch. The expression has achieved quite a vogue in popular culture. It's the name of a book on popular science (by Joe Schwarcz in 2004) and of two novels—by Alice Thomas Ellis in 1990 and by Anne Fine in 2008. And in pop music it turns up as the name of a pop group, the name of a disc recorded in the 1990s by the US rock band AFI, and the name of at least two songs—one recorded by Rod Stewart, and the other by Ian Dury and the Blockheads.

All dictionaries cite the King James Bible as its source. Yet it doesn't actually appear there with those exact words. What we find, in Ecclesiastes 10:1, is this:

Dead flies cause the ointment of the apothecary to send forth a stinking savour: so doth a little folly him that is in reputation for wisdom and honour.

The annoyance caused by flies that end up in a sticky substance, such as food or ointment, is presumably as old as humanity itself. Doubtless there were Anglo-Saxon equivalents for 'Waiter, there's a fly in my soup'. So why did this particular association of ideas catch the public imagination? Why did people remember it? And why did they adapt it?

It must be something to do with the properties of ointment. *Ointment* today has a medicinal or cosmetic meaning, but in earlier centuries it also had a strong association with religious ceremonial. It comes from a Latin word meaning 'anoint'. The link with anointing was clearer in Middle English, where there was a splendid verb: to *oint*. An early fourteenth-century psalter talks about the *ointing* of the Holy Ghost, and in one of the medieval accounts of creation from that time we read:

Of oyle taken yow some del, Wherwith ye mowen oynten me wel.
(Of oil take you some deal, wherewith you must anoint me well)

It's a shame that *ointing* seems to have left the language—though the *Oxford English Dictionary* does have a quotation from as recently as 1930, so perhaps some people still use it. To treat a swelling, it says there, we are advised to 'oint the part affected'.

Positive associations pervade the biblical uses of *ointment*. The adjectives associated with it in the Bible are *holy, precious,* and *good,* and the associated nouns are all sweet-smelling. 'Ointment and perfume rejoice the heart' says one of the verses in Proverbs (27:9). 'Because of the savour of thy good ointments thy name is as ointment poured forth, therefore do the virgins love thee', says the Song of Solomon (1:3). That's quite an accolade.

The message is clear. Flies can get away with landing on most substances without getting a bad press, but they shouldn't mess with ointment! And especially they shouldn't interfere with ointment in a sacred context. Not just because they were dirty; they were evil. Flies were thought to be a favourite hiding-place for devils, who found it easy to assume their shape. A fly is called 'a divill or familiar' in a 1584 book on witchcraft. For flies to appear, alive or dead, in holy ointment, is truly desecrating. In addition, it's unusual to have a reference to flies in the Bible. Apart from in Exodus (8:21), where a swarm of flies attack Egypt, the recollection of this event in Psalms, and a mention of their possible arrival in Isaiah (7:18), flies simply don't figure. So when they do turn up, even if dead, they are conspicuous—not just for what they are, but for what they do. They turn a savour into something stinking. That's unexpected too.

In the early books of the Bible, the only adjective used of *savours* is *sweet*. 'The Lord smelled a sweet savour' in Genesis (8:21). Throughout Exodus, burnt offerings repeatedly make a 'sweet savour' (e.g. 29:18). Savours are sweet, sweet, sweet. Then suddenly, in Ecclesiastes, the savour stinks. It's a dramatic and vivid way of capturing the impact a brief moment of foolishness can have on the reputation of a wise and honourable man.

For these reasons, the association of dead flies and ointment must have been especially memorable to seventeenth-century listeners and readers. It would have been picked up by many preachers and applied to the daily circumstances of the congregation, who would in turn have used it in a variety of situations. Other phrases with related meaning might have helped it to take hold. Insects were known to have been preserved in amber, and the phrase *flies in amber* would also eventually come to be used in English. The parallel would have been reinforced by the meaning of *amber*, which historically derived from *ambergris*, itself a substance used in perfumery.

The striking association would also have been strengthened by the similar vocabulary in other biblical translations. Geneva, for example, has *Dead flies cause to stink, and putrefy the ointment of the apothecary.* Douai-Rheims has *Dying flies spoil the sweetness of the ointment*. But notice how these translations separate the two critical words. By contrast, in King James the words are brought into close relationship with *flies cause the ointment*. It is not a great step from here, rhythmically speaking, to *flies in the ointment*. And rhythm always plays a crucial role in the memorability of phrases, as we have seen in earlier chapters. We see it pulsing out in the lyrics of the Ian Dury song:

> Fly in the ointment
> Stain on the character
> Dust on the wainscot
> Hair on the gate.

It's one of the most widespread rhythmical patterns in English idioms, several of which use *in* as the linking preposition—*bee in the bonnet, bats in the belfry, head in the sand*, and so on. One of the reasons why people have taken so much to *fly in the ointment*, I suspect, is because it slots neatly into their linguistic consciousness. It trips easily off the tongue and easily into the memory.

There's no hard evidence from the seventeenth century of these processes in operation, but that's hardly surprising. The changes would have emerged out of the dynamic of everyday listening and speaking, and it would have taken quite some time for them to be recorded in writing. In fact it's almost a century before we find the first recorded instance of *fly in the ointment*. In 1707, John Norris, the Rector of Bermerton, near Salisbury in Wiltshire, published a tract called *A Practical Treatise Concerning Humility*, and on p. 198 he quotes Ecclesiastes 10—or, rather, misquotes it, for it appears as a paraphrase:

Fly in the ointment

'Tis that Dead Fly in the Ointment of the Apothecary which causes it to send forth an ill savour.

What is interesting is the way the original expression seems to have transmuted into an idiom, forcing him to rethink the structure of the sentence as a whole. If *fly in the ointment* was a fixed phrase in his mind, he could no longer separate the words by the word *cause,* so he had to recast the syntax of the rest of the sentence.

Over a century later we find another piece of evidence that the expression has become an established idiom. In his *Essays to Elia* (1833), Charles Lamb asserts that *A Poor Relation is … a fly in your ointment.* Here we see someone now beginning to play with the idiom. It is a writer aiming for a stylistic effect. It's the sort of thing we often see these days, especially in newspaper headlines. On 7 March 2004, the *Observer* ran the headline *Bush is the fly in Blair's ointment.* On 20 July 2004, the Salt Lake City *Desert News* carried this one: *Fly in Congress' ointment.* And on 4 February 2008, you would have read this in the *Sydney Morning Herald*: *Frequent fly in Qantas ointment.* Each one needs a contemporary gloss. To make sense of the last headline, for example, we need to know that the newspaper article was about the trillions of unused frequent flyer points inside the global airline market. But note: it is the context which needs explaining, not the idiom. We take the meaning of the idiom for granted.

The wheel can turn full circle. On 1 November 2004, the website *Innovation Canada* had a headline which read simply *Fly in the ointment.* When we read on, it transpired that the joke lay in this being the literal sense of *fly* as 'insect'. The piece described a rare genetic disorder which leaves children with abnormally large bruises, and reported on a DNA research programme which aimed to provide new treatments using—the fruit fly.

Chapter 20
No peace for the wicked

No modern idioms emerge from the love story which is the Song of Solomon, with its highly poetic diction and various allegorical interpretations. But Isaiah more than makes up for it. Isaiah has been the most influential of the prophets, thanks largely to his annual appearance as part of the Festival of Nine Lessons and Carols at Christmas time, and his dominant presence in Handel's *Messiah*. Many people are familiar with these words:

9:2 The people that walked in darkness have seen a great light

9:6 For unto us a child is born, unto us a son is given

40:4 Every valley shall be exalted

53:3 He is despised and rejected of men; a man of sorrows, and acquainted with grief

For most of us, these have the status of quotations. Just occasionally we find some playful adaptation. Birth announcements, especially, like to play with 9:6: *Unto us a grandson* (etc.) *is born.* And the birth applies to more than humans. *Unto us a blog is born. Unto us a film is born* (about the Nativity).

But Isaiah gives us far more than popular quotations. Several passages have transmuted into idioms. We find one in 2:4:

115

No peace for the wicked

And he [the Lord] shall judge among the nations, and shall rebuke many people: and they
shall beat their swords into plowshares, and their spears into pruninghooks

The same expression turns up again in Micah (4:3), and there is
a nice rhetorical reversal in Joel (3:10):

Beat your plowshares into swords and your pruninghooks into spears: let the weak say, I am
strong.

Either of the two weapon transformations might have been
linguistically influential, but it was *swords into plowshares* (or
ploughshares) which carried the day. It's perhaps surprising,
given that swords and plowshares are no longer an everyday
experience for most people, that the expression continues to be
so popular. But the collocation of *swords* and *plowshares* has
had a widespread appeal, appearing as the title of several works
dealing with the 'war and peace' theme. A 2007 book by British
politician Paddy Ashdown was called *Swords and Plowshares*—
its subtitle *Bringing peace to the 21st century*. I had thought that
the word order, reinforced by the iambic rhythm, would never
be altered. But then I encountered a 2004 song by the American rock band E. Town Concrete called 'Plowshares and
Swords'. With language, the only safe aphorism is 'never say
never.'

The full form, *beating* (sometimes *turning*) *swords into plowshares*, is often adapted. The *sword* element is frequently replaced
by a more modern weapon: entities that have been turned into
plowshares include *bombs*, *plutonium*, *rockets*, and *AK-47s*.
Sometimes we see a more figurative adaptation: *Beating scientists into plowshares* headed an article about the way certain
industries were downsizing their science laboratories and providing funding for academic research projects.

The *plowshare* element also varies. Again, the military spirit of the phrase is never far away. Laser space weapons technology (developed during the so-called 'Star Wars' era in US politics) is now being used for other purposes, hence the headline *Beating swords into telescopes*. The reduction of paramilitary activity in Colombia and the rise of local literature elicited *Beating swords into pens*. A story about the opening of a guesthouse on the site of a former battleground in Thailand led to *Beating swords into teacups*. And a pun on *shares* is inevitable when someone adapts military technology for marketable products. Glenn E. Schweitzer wrote a book in 2000 called *Beating swords into market shares*. An article about political and economic changes in Libya led to the headline *Beating swords into oil shares*.

Isaiah also gives us a nice example of a modern usage which comes from a clear conflation of Old and New Testament texts. In 22:13 we read: *let us eat and drink; for to morrow we shall die*—a phrasing echoed in 1 Corinthians (15:32). And in Luke 12:19, we read in one of Jesus's parables about a rich man who tells his soul: *take thine ease, eat, drink, and be merry*—a line reinforced soon after in the parable of the prodigal son (15:23): *let us eat, and be merry*. The phrasing is similar in all Bible versions, though the translations sometimes differ over 'be merry': *make feast* (Wycliffe); *make good cheer* (Douai-Rheims), *take thy pastime* (Geneva). But the point is that the expression which has entered English-speaking consciousness is a combination of Isaiah and Luke: *eat, drink and be merry, for tomorrow we shall die.*

The two parts are often separated in modern usage. Restaurants, pubs, and food stores often use the first part in their advertising—but not the second, the assumption being that readers will somehow suppress the sequel. And yet awareness of that sequel is taken for granted in many other settings, as this selection of headlines illustrates:

Eat, drink, and be merry, for tomorrow we diet

Eat, drink, and be merry, for tomorrow we retouch [on plastic surgery]

Eat, drink, and be merry, for tomorrow we devalue the pound

Eat, drink, and be merry, for tomorrow we die on Flickr [knowing that embarrassing photographs are about to be posted there]

Eat, drink, and be merry, for tomorrow you may be in Utah [because of its strict alcohol laws]

Rhetorically effective are instances which elide part of the second element, as in this one reflecting on the future of the planet:

Eat, drink, and be merry, for tomorrow...

or dispense with it altogether, while using punctuation to remind us that it is there, as in this heading about obesity:

Eat, drink and be merry?

And it's difficult to beat the rhetorical force of this one, about the differences between the rich and the poor in Mugabe's Zimbabwe (in *The Tablet*, 16 December 2008):

Eat, drink and be merry, for it's others who die.

The case of Isaiah 40:3 is interesting because of the way it now appears in several variations. The original text reads:

The voice of him that crieth in the wilderness, Prepare ye the way of the Lord

Its popularity is reinforced by its recall in all four Gospels (Matthew 3:3, Mark 1:3, Luke 3:4, John 1:23), where it appears as *the voice of one crying in the wilderness*. Today, we most often find the expression in its full form as *a voice crying in the wilderness*, as well as in elliptical form as *a voice in the wilderness* and *crying in the wilderness*. It is no longer a single-person situation: there can be *voices* too. In all cases, it is the negative outcome that is being emphasized; the sense is of a voice not being heeded. It can thus be used of anyone trying (and failing) to get a point of view across, or even of someone repeatedly trying to get a reaction from an unresponsive company: 'Nobody's listening!' Adaptations are unusual, for the expression is vivid as it stands, especially in a part of the world where wildernesses are unfamiliar. But the memory of the original is strong enough to fuel a few variants, such as *a voice crying in the metropolis* and *a voice crying in the wickedness*.

It's difficult to be sure what the direction of influence is for this next expression:

> 48:22 There is no peace, saith the Lord, unto the wicked.
>
> 57:21 There is no peace, saith my God, to the wicked.

The same variation in prepositions is found also in Geneva. (Bishops avoids the prepositional issue altogether, having *As for the ungodly, they have no peace* and *the wicked have no peace*.) *To* is the preferred form, occurring also in Wycliffe and Douai-Rheims:

> Peace is not to wicked men
>
> There is no peace to the wicked

And if we were to suggest a direct influence on modern English, it would surely be here, for these are the two versions which do not separate the expression by a 'saith' construction. And yet, the conflation of separated words into a single expression is not unusual, so the King James version may nonetheless have had a role in influencing the modern usage.

There are two puzzles. The modern expression is *No peace for the wicked*. Where did the *for* come from? The norm was *to* throughout the seventeenth century. The *Oxford English Dictionary* first records *for* in 1732, and from then on that is all we find. Also puzzling is why *rest* has usually replaced *peace*. The word does appear in Isaiah, in the immediately preceding verse, but as a verb not a noun (*the wicked are like the troubled sea, when it cannot rest*). And there's a huge time gap before we find *no rest for the wicked*: the earliest instance in the *Oxford English Dictionary* is 1935. It definitely appeared two years earlier in the US, when Harold Gray used it as the title of one of his widely syndicated 'Little Orphan Annie' cartoons (5 January 1933). Perhaps this helped to spread the usage.

Whatever the reasons, today *rest* is far more common than *peace*. While we should never take search-engine frequency statistics at face value (they contain a great deal of duplication, and it's never clear what time-frame is covered), there does seem to be a real difference—600,000 of *no rest*...vs 24,000 of *no peace*...(Google, 2009). For both expressions, of course, the meaning has radically changed. It is never used literally, with reference to a really evil person, but always ironically or humorously among friends or acquaintances.

Several other expressions derive from Isaiah, though they are not usually unique to King James. *Behold the nations are as a drop of a bucket* (40:15) has given us *drop of/in a bucket* (especially in American English), but the phrase was also used by Wycliffe, Geneva, and Douai-Rheims; *drop in the ocean* is far more widely used now. Similarly, *they shall see eye to eye* (52:8) is also found in Geneva and Douai-Rheims, with Wycliffe very similar (*see with eye to eye*). The connotations of directness, openness, and integrity have given it a modern appeal, so that we find it used as the name of serious-minded television talk shows or companies advocating an open-door policy. In everyday speech, the usage is typically negative: *we **don't** see eye to eye.* A King James phrasing is however found in 38:1, when Isaiah warns Hezekiah:

Set thine house in order; for thou shalt die, and not live.

This is in none of the other early translations. Bishops and Geneva have ... *in an order*; Douai-Rheims has *give charge concerning thy house*; Wycliffe has *command to thine house*. Today, the expression is widespread, with *put*, *get*, and *keep* used alongside *set*. *Banks struggle to put their house in order* was a typical 2008 example. We often see it used after a focal noun: *Insurance: is your house in order?* It's the *house ... in order* part which is the basis of the idiom. Advertisers in particular are always asking us whether we have *put our life/tax affairs/portfolio/finances/website in order.*

Finally, in Isaiah, we encounter this familiar expression (in 65:5):

Stand by thyself, come not near to me; for I am holier than thou.

This is an unusual one, for there is no record of *holier than thou* being used outside this biblical context until the twentieth century. In the *Oxford English Dictionary* the first recorded usage as an adjective (meaning 'hypocritically pious') is 1912. I wasn't expecting there to be much playful adaptation for this expression, because the effect of the original disappears once *thou* is replaced. *Is Obama holier than Bush?* asked one blog. The echo of Isaiah is lost. (A rhyme helps to restore it. A food quiz has been called *Holier than chow.* A piece on the stock markets was headed *Holier than Dow.* An arts article began *Holier than highbrow.*) What surprised me was to find the *than thou* element retained as an echo in its own right. An amazing number of enterprises use it:

hippier than thou
prettier than thou
funnier than thou
healthier than thou
funkier than thou
geekier than thou

this last forming a T-shirt slogan. It is even possible to leave the *-ier* ending behind, as in *greener than thou* and *more progressive than thou.*

Two of the most creative echoes of the expression use the original without change. The huge statue of Christ the Redeemer looks out over Rio de Janeiro. Now a small town in Brazil wants to erect an even bigger Christ statue. The newspaper report was headed *Holier than Thou?* That was where I was intending this chapter to end. Then I discovered a candidate for the worst pun in this book. Studios for tattooing and body piercing. Called *Holier than thou.*

Chapter 21
Be horribly afraid

The remaining sixteen books of the Old Testament contribute next to nothing by way of an English linguistic legacy. In eleven of the books (Lamentations, Obadiah, Joel, Amos, Jonah, Micah, Nahum, Habbakuk, Zephaniah, Haggai, Zechariah) I could find nothing at all. And the others provide only sporadic and indirect evidence.

There are several familiar expressions in Jeremiah and Ezekiel, but virtually all of them were in use long before the King James Bible. Take this one, in Jeremiah 15:16:

Thy words were found, and I did eat them

'Eating someone's words', in the sense of feeding upon them, or treasuring them, we find in Wycliffe, which is actually cited by the *Oxford English Dictionary* as the first instance of this expression. In the sense of 'retract what someone has said in a humiliating manner', we find a first recorded instance in 1571. Sir Walter Raleigh has a nice illustration of the modern sense: *we'll make you…eat your own words* (1618). So the usage seems to have been well established before 1611. It is in fact but one of several figurative uses of *eat* during the sixteenth century. People talked of *eating iron* (i.e. being stabbed). Shakespeare's Hotspur is described as *eating the air* (i.e. being fed on promises) in *Henry IV Part 2* (I.iii.28). With 'eating words', as in many other expressions, the Bible would have been a popularizer rather than an originator.

The same point applies to Jeremiah 31:29 (echoed in Ezekiel 18:2):

In those days they shall say no more, The fathers have eaten a sour grape, and the children's teeth are set on edge.

This isn't the source of the modern expression *sour grapes* ('pretending to dislike something one really desires', 'being a bad loser'); that goes back to one of Aesop's *Fables* ('The fox and the grapes'). And *setting teeth on edge* was also in common usage before 1611. Here is Hotspur again (in *Henry IV Part 1*, III.i.127), reflecting on the horrible noise of a dry wheel grating on its axle:

> And that would set my teeth nothing on edge,
> Nothing so much as mincing poetry.

The biblical tradition can be traced back to Wycliffe, so King James is one voice among many, here.

Ezekiel 21:32 gives us another candidate:

Thou shalt be for fuel to the fire; thy blood shall be in the midst of the land; thou shalt be no more remembered

The expression *fuel to the fire* was well known before 1611. Poet Michael Drayton has a line *My blandishments were Fuell to that fire*—that was 1596. The modern idiom is *add fuel to the fire*, meaning 'make a bad problem worse.' *Fuel* is often replaced—we can add *oil*, *coals*, and other burnable things to a fire. And *fire* is often replaced, usually by *flame(s)*, but also by anything which has metaphorical heat: writers have added fuel to the *debate*, *fight, arguments,* and *controversy,* for example. Indeed, fuel can be added to anything controversial, such as a *legend, rumour,* or *claim.* Playful headlines, relying on the expression to motivate a rhyme, include *Manufacturers add fuel to the jobs pyre (Guardian,* 2000) and *Gas prices add fuel to the ire (Denver Post,* 2008).

Three expressions from these books do seem to be genuinely biblical in origin. Jeremiah 13:23 gives us this:

Can the Ethiopian change his skin, or the leopard his spots?

Geneva and Douai-Rheims have this phrasing too, and the expression quickly caught on. At the beginning of Shakespeare's *Richard II* (III.i.174), King Richard tries to stop an angry exchange between Mowbray and Bolingbroke. *Lions make leopards tame,* he tells Mowbray, who replies, *Yes, but not change his spots.* Four hundred years on, we find the image just as popular, and often adapted:

Can socialism change its spots?

Congress will not change its spots

Can Kennel Club change its spots over new dalmatian?

Can an old leopard change its silk pajamas?

The last mentioned is from the *New York Times* in 2009, when Hugh Hefner appointed a new editorial director to *Playboy.*

Wheels within wheels seems to derive from Ezekiel, though that expression doesn't actually appear in any translation. The writer (10:10) has a mysterious vision in which four cherubs each hold a wheel, but he has difficulty describing what he sees:

as if a wheel had been in the midst of a wheel.

All the early translations say something similar. People must have been impressed by Ezekiel's uncertainty, for the modern idiom has homed in on the notion of hidden, complex motives or plots. The first recorded use of *wheels within wheels* is in 1709.

Jeremiah 2:12 yields a particularly interesting example:

Be astonished, O ye heavens, at this, and be horribly afraid, be ye very desolate, saith the Lord.

It is echoed in Ezekiel (32:10), and *horribly afraid* is also used in Coverdale's Psalms (119:53), though not in King James (which has *Horror hath taken hold upon me*). None of the other translations of the time has anything like this, and there seem to be no other precedents. We find *be afraid and utterly confounded* in Geneva; *be afraid and abashed* in Bishops; and Douai-Rheims talks only of being *very desolate*. Something in the King James version obviously appealed to the popular ear, for it has come down to us not only as it stands but also in reduplicated form:

Be afraid, be horribly afraid.

I can't think of another biblical expression which reduplicates like that. Today, it is used as a mock-heroic warning. We find it introducing any dangerous enterprise, such as an ocean sailing trip or a journey to one of the Poles. Films and video games love it, especially if they're about monsters and demons. And newspapers make use of it, especially when they're advising their readers to fear the worst following the election to power of someone they disapprove of. Dropping off my son for his first term at a British university, I drove into the campus to be greeted by the sign: *PARENTS. Be afraid. Be very afraid.*

Idioms deriving from Daniel are all adaptations. *The writing is on the wall*, for example, derives from the account in 5:5 of a strange happening at the feast of King Belshazzar:

In the same hour came forth fingers of a man's hand, and wrote over against the candlestick upon the plaister of the wall of the king's palace: and the king saw the part of the hand that wrote.

It is a portent of doom (the king will be killed later that night), and the expression eventually entered the language in that sense: 'a sign of an impending decline or end.' *Is the writing on the wall for X?* is a popular media headline, where X can be a politician (coming up to an election), a company (in financial trouble), a football team (facing relegation), or anyone whose position is precarious. But nowhere in any translation do we find this exact phrase.

In 2:33 we read of a statue which had legs of iron, *his feet part of iron and part of clay.* All the early translations say something similar (though Wycliffe has the feet partly made *of earth*), but again, *feet of clay* doesn't appear in any translation. The first recorded usage by the *Oxford English Dictionary* is as late as 1814, in Byron's *Ode to Napoleon*. It became very popular in the twentieth century, titling many artistic works, from an early Cecil B. DeMille film (1924) to Terry Pratchett's nineteenth *Discworld* novel (1996). It also became a favourite phrase in the media, which became increasingly concerned with publicizing the failings or weaknesses of personalities. *Pop idol with feet of clay* ran the headline in the *Guardian*, shortly after the death of Michael Jackson in 2009.

In Daniel 6:12 the people ask the king:

Hast thou not signed a decree, that every man that shall ask a petition of any God or man within thirty days, save of thee, O king, shall be cast into the den of lions?

This is the usual biblical translation (though not in Wycliffe, which has *lake of lions*), and *den of lions* has come down to us in the sense of any threatening situation. Today the grammatical preference is for animate nouns to have a premodifying genitive (*my uncle's car* rather than *the car of my uncle*) and for inanimate nouns to have a postmodifying genitive (*the door of the house* rather than *the house's door*). This pattern became firmly established during the seventeenth century, which is why the usual modern phrasing is *lions' den* or *lion's den* (depending on how many entities are involved in the anticipated encounter).

Lions' den has become a fixed phrase, hardly ever varied or played with. We don't routinely find such expressions as *into the chickens' den*, or the like. This is not the case with the example from Hosea, which does yield a great deal of creativity. It appears in 8:7:

For they have sown the wind, and they shall reap the whirlwind

This vivid pair of metaphors, first found in Wycliffe, plainly impressed everyone, as it became the translation norm for this verse. The meaning is wide: from 'anything which rushes like a strong wind' it came to be applied to 'any violent or destructive agency' and thence to 'any confused or tumultuous state of affairs'. Today it is used of anyone who must suffer the consequences of reckless or bad behaviour.

It's another case which is commonly abbreviated to the last three words, as in the title of the *Star Trek* novel by David Mack (2007) or in this headline from the financial press *Speculators reap the whirlwind*. Many writers are a bit vague about what it is that is being reaped: we find people reaping *storms, tempests, hurricanes*, and *tornadoes*, for example. Occasionally, we find the whole expression used, but this is usually when the writer wants to adapt it to make a point—in this case, about the desirability of windfarms: *Sow the wind, reap cleaner energy!*

After Hosea there is a 10-book-long wilderness, and I was beginning to think my project would have no further Old Testament examples. Then, in the very last book, I found this (Malachi 4:1):

For, behold, the day cometh, that shall burn as an oven; and all the proud, yea, and all that do wickedly, shall be stubble: and the day that cometh shall burn them up, saith the Lord of hosts, that it shall leave them neither root nor branch.

Root nor branch. Other translations use this phrasing too. The modern expression is *root and branch*, used adjectivally to characterize the thorough or radical nature of some activity. To *destroy something root and branch* means 'destroy it totally'. It's an interesting example, because it's one of the few cases where we can say with some confidence how it became a part of general English usage.

In 1640, Londoners put together a petition for the abolition of episcopal government. It was called 'The Root and Branch Petition', from the phrasing in an early paragraph:

We therefore most humbly pray, and beseech this honourable assembly, the premises considered, that the said government with all its dependencies, roots and branches, may be abolished, and all laws in their behalf made void, and the government according to God's word may be rightly placed amongst us.

A similarly named bill was placed before Parliament the following year, and its supporters came to be known as the *root-and-branch party*. Since then, the phrase has been widely associated with political change. There's a strong collocation with *reform* and *review*, as in these headlines: *Root and branch reform call for the World Bank*; *Time for a root-and-branch review of public spending*. And, of course, the literal meaning has been borrowed back by genealogy sites and gardening centres, for whom *Root and Branch* provides an apposite name.

Interlude

With the New Testament we enter a new linguistic world. In the Old Testament, there are whole chapters, and even books, where plausible candidates for a role in modern English are conspicuous by their absence. With the four Gospels, the candidates appear in every chapter, sometimes even in a series of verses. The 'sayings of Jesus' echo down the centuries, permeating Christian intuition. People who try to live like Jesus will inevitably to some extent speak like him, and we might expect the King James New Testament to play its part in forming their linguistic intuitions. So, to avoid being swamped by examples, we need to distance ourselves from the language preferences of the practising Christian, and try to maintain the distinction between personal quotation and idiomatic common usage that I made in an earlier chapter (p. 89).

If a New Testament expression has genuinely entered English, we will expect to find it in the everyday speech or writing of native speakers who are only nominally Christian, not Christian, or who have no religious belief at all. It will be used outside a religious frame of reference, often with a change in meaning from its original biblical sense, and will be found frequently adapted to express a special (often playful) effect. Quotations, by contrast, are expressions which are used only in settings where the religious application is relevant, maintaining their original biblical sense, and sticking closely to the translators' language. A clear example of a verse which has resulted in a common idiom is Matthew 15:14 (see further, Chapter 22):

Let them alone: they be blind leaders of the blind. And if the blind lead the blind, both shall fall into the ditch.

A clear example of a verse which is known only as a quotation is Matthew 1:23:

Behold, a virgin shall be with child, and shall bring forth a son, and they shall call his name Emmanuel, which being interpreted is, God with us.

Other cases that are clearly quotation include most of the opening two chapters of Luke (the Christmas story) and the words of the Lord's Prayer (Matthew 6:9–13, Luke 11:2–4). The distinction works well enough, though there are some interesting cases which fall between these two types. A few expressions, for the most part used as quotations, have begun to attract a certain amount of playful adaptation. *Give us this day our daily blog*, for example, headed a 2010 report about the Pope's wish for the Catholic church to have more online presence.

Another difference with the Old Testament arises from the unique position held by Jesus in Christian belief. Until relatively recently, the law of blasphemy made it a serious offence to expose the Bible to contempt or ridicule. The law was primarily intended to protect (as an 1838 case put it) 'the tenets and beliefs of the Church of England', so the language of the King James Bible was of central concern. It is easy to see, therefore, how any popularization or adaptation of the words of the Bible could be interpreted as an offence. This would apply to both the Old and the New

Testament, but the words of Jesus would be especially sensitive to manipulation. It is difficult to imagine lines from the Lord's Prayer, for example, being altered simply to make a 'clever' effect. This reluctance to tamper with the sacred probably accounts for the lack of idiomatic development in the use of New Testament language between the seventeenth and nineteenth centuries. The reduction in force of the blasphemy laws since then has radically changed this situation. But there are still many passages held in such high emotional regard by believers that any attempt to manipulate them would result in an outcry. This is why so many well-known New Testament passages have remained under the heading of quotations. Although we will encounter the occasional daring adaptation on the internet, the effects obtained have not (as yet) influenced the character of the language as a whole.

A further difference with the Old Testament is that it makes no linguistic sense to treat the books of the New Testament as a sequence of entities. For example, the expression about 'a prophet not being honoured in his own country' turns up in three places:

Matthew 13:57 And they were offended in him. But Jesus said unto them, A prophet is not without honour, save in his own country, and in his own house.

Mark 6:4 But Jesus, said unto them, A prophet is not without honour, but in his own country, and among his own kin, and in his own house.

Luke 4:24 And he said, Verily I say unto you, No prophet is accepted in his own country.

Given the way the expression is used today, in several variant forms (see Chapter 35), it is not possible to identify a specific source in one or other of these texts. Rather, we must acknowledge that the texts have been recalled serendipitously to highlight a sentiment that has had great subsequent appeal. I worked my way through the Old Testament books in their traditional ordering, but I will use a thematic principle of organization for my New Testament chapters.

Chapter 22
Seeing the light

Innumerable New Testament quotations testify to the importance of the metaphor of light, continuing a theme which can be traced back to the very beginning of the biblical story (as illustrated in Chapter 2):

Matthew 5:14 Ye are the light of the world.

Matthew 4:16 The people which sat in darkness saw great light;

John 1:4 (and following verses) In him was life; and the life was the light of men

John 8:12 I am the light of the world.

Not surprisingly, then, a number of biblical light idioms have entered the language as a whole, one of the most widely used being from Matthew 5:15:

Neither do men light a candle, and put it under a bushel, but on a candlestick

All early translations use the phrasing, and it seems to have become proverbial by the sixteenth century. It must have been quite a vivid phrase. The vessel used as a bushel measure was large (holding eight gallons), so a light placed under it would certainly be invisible. It's surprising that the expression has continued in use, given the demise of the imperial measure system.

Many people who use the phrase nowadays, I imagine, have no idea what a *bushel* is—which is presumably why so many of the online citations replace it by another *b-* word: *barrel, bowl, box, bush, basket,* or *bucket* (though I rather like the one which bucked the trend and said *lampshade*).

Bushel is nonetheless the dominant word still, and virtually anyone or anything, it seems, can hide their light under one now. People: *Is David Cameron hiding his light under a bushel?*, asked one British newspaper of the Tory leader. Places: *Has Preston been hiding its light under a bushel?* was a commentator's query about the city's regeneration project. Organizations: *The markets are holding their light under a bushel,* said a financial report. Things: *The New Jaguar XJ is one car that can be described as hiding its light under a bushel* began a car advertisement.

The modern equivalent to the biblical candlestick seems to be a blog, according to several online enthusiasts, who cite the second part of the Matthew verse in recommending people to take up that medium of communication: *Let it shine in a blog.* On the other hand, not everyone is enamoured: *Don't hide your light under a browser.*

Another modern expression derives from the very next verse (Matthew 5:16):

Let your light so shine before men, that they may see your good works.

The phrasing is virtually the same in all early translations, and has entered modern English chiefly as advice to people with a particular ability or gift: *let your light shine.* The expression has been varied quite a bit—*let your light shine bright,... shine on,... shine in,* and the pronouns can change: *let my light shine,* and so on. It's unusual to see it used in non-religious settings, though it does tend to be trotted out when it's time for Christmas decorations. And it was once quite an effective slogan for a road safety campaign focusing on car headlamps.

The same Matthew sequence yields another example, in 15:14:

Let them alone: they be blind leaders of the blind. And if the blind lead the blind, both shall fall into the ditch.

Luke (6:39) repeats the sentiment, but phrases it rather more dramatically:

Can the blind lead the blind? shall they not both fall into the ditch?

Similar phrasing is found in all early translations (though Wycliffe has *if a blind man lead a blind man*). The meaning is clear, and hasn't altered over the centuries: disaster looms when someone incompetent or lacking in knowledge is in charge of someone equally incompetent or lacking in knowledge. The 'falling into the ditch' part is generally taken for granted. A surprising number of circumstances motivate the use of the expression. It's the standard locution to describe the frustrated behaviour of two people jointly poring over the poor expository level of an instruction manual—a regrettably all-too-common experience. In the public domain, it's the expression of choice when all levels of management in an enterprise seem to have failed; and we saw it used repeatedly during the banking crisis of 2008.

Blind people have partially reclaimed the expression: it's a popular phrase to describe the operation of self-help groups for the visually impaired. But the general usage remains resolutely figurative. The repeated use of *blind* makes it resistant to playful adaptation, though we do occasionally find such lines as *the blind leading the clueless* or *the blind leading the banned*. The expression received an unexpected boost when Mick Jagger used it as a song title in the movie *Alfie*:

> Like the blind leading the blind,
> After the wine, the tears they are gushing,
> Just like the blind leading the blind,
> Time after time, You won't let the love in.

Elsewhere in the media, a somewhat desperate brainstorming for TV episode titles must have accounted for both *the blind leading the blonde* and *the blonde leading the blind*.

John 5:35 gives us another popular expression:

He was a burning and a shining light

Either collocation might have come down to us. In the event, it wasn't *burning light* but *shining light*, used in several early translations (though not in Geneva, which has *candle*, or Wycliffe, which has *lantern*), which won the day. The chief modern sense, 'a person of excellence in a particular context', has made it a favourite expression of obituary columnists. And some living people seem to particularly attract it: *Obama a shining light for us too*, said a Canadian newspaper at the end of 2008.

The expression is no longer restricted to people, however. Institutions, such as schools or university departments, which achieve above-average standards of excellence are likely to be called *shining lights*. Thus, *Newcastle Central Library a shining light of the North East*, said a newspaper reporting Andrew Motion, when the new facility was opened there in 2009. So are businesses. *Queensland chocolate factory a shining light in the industry*, said an Australian paper (because of its policy to eradicate child slave labour in the source countries). A company that continued to make profits in 2009 was called *a shining light in the darkness of the recession.* The arts can help too. *Music a 'shining light' in dark times,* said the *Irish Times,* reporting the opening of an Irish music festival the same year.

Light is a metaphor for understanding and knowing, and so it is perhaps appropriate to include in this chapter a highly productive expression, from Luke 23:34:

Father, forgive them; for they know not what they do.

All the early translations use this syntax, though the earliest ones have *wot* for *know.* Doubtless it is the monosyllabic simplicity of the expression which has given it such widespread appeal. Today, we can find a veritable conjugation of verbs:

I know not what I do [a line in various pop love songs]

You know not what you do [Cassius to Brutus, *Julius Caesar*, III.i.232]

Energy secretary knows not what he does [headline]

She knows not what she does [title of an episode of Australian TV series *The Strip*, 2002]

The government knows not what it does [headline]

We know not what we do in Afghanistan [headline]

You know not what you do [anti-EU politician to referendum voters]

Online pirates know not what they do [headline]

A metaphor of seeing has also proved highly productive, from 1 Corinthians 13:12:

For now we see through a glass, darkly; but then face to face

Thousands of books, articles, and headlines have used it as a title, in all kinds of genres. *Olympic Games show China through a glass, darkly,* said the *Times* in 2008, discussing the restrictions imposed on foreign journalists. Exhibitions on painting, sculpture, and photography love it. *The past, through a glass darkly*, said the *Guardian*, reporting a Turner Prize winner who uses a lot of glass in his work. The most famous title of all, I suppose, is Ingmar Bergman's 1961 film.

The appeal of the expression has been so great that it's surprising to see it varied at all. The same phrasing is shared by Geneva, and the other early variants have had negligible influence: Tyndale and Bishops have *we see in a glass, even in a dark speaking*; Douai-Rheims has... *in a dark manner*. But we do nonetheless find people today seeing darkly through *veils, mirrors, lenses*, and other optical devices. *Mirror* shows the influence of Wycliffe, who has *and we see now by a mirror in darkness*. A nice variant appeared in an article on research into the Shroud of Turin: *Seeing through a shroud, darkly*.

By contrast, the *mote* metaphor from Matthew 7:3 (repeated in Luke 6:41) has had little influence outside a religious setting:

And why beholdest thou the mote that is in thy brother's eye, but considerest not the beam that is in thine own eye?

It appears in all the early translations, and later usage has kept the original meaning: 'a minor fault observed in another person by those who ignore a greater fault in themselves.' Outside a religious frame of reference, literary and rhetorical settings predominate, such as Theodore Roosevelt's powerful use of the expression in his speech 'On human rights in foreign policy' in 1904: *There must be no effort made to remove the mote from our brother's eye if we refuse to remove the beam from our own. Mote* is such an unusual word that it's hardly ever used without that sort of full accompanying context; we don't find people saying such things as *Your problem is your mote.*

Matthew 16:3 provides the final example for this chapter:

O ye hypocrites, ye can discern the face of the sky; but can ye not discern the signs of the times?

Signs of the times is in all the early translations except Wycliffe (who has *the tokens of times*), and it has retained its meaning over the years: 'indications of current trends'. Since the early twentieth century, the singular form has been popular: *a sign of the times*. It has kept its strong biblical associations, being used as the name of several religious publications, but its present-day use is predominantly secular, usually heard as an everyday comment, mildly pejorative in character, about changes taking place in society. The usage is well established: Thomas Carlyle wrote an essay under this heading in 1829.

The many meanings of the word *sign* have led to an extraordinary diversity of applications. The signage industry has happily adopted it for the names of magazines and companies. *Signs of the Times* is the name of one such firm which supplies bespoke house signs, street signs, letterboxes, commemorative plaques, and street furniture. Newspapers which have *Times* in their masthead also readily adopt it. *The Times* of London, for example, capitalizes on the fruitful wordplay with its 'Signs of the Times' competitions to find the most humorous public signage.

Other meanings of *sign* compete. The expression has been used in relation to advertising, medical symptoms, climate change, crop circles, deaf sign language, astrology (modern interpretations of the zodiac), autograph collections, and semiotics (the science of signs). The email @ symbol has been called 'a sign of the times'.

Many words rhyme with *sign*—a fact which has not gone unnoticed by the copywriters wanting to catch a reader's eye. Here's a small selection, each with a brief contextual gloss:

wines of the times [the latest vintages]

whine of the times [a newspaper agony column]

shine of the times [a new hair-care product; also a new LED indicator light]

spine of the times [the latest treatment for back pain]

swine of the times [on the swine flu virus]

and, a favourite for any linguist:

Strine of the times [changes in Australian English].

Chapter 23
Eyes, ears, cheeks

The parts of the body have yielded a few modern idioms, though it isn't always clear whether they originate in a Bible translation. The problem is clearly illustrated with 1 Corinthians 2:9:

Eye hath not seen, nor ear heard, neither have entered into the heart of man, the things which God hath prepared for them that love him.

Shakespeare was the first I'm aware of to dare to play with this verse, when Bottom recounts his dream in *A Midsummer Night's Dream* (IV.i.209):

The eye of man hath not heard, the ear of man hath not seen, man's hand is not able to taste, his tongue to conceive, nor his heart to report what my dream was!

Many others took up the conceit, though whether the writer is following the Bible or Shakespeare usually isn't clear. What is Byron doing, for example, when he writes in a letter (9 December 1811) about a theatre visit at the Haymarket?

Oh, Captain! eye hath not seen, ear hath not heard, nor can the heart of man conceive to-night's performance.

Is this Shakespeare or King James talking? None of the early translations have *conceive*. It seems to be a mixture of both.

Outside of the religious setting we encounter the sentence more often in truncated form, with one or other of the *hath* phrases used alone. Here is a writer using the *ear* element. Thomas Carlyle in *Past and present* (1843, Chapter 12) talks of

The unborn Ages; the old Graves, with their long-mouldering dust, the very tears that wetted it now all dry,—do not these speak to thee, what ear hath not heard?

And a more modern voice, in *Time* (1926), begins an article about an impending Arctic expedition using the *eye* element:

There remains to this day a place on earth which eye hath not seen.

The complex rhetoric of the original tends to restrict modern adaptations to literary contexts.

A similar uncertainty over sources arises in 1 Corinthians 15:52:

In a moment, in the twinkling of an eye, at the last trump

Should I include *in the twinkling of an eye* in this book? All the early translations use it, but so do many other works, the earliest *Oxford English Dictionary* citation dating from 1303. The construction was syntactically various: we find *in a twinkling...*, *with a twinkling...*, and *with the twinkling...*, as well as the King James usage, and this suggests the expression was widely used. It's one of those cases which make it impossible ever to decide exactly how much influence biblical translations had on English—though, thanks to its use in Handel's *Messiah* ('The trumpet shall sound'), we must surely attribute some of our present-day awareness of the phrase to a biblical source.

Adaptations certainly abound, whatever the source. An article on quantum teleportation (such as when people are 'beamed up' in *Star Trek*) was headed *In the twinkling of an ion*. One on obsolescence in computers was called *In the twinkling of an IT*. A review of a production of Shakespeare's *A Winter's Tale* talked about *the twinkling of an act-break*—referring to the time-jump of sixteen years which takes place in the middle of the play. Astronomers, used to huge time-frames, sometimes play with the phrase: *In the twinkling of a million years or so*. And several creative writers have noticed the possible pun: *We shall be changed in the twinkling of an 'I'*.

The problem of provenance arises again with 2 Timothy 4:3:

For the time will come when they will not endure sound doctrine; but after their own lusts shall they heap to themselves teachers, having itching ears.

In the sixteenth century we find *itching* used figuratively with several body parts. Brutus accuses Cassius of having an *itching palm* in Shakespeare's *Julius Caesar* (IV.iii.10). Sir Philip Sidney observes, in *An Apology for Poetry* (published in 1595, folio G2v), *there is nothing of so sacred a majesty but that an itching tongue may rub itself upon it*. An *itching elbow* was used of those who had a passion for gambling. And all the early Bible translations collocate *itch* and *ears*, expressing the idea of a craving to hear something new, or something that doesn't require any change of heart. There's no nonbiblical example in the early *Oxford English Dictionary* citations, but this may be fortuitous.

Today the phrase tends to be used more with reference to casual or trivial subject matter. People who like to hear the latest gossip are said to have *itching ears*, as are those who listen in surreptitiously to other people's conversation. *Watch out—itching ears*, someone might say, having noticed an unwanted listener. However, the negative sense is these days being balanced by a positive sense of *itching* meaning 'desiring' (as in *my ears are itching to hear that piece of music again*). An opinion column in 2009 was headed *Obama tickles the world's itching ears* (in his speeches). The writer was suggesting that the world was listening enthusiastically. There's thus a certain ambiguity in the expression now.

Biblical references to other parts of the body have on the whole had a limited impact on modern English. There are two relevant mentions of *hair*, which vary little in the early translations:

Luke 21:18 But there shall not an hair of your head perish.

Matthew 10:30 But the very hairs of your head are all numbered.

Both have some present-day use, especially when people talk about *not hurting* or *harming a hair of your head*. The Matthew expression is less often encountered, apart from in hair-care literature, but I did find one adaptation heading an article on disease checks in poultry: *The very hens in your flock are all numbered.*

The *hands* have two relevant references also:

Matthew 6:3 But when thou doest alms, let not thy left hand know what thy right hand doeth:

Matthew 27:24...he [Pilate] took water, and washed his hands before the multitude, saying, I am innocent of the blood of this just person.

Both expressions appear in all the early translations, and have come down to us with hardly any change. The first is of course no longer restricted to alms-giving. Any organization that gives conflicting advice, or functions inconsistently, is likely to attract the comment, either in its full form (such as *the left hand's no idea what the right hand's doing*) or abbreviated (*it's a case of left hand–right hand*). The order of elements is often reversed as *right hand... left hand*. Adaptations are unusual, but not impossible, as shown by a clever piece in 2009 from BBC Radio Oxford, using the one-sided paralysis that often follows a stroke to publicize Stroke Awareness Month: *The right hand doesn't know what the left is doing.*

The other *hands* expression is very common: people say they *wash their hands of* something, meaning they disown personal responsibility for it, or refuse to have any further connection with it. All pronouns and tense forms are used. The search engines also display several examples of the type *he washed his hand*, in the singular, which is strange; it may be a predominantly non-native speaker usage. It's difficult to tell, on the anonymous internet. But, singular or plural, this is one of the few biblical idioms where there is no playful adaptation—at least, none that I've yet found.

There are two cases where the body as a whole has introduced a modern phrase. One is in Matthew 16:17, when Jesus praises Simon for knowing who he is:

flesh and blood hath not revealed it unto thee, but my Father which is in heaven.

Flesh and blood is in all the sixteenth-century translations, and indeed well predates them, for the phrase can be found in the Old English Gospels and in the devotional literature which followed them. From its original sense ('human beings'), it developed several general meanings—'close relatives' (*they're my own flesh and blood*)—as well as some particular senses ('bodily form', 'affected by human feelings and weaknesses'). *Men are flesh and blood*, says Shakespeare's Julius Caesar dismissively, talking about everyone bar himself (*Julius Caesar*, III.i.67). All these senses are found today.

The other instance is in Philippians 3:21:

[Christ] shall change our vile body, that it may be fashioned like unto his glorious body

The expression is in several translations, though not Wycliffe (who has *the body of our meekness*) or Douai-Rheims (*the body of our lowness*). I doubt if our present-day awareness of the phrase would be profound if it hadn't been for Evelyn Waugh's highly successful 1930 novel about decadent London high society *Vile Bodies*. Certainly, it's the plural form (found in Tyndale) which we now encounter most often when people present the human body in art. Several photographic exhibitions have attracted the phrase as a title—not to mention several pornographic sites.

The most productive biblical expression in the 'body' category comes from Matthew 5:39 (echoed in Luke 6:29):

But I say unto you, That ye resist not evil: but whosoever shall smite thee on thy right cheek, turn to him the other also.

There's no question about this one coming from the Bible. It's first recorded in all the early translations (though Wycliffe has *show* rather than *turn*), and the sense—offering no retaliation for an insult or injury—hasn't changed over the centuries. Strangely, the *Oxford English Dictionary* has citations dating only from 1850, but I expect earlier ones will emerge in due course. It's certainly been a highly popular turn of phrase in recent times, and I can't imagine this wasn't the case in the seventeenth and eighteenth centuries also.

It appears in relation to all kinds of confrontation, often in a reduced form as *turn the other cheek*. In football, for example, we find it used to answer the question of how David Beckham should deal with offensive fans. Not all footballers would agree: the tough-tackling Paddy Crerand called his autobiography *Never*

Turn the Other Cheek (2007). Nor would cowboys agree. The title of the spaghetti western *Viva La Muerte…Tua!* (1971) was translated into English as *Don't Turn the Other Cheek*. Perhaps footballers and cowboys need to read Suzette Haden Elgin's book, *How to Turn the Other Cheek and Still Survive in Today's World* (1997). Perhaps we all do.

The expression turns up in some extraordinary contexts. A 2007 *Times* article on the changes in cheek-kissing patterns in France resulted in this headline: *French unsure when to turn the other cheek*. And the phonetic similarity of *cheek to* other English words has generated a swathe of puns:

Turn the Other Chick (fantasy novel by Esther Friesner, 2004)

Turn the Other Sheik (adult novel by Troy Conway, 1970)

Turn the other chic (ad for a fashionable new mobile phone)

Turn the Other Check (article about effective marketing)

Turn the Other Chico (article about change in the town of Chico, CA)

This is a respectable book, so I will leave to your imagination the punning use of this phrase when *cheek* is made to refer to a different part of human anatomy.

Chapter 24
Speaking, shouting, wailing, writing

The Gospel of John begins with a powerful linguistic metaphor: *In the beginning was the Word*. The expression has generated countless imitations. Some make a serious point: *In the beginning was the Big Bang*. Others make a historical point about a particular area of knowledge: *In the beginning was the IBM card* (in computing); *In the beginning was the worm* (in zoology). Others are just trying to be funny: *In the beginning was the verb/the vowel/the joke*.

The dramatic central moment of John's opening chapter, *And the Word was made flesh* (1:14), hasn't escaped adaptation. The biblical theme is sometimes present, as in a 2005 article in the *Economist* about the project to scan the Codex Sinaiticus using a technique called hyperspectral imaging: *And the Word was made flash*. But usually we find the expression used with reference to language as a whole, especially in written form. *And the word was made fresh* headed a report on neologisms entering the English language. *And the word was made electronic* was talking about the arrival of the Kindle reader. The *Washington Post* ran a piece in 1994 on the financial success of large-scale book festivals: *And the word was made*. Of course, the expression was a gift for copywriters when Microsoft's computer program *Word* arrived in the 1980s, so much so that it sounds clichéd when we encounter it in that context now. Indeed, the limited possibilities for adapting the expression seem to have made it far less popular these days.

The same is true of Matthew 24:35 (echoed in Mark 13:31):

Heaven and earth shall pass away, but my words shall not pass away.

Just a few writers have played with the second part of the expression, replacing *words* by another term that identifies their interest. We find romantic expressions such as *love* and *marriage*, and also the not quite so romantic, illustrated by the man who wrote glumly... *but my marriages shall not pass away.* Artists quite like the expression because of its emphasis on permanence:... *but my paintings shall not pass away.* Even people who are proud of their domestic creativity use it:... *but my pancakes shall not pass away.* A financial analyst, writing in 2009 when public criticism of city salaries was at its height, affirmed belligerently:... *but my bonus shall not pass away.*

There are several 'speaking' expressions in the New Testament, but few have been influential. *Speak in tongues* (Acts 2:4 has *speak with other tongues*), for example, is widely used, but only in relation to the charismatic phenomenon known as *glossolalia*. Other religious formulations are found, such as *listening, praying, talking,* even *whistling in tongues,* but again, always within a religious frame of reference. Very rarely do we see the expression adapted for other contexts: an example is *programming in tongues,* referring to different computer languages.

Rather more influential is this usage in Matthew 10:27:

What I tell you in darkness, that speak ye in light: and what ye hear in the ear, that preach ye upon the housetops.

Luke (12:3) is similar, except that it ends *shall be proclaimed upon the housetops*. The *housetops* of the King James version is found also in Tyndale and Douai-Rheims. Wycliffe, Bishops, and Geneva have the much less vivid *houses*. The collocations vary somewhat. We can also *declare, cry,* or *shout it on* or *from* the *housetops* or *rooftops*. *Shout* is by far the commonest choice. The *it* is optional in the earliest references, but is hardly ever omitted today. The noun is usually plural, though we do find the occasional singular *housetop/rooftop*. The original meaning ('publicly and forcefully proclaim something') has stayed, over the centuries, but a secondary meaning has emerged: 'blab about something to everyone.' In this latter sense, we can go around *shouting something from the rooftops* without actually using a very loud voice.

There's a lack of references in the *Oxford English Dictionary* until 1870, where the expression is listed in Brewer's *Dictionary of Phrase and Fable*—which suggests it must have been around for an appreciable time before that. Since then, it has increased its range of collocations. Today we can find people *screaming, yelping, howling, bellowing, roaring, yelling, singing*—virtually any verb of noisy communication—*from the rooftops*. Indeed, not only 'noisy': some cautious announcements use an oxymoron and *whisper from the housetops*.

The expression still has a strong association with religious expression. It's a common title for books and articles on preaching—whether by theists or equally evangelical atheists. Playfulness is unusual, though its rarity makes it quite effective when it appears. Two examples. *Shout it from the rooftops* headed an announcement that a Flemish company was encouraging businesses to generate electricity using rooftop solar panels. And a company that specializes in planting grass and other greenery on the tops of houses told us all to *Sprout it from the rooftops*.

There's another fruitful speaking expression in Matthew—if 'speaking' is the right word. The modern expression is *weeping and wailing and gnashing of teeth*, but that exact combination is nowhere to be found in the Bible. Rather, we get various pairings all expressing the idea of total misery. Matthew provides us with *weeping and gnashing of teeth* (8:12, 22:13) as well as *wailing and gnashing of teeth* (13:42, 50), and the two expressions are perhaps reinforced by the *weeping, and wailing* of Esther (4:3) in the Old Testament. The words are found in all the translations, though Wycliffe has *grinding* or *biting together* instead of *gnashing*. Somehow, a synthesis of all three verbs took place, resulting in the full form of the modern expression. 'Choose any two out of three' is still an option, however. We find *weeping and wailing* most commonly, but also *weeping and gnashing* and *wailing and gnashing*. Reversing those word orders is rare.

It's unusual today to see people giving any of these expressions their original semantic force. Rather, they are used hyperbolically. Sometimes quite minor (in the great scheme of things) events elicit the description, such as when a trip to the seaside is cancelled because of the weather. There's usually an ironic or jocular intent, which can often be seen in a manipulation of the original phrasing. People replace *teeth* by something dentally more specific, such as *molars*, *incisors*, or *expensive dental work*. Or they leave teeth behind altogether, as happened in these instances:

> there will be a wailing and gnashing of forks [because a favourite restaurant is closing]
>
> there will be a weeping, wailing, and gnashing of gears [describing the start of a motor-racing Grand Prix]
>
> there will be a digital weeping, wailing, and gnashing of circuits [as 2000 approached, and people anticipated global computer meltdown because of the millennial calendar change]

Woe is me! might be the plaint of anyone weeping and wailing. This unusual word order is found several times in King James, occurring first in Psalms 120:5:

Woe is me, that I sojourn in Mesech, that I dwell in the tents of Kedar!

The same words are in Coverdale, and also in Douai-Rheims, but the other translations lack the succinctness: Bishops *woe be unto me*; Geneva *woe is to me* (Wycliffe has *Alas to me*). Job uses a similar expression (10:15: *If I be wicked, woe unto me*), but that version never caught on, perhaps because 'woe to come' is less urgent than 'woe present'. *Woe is me* is often said to be a biblical phrase. In fact it merely reflects a usage that is found throughout Old English. *Woe* was one of the first words to be recorded in the English language (in the eighth-century *Corpus* glossary), and *wā bið þǽm* ('woe be to them') is found, for example, in *Beowulf* (line 183).

We might include two other expressions in this 'language' chapter. One is in 1 Timothy 4:7:

But refuse profane and old wives' fables

All the early translations talk about *old wives' fables*, apart from Wycliffe, who has *old women's fables*, and *fables* continued to be used in this way into the 1700s. But by the end of the sixteenth century there was an alternative expression, *old wives' tales*, and this is the one that is chiefly used today. It's unclear whether the *tales* version was directly influenced by the Bible or whether it was an independent development. *Old wives* (without any derogatory force) and *tales* are both mentioned in Anglo-Saxon texts, so it would have been natural to bring them together. (Interestingly, in the sixteenth century, an *old woman's tale* was also known as a *Canterbury tale*.)

The other is in John 19:22, at the point when Pilate replies to critics of his description of Jesus as *King of the Jews*:

What I have written I have written.

This is always used as a quotation, but it can turn up in some unexpected places. Several authors have used it as part of their response to criticism of their work. Anthony Burgess was one. In 1986, he wrote an essay called 'A clockwork orange resucked' (1986), in which he explains (and castigates) his American publishers and Stanley Kubrick for omitting the final chapter of the novel. He concludes by saying that, whether the last chapter works or not, *'What I have written, I have written'. We can destroy what we have written but we cannot unwrite it.*

Chapter 25
Shaking, turning, moving

Several 'movement' metaphors have come down to us from the New Testament. Mark 6:11 gives us this:

> And whosoever shall not receive you, nor hear you, when ye depart thence, shake off the dust under your feet for a testimony against them.

To *shake (off) the dust from (under) one's feet* is found in the Bible translations which date from Anglo-Saxon times, with very little variation (apart from Wycliffe, who has *powder* for *dust*). Today, the reference to *feet* is either redundant or irrelevant, for the meaning has developed into 'leave an undesirable situation behind', regardless of whether we leave it by walking or in some other way. The geographical setting remains when we encounter such usages as *I shook off the dust of Glasgow and set out for Edinburgh*. But the vast majority of modern instances have no such regional implication.

Virtually anything can have the dust shaken off it. All that's needed is a radical change. A new film adaptation of *Pride and Prejudice* was said *to shake the dust off the novel*. The entities don't have to be physical: we find people, organizations, or countries shaking off the dust of *colonialism, exile, poverty, complacency, idleness*, and *failure*. A website for women poets in India proved successful, and the report began: *Women writers shake off the dust of neglect*. A stock-market recovery was greeted with *US markets shake off the dust of losing streak*. We can use the idiom for times too: *we need to shake off the dust of winter*.

It isn't always clear whether the more literal 'shaking off of dust' has been influenced by the biblical idiom or not. If a museum has a period of renovation, or puts some artefacts on display after keeping them hidden for a long time, the announcement might well use this phrasing. *Berlin's scientific treasure-house shakes off the dust* was one such announcement in 2004. *Maxol's link with Marks & Spencer set to shake the dust off oil company promotional schemes* was another. *Shake off*, meaning 'get rid of with an effort', long predates the Bible era. The verb *shake* is Anglo-Saxon. This may well be a separate development.

Galatians 5:4 gives us this:

Christ is become of no effect unto you, whosoever of you are justified by the law; ye are fallen from grace.

The phrase *fallen from grace* was popular, with most early translations using it, and it has stayed in regular use, though without the theological overtones. I'm amazed at how many pop songs have used it as a title (at least ten), and it is found in films, books, and other art forms. The media love it as a byline whenever someone famous is rocked by scandal, drops status, or loses a job—politicians, footballers, filmstars, company bosses, and so on.

Acts 17:6 gives us this:

These that have turned the world upside down are come hither also.

Today we say *turn the world upside down* without thinking, but it wasn't a natural expression in the sixteenth century. Wycliffe translates the sentiment as *move the world*; Tyndale and Bishops as *trouble the world*; Geneva as *subverted the state of the world*; Douai-Rheims as *set the city in an uproar*. The explanation lies in the curious etymology of *upside-down*. It was originally (in early Middle English) *up-swa-down*, i.e. 'up so down', meaning 'up as if down', and spelled in various ways, such as *upsadoun* and *upsedoun*. People evidently had trouble making sense of this, so over the years they altered it to something more intelligible. We find *up-set-down* and, gradually during the sixteenth century, *upside-down*. The early Bible translations use it sporadically, but by 1611 it must have been the norm. It appears half a dozen times in King James, only in this form.

Acts also gives us *no small stir* (12:18, and also 19:23):

Now as soon as it was day, there was no small stir among the soldiers, what was become of Peter.

This is one of the few cases where we can say with some certainty that we are dealing with a King James phrase. The other early translations hardly use it. Tyndale and Bishops have *no little ado*; Wycliffe has *not little troubling* and *a great troubling*; Geneva has *no small trouble*. Douai-Rheims does use it in 12:18 but has *no small disturbance* in 19:23. The *Oxford English Dictionary* first recorded usage outside the Bible is 1671: *There are many things we make no small stir about*. The phrase has a rather literary ring to it today.

Also somewhat literary is the phrase that comes from Matthew 21:21:

If ye have faith, and doubt not, ye shall not only do this which is done to the fig tree, but also if ye shall say unto this mountain, Be thou removed, and be thou cast into the sea; it shall be done.

It was a paraphrase of this verse which eventually entered English: *faith can move mountains* or *a mountain*. The same sort of language is in all the translations of the time, apart from Wycliffe, who talks about faith moving a *hill*, and it is echoed by St Paul (in 1 Corinthians 13:2). Outside of the religious context, the expression is used to affirm belief in the ability of someone or some group to get a difficult task done. It was being used with that general meaning as early as the sixteenth century, and its enduring popularity can be judged by the success of the pop song *Faith can move mountains* in 1952–3. Nat King Cole, Johnny Ray, and Jimmy Young all had versions of it, and all did well in the charts.

Today it is not only faith that can move mountains. *Love, prayer, hope, words, dreams*, and other such notions are all said to do so. *A united front* will do so, according to one political commentator. *Confidence* will too, according to a supporter of a football club languishing at the bottom of a league. The expression gets a neat syntactic twist in a *Guardian* report in 2009 about the social impact of buying Fairtrade goods: *Produce sold in good faith can move mountains.* The physical attribute of mountains is echoed in the headline about an American congregation that wanted to move its church building to a new location: *They say that faith can move mountains, but can it move a church?*

Another paraphrase has taken place with Matthew 5:41:

And whosoever shall compel thee to go a mile, go with him twain.

Go with him twain. The expression is shared with Tyndale, Geneva, and Bishops; Douai-Rheims has *go with him other two*; Wycliffe rather reduces the force by having *a thousand paces* instead of *a mile*, so that *other twain* doesn't seem to add very much. Today we say *go* (or *walk* or *travel*) *the second* or *extra mile*. The core sense is to expend more effort in performing an activity or achieving some goal than is strictly necessary, especially as a sign of goodwill. The earliest *Oxford English Dictionary* reference is quite late: 1854.

A great deal of movement is acknowledged in the parable of the prodigal son (Luke 15:13), and one part of it contains a modern expression:

And not many days after the younger son gathered all together, and took his journey into a far country, and there wasted his substance with riotous living.

Tyndale, Geneva, and Bishops all use the phrase: Douai-Rheims keeps the collocation but alters the grammar (*living riotously*); only Wycliffe does something different (*living lecherously*). However, this is not a biblical original; the phrase is found in English much earlier. *Riotous* entered the language from French in the early fourteenth century, and by 1389, in the ordinances of the Carpenters' Guild of Norwich, sent to King Richard II, we read:

if any brother or sister of this gilde falle in any meschef or pouert, be godis sendyng, or be any chaunce of the werld, and nat be his owne folye ne ryotous lyuyng, and he may nought withe his craft ne with his godis helpen him self, he shal han, of eueri brother and sister of this gilde, eueri woke, a ferthyng, lestyng his meschif.

(if any brother or sister of this guild fall into any misfortune or poverty, through an act of God, or through any vicissitude of the world, and not through his own folly or riotous living, and is unable to help himself using his skills or goods, he shall have, from every brother and sister of this guild, every week, a farthing, reducing his misfortune.)

Once again, we see the Bible as a medium through which an expression was popularized. References to its use in the parable increase greatly after 1611, and it begins to be found in nonbiblical literary settings. It is a running head in Tobias Smollett's *Humphry Clinker* (1771), for example.

The movement of stars, described in Jude 1:13, has provided another modern expression:

Raging waves of the sea, foaming out their own shame; wandering stars, to whom is reserved the blackness of darkness for ever.

Apart from Wycliffe, who has *erring stars* (following the Latin *stellae errantes*), the early translations agree on *wandering stars*. For many people, the collocation was fixed in their mind for ever by filmstar Lee Marvin in 1969, whose recording of 'I was born under a wandering star' was a surprise hit. But the expression had already achieved a wide range of applications. It has a certain romantic image, and thus appears quite often as the name of a company selling (if the *star* element is primary) jewellery or the arts, or (if the *wandering* element is primary) holidays or relationships (such as contact agencies). The personification of *star* has led to the expression being used in articles about footballers who have played for several clubs, or pop stars who have homes in several countries. After all this, it's something of a relief to find it also being used in its original physical context as the name of a company that deals in meteorite fragments.

Luke (4:8) gives us a further dynamic expression:

Get thee behind me, Satan.

The utterance is repeated in Matthew (16:23) and Mark (8:33), when Jesus rebukes Peter. The King James is the only version that has this phrasing and keeps the same words in all three texts. Others vary. We find, in various combinations, *go after me*, *go behind me*, *come after me*, and *hence from me*, none of which have had the same appeal. Today we find the expression, often without the *thee*, in a remarkable range of settings. The temptation theme has given it iconic status in the world of romance, especially in song, thanks mainly to Irving Berlin's lyrics:

Get thee behind me, Satan
I want to resist
But the moon is low and I can't say no
Get thee behind me

not least as sung by Ella Fitzgerald. But temptation is everywhere, in sales catalogues, ice-cream parlours, and restaurant menus, so it is widely heard. And seen. It is a favourite T-shirt motif. The underlying message, to reject something that is bad, allows the expression to appear with the name replaced: *Get thee behind me, N*—where *N* can be a friend, a sales assistant, or anyone offering something that is naughty but nice. Political rhetoric can be treated in the same way, where *N* is the persuasive politician. Sometimes there is an agenda. *Get thee behind me, Santa* argues for a less material Christmas—with nice effect, when we recognize the anagram.

Personifications are allowed too. Among the things that have been addressed in this way are fat, depression, and stains (in an advertisement for cleaning fluid). *Get thee behind me, Facebook* headed a news item in 2009, when a bishop warned of the dangers of social networking. A neat pun accompanied a piece by someone who didn't like wheat gluten meat substitute: *Get thee behind me, seitan.*

Jocular variants of the preposition are also common. *Get thee before me, Satan* is the riposte of choice when entering the ice-cream parlour. Political manoeuvring leads to such expressions as *Get thee to the left of me.* And Paul Magrs, in his black comedy *Hell's Belles* (2009), includes a horror movie called *Get thee inside me, Satan.* The mind boggles.

Chapter 26
Many and few, first and last

We might not expect expressions of quantity, being so commonplace in everyday language, to be much affected by biblical usage. But it is the rhetorical context in which they are used which has appealed to people down the ages. Take Matthew 22:14:

For many are called, but few are chosen.

The succinctness and rhetorical balance of this statement, found with only minor variations in all the early translations, have made it a memorable expression. It might be the motto for this book—or for any project which has to make a selection from candidate entries. And certainly today, we find it most often used in relation to domains where choices have to be made, such as the number of people applying for a particular job or entry into a particular course. Not only people are called. The expression once headed a news interview with the editor of the *Oxford Book of Quotations*, whose main problem (as in the present book) was to decide what to include and what to exclude. Rather cheekily, in view of the creation/evolution debate, it was used in one scientific journal to headline a study of natural selection.

Adaptations of the second element are very common. *Many are called, but...*

few are choosing [on the shortage of candidates for the priesthood]
few are called back [on getting an audition in the performing arts]
few are frozen [on quality checks in retail frozen foods]
few are at their desks [an established jocular aphorism]

Less often the first element is affected. *Many apply* [for jobs] *but few are chosen. Many are culled but few are chosen* [from competition entries]. *Many are cold but few are chosen* [ideas for new kinds of ice-cream].

Many turns up again in Mark 5:9:

My name is Legion: for we are many.

This use of *Legion*, to name a demon, is found in Tyndale and all later translations, with hardly any variation in the syntax. (Wycliffe is the exception, with the reverse word order: *A legion is my name.*) The name has had an enormous appeal in popular culture, doubtless because the notion of an army of demons attracts the fantasy mentality which has fuelled so many contemporary films, novels, comics, songs, and video games. Innumerable beings have been called *Legion*, typically shown with multiple personalities, identities, or powers, and many of them use the expression as their character note.

The expression has also found several homes on the internet. A computer virus used the name, and the *many* element has appealed to those who engage in the production of internet spam. Huge numbers of messages of the form 'X is Legion, for we are many' are in circulation, some of them revoltingly obscene. And there is a predilection for the phrasing 'My name is X, for we are many'. *My name is anonymous, for we are many* illustrates the genre. Often one searches in vain for any kind of sense behind the usage. In many instances, it seems to be no more than a piece of language play, motivated by the desire to be different or to shock. Biblical allusions, it appears, turn up in some very strange places. Having said that, there's something rather appropriate about this particular demon causing internet havoc.

A contrastive rhetorical power is also seen in Matthew 20:16:

So the last shall be first, and the first last

The expression is echoed in Matthew 19:30, and also in Mark 9:35 and 10:31, and is in all the translations. The situation being described is a very specific one, and this, along with the balanced rhetorical reversal (an example of the figure of speech known chiasmus), we might think would make it difficult for the expression to appear in general use. But that is to underestimate popular linguistic ingenuity.

And the first shall be last said an online article, when the crew of *Apollo 7* (NASA's first manned mission in 1968) were honoured in 2008 with the space agency's highest award, the NASA Distinguished Service Medal. *And the first shall be last as the economic boom fades in New England*, said the *Boston Globe* in 1990, referring to the region as the first to be permanently settled by Europeans. *The first shall be last*, claimed a 2005 research study, reporting that participants in *American Idol* who appear towards the end of the competition do better than those who perform at the beginning. *The first shall be last* described one of the events held at London's Tate Modern in the 2008 Fluxus Olympiad—a bicycle race in which competitors raced to see who was the slowest. It's unusual to find the expression used with the words altered, but one such instance headed a story about an athlete who was disqualified after a drugs test: *the first shall be second*.

Matthew 18:1 provides an unusual example of rhetoric in practice:

At the same time came the disciples unto Jesus, saying, Who is the greatest in the kingdom of heaven?

Here we have a sentence that is only ever used as a quotation in its original form, but which is adapted quite often when *greatest* is replaced by its opposite. We don't usually find people describing themselves (or being described) as *the greatest in the kingdom of* such-and-such. But the opposite is common enough when someone is apologizing for a lack of expertise: *I may be the least in the kingdom of advertising, but*...

By contrast, the expression in Romans 13:1 has truly entered the language:

the powers that be are ordained of God.

Tyndale was the first to use it, and it was reinforced by Bishops and Geneva (Wycliffe's *those things that be* is bland, as is Douai-Rheims' *those that are*). It has become a very popular way of referring ironically to those in authority, and is regularly encountered in comedy routines, sitcom episodes, satirical journalism, and suchlike, presumably because it appeals to the subversive instincts of the writers. As a title, the ambiguity in the word *power* has motivated some novel applications, such as Scott L. Montgomery's *The Powers That Be* (2010), where the subtitle explains all: *Global energy for the twenty-first century and beyond*. Adaptations are rare, partly because there are few words that rhyme with *powers*, but also because the subjunctive verb fossilizes the phrase. Nonetheless, I've found a wedding site emphasizing the importance of selecting the best blooms for the occasion using *the flowers that be*; a complaint about male bias in sports reporting which referred to *the manpowers that be*; and a dismissive comment in a *Guardian* football report talking about the *showers-that-be*.

Matthew 5:18 provides an example of the opposite extreme, in terms of importance:

For verily I say unto you, Till heaven and earth pass, one jot or one tittle shall in no wise pass from the law, till all be fulfilled.

This unusual phrase appears in all the early translations (though Wycliffe has *letter* for *tittle*). *Jot* is from *iota*, which was the smallest letter in the Greek alphabet, and had come to mean a 'very little part' of something. *Tittle* was a small distinguishing mark used in writing or printing, such as the dot on an *i* or the horizontal stroke on a *t*. The idiom, used with *and* and *or*, has passed into modern English with the sense of 'every little detail'. Sometimes it appears in reverse order as *tittle and jot*. It makes a cute company name—though it would only be appropriate for companies that pay attention to detail or where detail is an important part of the product, such as one that carries out legal proofreading or makes doll's houses.

Little has been influential in the phrase *little children*, which is found in Luke 18:16:

Suffer little children to come unto me, and forbid them not: for of such is the kingdom of God.

It appears also in two of the other evangelists. Mark (10:14) has *suffer the little children*. Matthew (19:14) splits it in two: *Suffer little children, and forbid them not, to come unto me*. Only King James has *little*; the others have *suffer children* or *suffer the children*; Geneva has *suffer the babes*. We've now largely lost the old sense of *suffer* meaning 'permit'. As a result, the expression has been partly kept alive by its jocular misinterpretation—such as *we suffered the little children all right!* (following a church service in which some of the babies had been especially vocal). It received a poignant application when The Smiths used it as part of a 1984 pop song about the Moors murders in England. And it was given a heavily ironic application in 2009 when several children's authors in the UK (such as Philip Pullman) protested strongly against government proposals to vet all adults who were going to have regular contact with children in schools. One writer put it like this: *Suffer the little children to come unto me, for I've been checked by the ISA* [i.e. the Independent Safeguarding Authority].

Little has also been influential in the expression *O ye of little faith*, as in Matthew 6:30:

Wherefore, if God so clothe the grass of the field, which to day is, and to morrow is cast into the oven, shall he not much more clothe you, O ye of little faith?

Matthew uses it twice more (8:26, 16:8), and Luke again in 12:28. Matthew also has it with a *thou* in 14:31, when Jesus addresses a single person. The repeated use, plus the fact that it appears in all the translations of the time (though Wycliffe drops the *O*), has made it a popular saying. The sense has been generalized well beyond the notion of religious belief. It's now used as a good-humoured riposte which we can make to anyone who doubts our claimed ability to do something.

The humour begins to disappear in the adaptations, especially when *faith* is replaced by such words as *imagination, shame, humour, patience, memory,* or *vision.* The expression takes on a dismissive force, which at its strongest can amount to quite an insult, as in *O ye of little brain!* The irony returns when *little* is replaced, as in these examples:

O ye of literal faith [on issues of biblical interpretation]

O ye of liberal faith [on party political policy]

O ye of too much faith [on placing trust in marketing predictions]

O ye of limitless faith [on continuing to support a team that isn't playing well]

And the humour is totally restored when the opening word is replaced. In a *Simpsons* episode (16 December 2001), Lisa looks for a new religion, after Homer and Bart inadvertently burn down the local church. The episode is called *She of Little Faith*.

Chapter 27
Fights, foes, fools, friends

Faith appears again in another expression, from 1 Timothy 6:12, which has resounded down the centuries as a religious wake-up call:

Fight the good fight of faith

It is in all the early translations apart from Wycliffe (who has *strive thou a good strife*), and it was soon being varied. John Milton, for example, has this in *Paradise Lost* (1667, Book 6, line 29):

> Servant of God, well done, well hast thou fought
> The better fight

Fight the good fight will be seen on many a gravestone. And the expression has had a musical incarnation since John Monsell extended the rhyme in his 1863 hymn *Fight the good fight with all your might*.

Today the expression is widely used, even to the point of cliché. We often read of someone who has died after a 'long battle' against an illness, that *(s)he fought a good fight*. It's a standard comment made to (or by) a politician who has just lost an election. Oscar Wilde is one of many writers who have used it.

In a character sketch of the English author W. E. Henley, he wrote in 1897: *He has fought a good fight and has had to face every difficulty except popularity.* Journalists use it often. *Fight the good fight* headlined a *Guardian* article in 2002 advising Tony Blair to emphasize key human rights principles before entering Iraq. The *Jerusalem Post* in 2009 had the headline *Jewish groups ready to 'fight the good fight' in Geneva*—the inverted commas probably reflecting a sense of the expression's Christian origins.

Needless to say, *fight the good fight* turns up routinely whenever someone is literally fighting. It's almost certain to be used in relation to a boxing or wrestling match, or one of the other personal combat sports. And because *fighting* is one of the commonest metaphors of everyday life (we *fight disease, elections, emotions, the flab*, and so on) the expression turns up in all kinds of contexts. It has headed several articles about how to lose weight. It turned up on a BBC Gardeners' World site about how to combat weeds.

The fighting metaphor underlies Matthew 12:30, echoed in Romans 8:31:

He that is not with me is against me.

If God be for us, who can be against us?

The unadorned style appealed to all the early translators, and continues with little modification today. Other pronouns have appeared (*are you with us or against us?*) and *with* is often replaced by *for*; but the sense remains the same. It's often used in party politics to persuade people to make up their minds about an issue. The simplicity of the language, and the syntactic parallelism, makes it a difficult expression to adapt, and few have tried to do so. An early exception was Francis Bacon. In his

Advancement of Learning (Book 2, p. 241) he quotes it then reverses it: *He that is not against us, is with us.*

Fighting and conflict are implied by the expression which derives from Matthew 3:11:

he shall baptize you with the Holy Ghost, and with fire

All the early translations say something similar, and the force of the metaphor eventually gave rise to *baptism of/by fire*—though its first recorded use is not until the nineteenth century, when it referred to a soldier's first experience of battle. Today the media frequently use it for anyone experiencing a severe ordeal, especially during the first days in a new job. Footballers in their debut game, for some reason, seem to undergo such a baptism more than anyone else.

Romans 12:20 has more to say about friends and enemies:

Therefore if thine enemy hunger, feed him; if he thirst, give him drink: for in so doing thou shalt heap coals of fire on his head.

The *coals of fire* metaphor is in all the early translations, but they may simply be tapping into an expression that was already current in everyday speech. The notion of 'casting coals on one's head' is found in early Middle English. In William Langland's great allegorical poem *Piers Plowman*, we read about how to deal with an enemy (Passus 13, line 144):

Cast coles on his heed of alle kynde speche

(Cast coals on his head of all kind speech.)

The text was written in the 1360s, well before the earliest English Bible translation.

The expression feels somewhat dated today, but it was hugely popular when coalfires were in every home. The nineteenth-century novelists, in particular, loved it, for it provided a perfect metaphor to express one of their recurrent themes, that remorse can be engendered by requiting evil with good.

And your care of me is like coals of fire on my head! (Lucetta to Henchard in Thomas Hardy, *The Mayor of Casterbridge*, Chapter 29)

I felt impatient of him and out of temper with him; in which condition he heaped coals of fire on my head. (Pip of Joe in Charles Dickens, *Great Expectations*, Chapter 27)

See how the Lord has put coals of fire on my head! (Alice to Mary, in Elizabeth Gaskell, *Mary Barton*, Chapter 12)

I suppose you're heaping coals of fire on my head, you think? (Arthur to Helen, in Ann Brontë, *The Tenant of Wildfell Hall*, Chapter 47)

The metaphor has had less appeal in an age of central heating. *Cast* turns up again in John 8:7:

He that is without sin among you, let him first cast a stone at her.

All the early translations say something similar, but Tyndale, Bishops, and Geneva alter the word order to produce the modern expression: *cast/throw the first stone*. The usage with *cast* has generated a title for books and films, though it hasn't been taken up as widely as some other biblical expressions, probably because a proverb occupies the same semantic space: *people in glass houses shouldn't throw stones*. Whether there's any historical relationship between the two expressions is unclear.

Tension in relationships also appears in 2 Corinthians 11:19:

For ye suffer fools gladly, seeing ye yourselves are wise.

This expression originates in Tyndale, and other translators kept the punchy rhythm, apart from Douai-Rheims, which has *gladly suffer the foolish*. (Wycliffe had *suffer gladly unwise men*.) In popular usage it rapidly developed a negative equivalent—people who *don't* suffer fools gladly. Today, both positive (tolerant) and negative (intolerant) versions are heard, but the latter are very much more frequent. We hardly ever hear someone being described as a person who *does* suffer fools gladly. Some might see in this a linguistic reflection of a less patient or more egotistical society.

When the expression is adapted, we find both positive and negative forms. *Life insurers suffer fools gladly* was one headline, reporting the way some insurance companies pay out even when a claimant has done something really stupid. *Exposing fools gladly* was another, heading a bio piece about a man who specializes in exposing fraudulent scientific claims. But the majority of adaptations follow the trend, and are negative. An opinion editorial: *Don't suffer biofuels gladly.* A political commentary: *The CIA doesn't suffer threats gladly.* An arts review: *Why do we suffer bad singers gladly?*

Strong relationships are the keynote of Matthew 19:6 and Mark 10:9:

What therefore God hath joined together, let not man put asunder.

The King James and Douai-Rheims texts have the modern syntax and rhythm; other translations of the time vary it, having *coupled* instead of *joined* or changing the word order. Tyndale, for example, has *Let not man therefore put asunder that which God hath coupled together.* However, the influence of the Book of Common Prayer (1559) would have been critical in popularizing the expression that has come down to us, for the marriage service ends with *Those whom God hath joined together let no man put asunder.*

The expression has been adapted in countless situations, usually by varying the first element. An article on computer-dating produced *What the computer hath joined together, let no man put asunder.* A commentary about non-aligned nations began *What political convenience hath joined together, let no man put asunder.* One on ways of managing the economic crisis of 2009 began *What bankers hath joined together, let no man put asunder.* A wry riposte to a critic of social networking gave us *What Facebook hath joined together, let no man put asunder.* These examples all had the second element spelled out in full. The *Observer* in 1999 used continuation dots in its headline and left the rest to the reader's imagination: *What Europe hath joined together*...

Both first and second elements can be altered. Sometimes it is a simple gender switch to *let no man or woman* or even *let no woman*. An article on land management in river basins went further: *what nature hath joined together let not science put asunder.* Rather more radical was the comment I heard when the sixth edition of the *Shorter Oxford English Dictionary* appeared in 2007. It transpired that some 16,000 compound words had lost their hyphens (e.g. *ice-cream* becoming *ice cream*). One conservatively minded critic felt this was going too far, observing that *what the hyphen hath long joined together, no dictionary editor should put asunder.* The most bizarre innovation I have seen was the one made by someone answering the question of whether garden gnomes should be allowed as part of the exhibits at the Chelsea Flower Show? Yes, he said: *What the gardener hath joined together, let gnome man put asunder.*

Chapter 28
Praising famous men

The male mindset of biblical times manifests itself in several expressions that have come down to us, though today the idioms are frequently altered by those who feel uncomfortable about a masculine generic noun being used to include women. Sirach (Ecclesiasticus) 44:1 is a classic case:

Let us now praise famous men, and our fathers that begat us.

Douai-Rheims has *men of renown*. (The other translations do not include this book.) The sentiment is a general one, with no especial religious content, and so we find the first part of this sentence used with reference to anyone or anything that might legitimately be described as famous. *Let us now praise famous cats, dogs, mice* (Mickey Mouse), *trees, gardens, bloggers, Tories, Muppets…* The titles of some iconic works keep the use of *man* in our minds, such as Vaughan Williams's 1923 anthem or the pioneering book of photo-journalism by James Agee and Walker Evans in 1941 about white tenant farmers in Alabama. In 1987, Andrea Fisher introduced a gender balance with her book about women photographers for the US government: *Let Us Now Praise Famous Women*.

The adaptations have largely relied on phonetic similarities with *praise*, as in these examples:

let us now raise famous men [article on short people who have become well-known]

let us now braise famous men [a critical view of the businessmen who caused the 2008 recession]

let us now gaze, famous men [a book about death masks]

Just occasionally, the expression is changed more radically. An article condemning the demolition of old buildings to provide space for new developments was headed *Let us now raze famous dens.*

Another popular *men* expression appears in 1 Corinthians 9:22:

I am made all things to all men, that I might by all means save some.

Wycliffe introduced the phrasing, but his reversal of the word order lessened the rhetorical effect of the parallelism: *to all men I am made all things.* Tyndale has *I fashioned myself to all men.* King James has the same text as Bishops, Geneva, and Douai-Rheims, and it is *all things to all men* that has come down to us, with the gender bias sometimes avoided through the use of *people.* An ad for a particular brand of car was headed *All things to all men (and women and vicars).*

The sense of an individual 'meeting all needs' has easily transferred to groups. *Men* is often replaced by another generic noun such as *customers, patients, diners* (in a restaurant review), and *drivers.* Non-humans aren't excluded: a new software development was introduced with the words *all things to all machines.* And the phrase as a whole is often applied to abstract notions. *The art of marketing: all things to all men* ran one headline. *Are museums all things to all men?* asked the writer of an article about the tension between their scholarly and popular functions.

Something interesting has happened with Mark 2:27:

The sabbath was made for man, and not man for the sabbath

All the early translations have this reversed parallelism (another example of chiasmus, p. 164), and this seems to have been the influential factor, for today it is the underlying syntactic pattern that has been adopted, rather than the specific reference to the sabbath: 'X was made for man not man for X.' A gender replacement is uncommon, though we do find the occasional observation, such as *the garment was made for woman not woman for the garment* (in a discussion about the need to adapt clothing to make it fit). For the most part, people use generic *man* without further thought.

The original expression is chiefly used nowadays in relation to any institution where the procedures have become an intolerable burden, and where people want things to change. A typical example is *technology was made for man, not man for technology*. At some point or other, someone has said the same about *industry, the state, morality, theology, martial arts, physics, art*, and *punctuation*—a small sample of enterprises where someone has said 'things must be this way' and someone else has said 'not necessarily'. Occasionally, the original *sabbath* usage is found, whenever an issue arises about the kinds of activity that should be permitted on a Christian Sunday or Jewish Saturday.

A literary instance occurred in a debate on what counted as poetry. Should poetry be metrical, and follow the rules of prosody laid down over the centuries? 'Yes', said one participant. 'No', said another, who then commented that *poetry was made for man, not man for poetry*. My favourite example, in this connection, occurred in an online discussion of *Star Trek* and its opening aphorism, *to boldly go*, criticized by language pedants for being a split infinitive. The writer observed: *The infinitive was made for man, not man for the infinitive.*

Behold as an imperative is recorded during the fifteenth century, but it is probably the reference to Jesus in John 19:5 which fixed the expression *behold the man* in people's minds:

Pilate saith unto them, Behold the man!

It appears in all the early translations apart from Wycliffe, who has *Lo the man*. Coming as it does at a particularly dramatic point in the Gospel story, it's not surprising to see it being used as the title of many books, paintings, and pieces of music, both classical and popular (memorably, for many young people, in a 2005 track by Michael Jackson). The twentieth century saw the expression move in new directions, notably in male art photography. *Behold the woman* also arrived. Gradually, the meaning weakened, so that now it is used to announce the arrival of anything special, as in a physics article which began with *Behold the pentaquark*. The word hasn't lost its stylistic charisma. Marketing people sense this when they use it to present a new product. *Behold the iPhone*. But the stylistic reverence is likely to dissipate as the expression comes to be increasingly used in less imposing contexts. *Behold the power of Twitter.*

The gender issue doesn't arise in Matthew 18:20:

For where two or three are gathered together in my name, there am I in the midst of them.

All translations have this phrasing (Wycliffe drops the *together*), and it also appears in the Morning Prayer in the Book of Common Prayer. Over the years it has proved a popular maxim for religious groups with few members, and its first element has been gradually extended to include any setting where speakers, faced with a small audience, use the quotation to break the ice.

Writers have taken it further, applying *Where two or three are gathered together* to any small-group activity. It's been used to introduce an article about one-teacher schools, and an advertisement for small-group travel programmes. It's a ready source of humour. *Where two or three are gathered together, grandparents will show pictures of their grandchildren!* A famous modern instance was the sketch on BBC television's *Not the Nine o'Clock News*, in which Rowan Atkinson, playing a bishop-cum-film-director, defends his New Testament film against a charge of blasphemy made by the Church of Monty Python, whose members treat the Python series as a gospel and John Cleese as a messiah. *Whenever two or three are gathered together in one place, then they shall perform the parrot sketch.*

Chapter 29
Sheep, goats, swine

Animal imagery provides a major biblical theme, and one animal in particular has been a fruitful source of modern idiom. Jesus calls himself a *good shepherd* (John 10:11); John the Baptist calls him *the Lamb of God* (John 1:29); people are described as *lambs* and *sheep* (John 21:15–16). These have remained with us as quotations. But the usage in Acts 8:32 is different, for it has given us *led as a sheep to the slaughter*.

This is a direct allusion to Isaiah 53:7, where we find *as a lamb to the slaughter*, and the Old Testament has two other references: Jeremiah 11:19 talks about a *lamb or an ox* going to the slaughter; and *lamb* appears again in 51:40. The result is that *sheep* and *lamb* have competed as the popular idiom, *lamb* (either singular or plural) today being about three times as common as *sheep*. *To the slaughter* has also become the norm, being preferred to earlier variants such as *for the slaughter, to slaying* (Wycliffe) or *to be slain* (Tyndale).

It's proved to be a popular twentieth-century idiom. Many people associate it with a film (Hitchcock's *Lamb to the Slaughter*, 1958) or a story (Roald Dahl, 1954). In real life, writers have found it appropriate for describing military campaigns where troops have been ordered to advance against overwhelming odds, such as the charge of the Light Brigade in the Crimean War or the trench warfare movements of World War I. World War II brought a different slant, in the context of the Holocaust. For long a favourite idiom to describe the genocide, it has been challenged by those who point to instances of active Jewish resistance. The debate has kept the idiom in the public eye, and it came to the fore again in 2008 in relation to the high level of troop deaths in Afghanistan.

Today, any enterprise where disaster looms can attract a *sheep/ lambs* description. *Koizumi cabinet sheep to the slaughter* headed an article in 2003 about (what the writer considered to be) a disastrous economic policy in Japan. Any political party doing badly before an election might be described in this way, as might people investing in a bad stock-market deal, or a lowly-placed football team about to be hammered by a top-division giant. Whether the about-to-be-slaughtered group is described as *sheep* or *lambs* depends very largely on the sympathies of the writer. When a popular individual is involved, *lamb* is much more likely. It was a favourite retrospective description of Princess Diana's entry into the Royal Family.

Sheep appear again as a result of Matthew 7:15:

Beware of false prophets, which come to you in sheep's clothing, but inwardly they are ravening wolves.

All the translations use *sheep's clothing* or its equivalent (Wycliffe has *clothings of sheep*; Douai-Rheims has *clothing of sheep*). The original expression isn't biblical at all: it's in Aesop's *Fables*, 'The wolf in sheep's clothing', and as Aesop was widely known in Europe, Wycliffe probably got it from there. Tyndale is the first to use the premodifying form *sheep's*, and by 1600 it is widely encountered—for example, Diggon, in Spenser's *Shepherd's*

Calendar (September), talks of wolves going 'in more secret wise, / And with sheepes clothing doen hem disguise' (i.e. 'do them disguise'). Today, the meaning is less one of danger and more one of caution. The expression usually refers to someone who appears friendly but who cannot be trusted.

In its many adaptations, the meaning has broadened somewhat, referring to anything that is not as it seems on the surface. There is always an element of masquerade. Virtually anything can be *in sheep's clothing*, as a consequence, not only animate beings. Headlines regularly use it to talk about products that the writer feels are pretending to be something they're not, such as a software program or a mortgage offer. The sense is not always negative: one motoring report of a test drive described a particular model of compact hatchback as being *a sporty little wolf in sheep's clothing*.

Adaptations are widespread. It's an obvious name for shops selling woollen goods. Stories about sheep go for it too. A report in *Scientific American* (1997) about Dolly the sheep was headed *A clone in sheep's clothing*. Politicians have attracted the phrase ever since Churchill famously described his Labour opponent Clement Attlee as *a sheep in sheep's clothing*. US presidential candidate John McCain and London mayor Boris Johnson are among those who have been similarly labelled. An animal variant headed an article in the *Economist* (2008) about the relations between the Dalai Lama and China: *A lama in sheep's clothing*. And even if you win the presidency, you don't escape the barb: Obama's speech in Cairo (2009), according to the *Guardian*, showed little change in US policy: the headline read *A Bush in sheep's clothing*.

Reversals are found too. A story about an average guy who made it into an elite military unit was headed *a sheep in wolf's clothing*. And the same words headed a 2008 report in the *New York Times* about how Japanese saké is being used to great effect to replace spirits by some restaurants who don't have a full liquor licence. (Being made from rice, it falls under a beer/wine licence category.) Some rather unbiblical lexical blends have been the outcome, such as *saketails* and *saketinis*.

A third popular sheep idiom is found in Matthew 25:32:

And before him shall be gathered all nations: and he shall separate them one from another, as a shepherd divideth his sheep from the goats:

Some translations (Geneva, Douai-Rheims) have *separate*, rather than *divide*, and both verbs are found in modern usage. There's quite a bit of variation: all possible combinations of the following can be found—*divide/separate (the) sheep and/from (the) goats*. (Wycliffe has *kids* instead of *goats*.)

The continuing popularity of the metaphor must be because 'good vs bad guys' can be found everywhere. They can be people, institutions, or even products. Poker players, according to one pundit, can be *divided into sheep and goats*, depending on how they behave when they're losing. And an investigation of our aptitude for computer programming led one analyst to divide everyone into sheep and goats. *Separating programming sheep from non-programming goats*, ran the headline.

Good banks and bad banks were described as *sheep and goats* in the 2008 world banking crisis. Political groups are often described in this way. *Which are the sheep and which are the goats?* asked one writer about the uncertain status of separatist movements within an African country. The same question was asked of the latest developments in computer software.

As for the beasts themselves, they haven't been forgotten. An animal physiologist once made a genetic study of 50 species of ruminants from the family *Bovidae* (cloven-hoofed mammals). She called it *Separating the sheep from the goats on the basis of their chromosomes*—an unexpected integration of the languages of science and religion.

Not all sheep expressions have proved so adaptable. I would have expected more to be made of Matthew 10:6:

But go rather to the lost sheep of the house of Israel.

It's used several times—again in Matthew (15:24), echoed in Luke (15:6), with antecedents in Jeremiah (50:6) and Psalms (119:176), the latter ensuring its use in the Book of Common Prayer. All the early translations use the phrase, with the exception of Wycliffe, who refers to the sheep as *perished*. Its sense is quite general—'one who has strayed from the right way'. And yet it has had very little use outside religious settings.

Other animals can be treated more briefly, as most references usually play no further role in English, other than in quotations, as in the description of Satan as *that old serpent* (John the Divine 12:9), which we might now find applied to any older male. Occasionally we do find a limited use outside religion, as when *fatted calf* (a specially fattened beast killed for a meal to celebrate the return home of a long-lost son, Luke 15:23) is used as a company name by charcuteries, burger stores, and butchers. Another instance is in Matthew 19:24 (repeated in Mark 10:25):

It is easier for a camel to go through the eye of a needle, than for a rich man to enter into the kingdom of God.

The analogy has prompted considerable biblical interpretation, so it's hardly surprising to find it little used outside a religious setting. We do encounter the occasional adaptation, however. A report on the economic disasters of 2008 led one writer to say: *It is easier for a Land Rover to go through the eye of a needle than for an Investment Banker to enter the kingdom of God.*

There's one big exception to the statement that animals other than sheep haven't been influential. It is in Matthew 7:6:

Give not that which is holy unto the dogs, neither cast ye your pearls before swine

The image of 'casting pearls before swine' caught the imagination in the Middle Ages, and has been with us ever since. The phrasing is in Tyndale and other translations (though not Wycliffe, who talks of *margaritis* instead of *pearls*), so the King James Bible can have had only a facilitating effect here. The expression has kept its meaning: 'to offer something of value to someone who is incapable of appreciating it.' And although it has a slightly clichéd ring about it nowadays, it continues to be used, sometimes reduced to simply *casting pearls*. It's been the title of many songs and TV episodes, and it even named a folk band during the 1960s. Many Americans will know it as the name of a widely syndicated newspaper comic strip by Stephen Pastis.

The usual media adaptation is to replace *swine* with something else, the writer being satirical at the expense of some target group. Pearls have been cast before *parliament, bureaucrats, customers, teenagers, immigrants*—indeed, before anyone who comes from a particular region, if the writer wants to make the point that the inhabitants don't deserve some benefit or other. *Casting pearls before Tennesseeans*, wrote one contributor to an online forum, disturbed that another contributor (from Tennessee) wasn't appreciating the points he'd been making. Occasionally, *pearls* is replaced: one stand-up comedian talked about *casting my jokes before swine* (though what his audience's reaction was isn't recorded). And the influenza epidemic of 2009 opened the floodgates to a string of puns, mostly to do with people abusing tamiflu treatment measures: *Don't cast pearls before swine flu.*

Chapter 30
Money, wages, pearls, mites

t's probably the perpetual relevance of the subject matter that has led people to adopt and adapt so many pecuniary phrases from the New Testament. Perhaps the most famous is in 1 Timothy 6:10:

For the love of money is the root of all evil

St Paul must actually be feeling a bit miffed at the way his phrase has been adopted. It's the *love* of money, he is saying, which is the root of all evil, not money *per se*. Other translations change the word but not the sentiment: *covetousness* in Wycliffe and Tyndale; *desire* in Geneva and Douai-Rheims. But that hasn't stopped the vast majority of people using the expression without its opening four words. For virtually everyone today, it is simply *money is the root of all evil. (Take it away, take it away, take it away.)*

If that last association of ideas means anything to you, it is because you are recalling the riff in the hit song by the Andrews Sisters in 1946 called *Money is the root of all evil*. Popular song has a hugely important role to play in consolidating a usage in the public consciousness, especially when, as in that song, the title line was repeated three times in the chorus.

All parts of the expression have been adapted. *Root* is sometimes changed to *route* or *roof*, though not always with much semantic point. Innumerable candidates have been suggested as an alternative opening word: *gambling, sex, idleness, boredom, technology*—even *poorly written SQL* can be *the root of all evil*. When the film *A Different World* came out in 1991, it had an associated strapline which provided one of the best puns based on this expression: *Monet is the root of all evil*.

Evil has also been replaced by hundreds of alternatives, depending solely on what the user feels to be evil, either seriously or in jest. A random sample produces *Money is the root of all divorce,...of all baseball,...of all Hollywood*. In most cases, the meaning is plain: the more money that is available for an enterprise, the more successful it will be—the implication being, of course, that this will be at the expense of other values. Sometimes the adaptation needs a gloss. *Money is the root of all maths* said one headline. The reference was to the need for investment in education if exam results in mathematics were to significantly improve. Sometimes the reference is so personal and obscure that it is unglossable. I have no idea what to make of *Money is the root of all email*, which appeared one day on Twitter. But the spirit of Timothy is there nonetheless.

These are all examples which accept the underlying sentiment. The expression is unusual, in biblical phraseology, for the way in which writers have sometimes dared to alter that sentiment, even at times to the point of reversing it. George Bernard Shaw is probably the best-known: *Lack of money is the root of all evil*.

Some writers have also tried to reclaim the distinctive phrase found in 1 Timothy 3:8:

Likewise must the deacons be grave, not doubletongued, not given to much wine, not greedy of filthy lucre.

Apart from Wycliffe (who has *foul winning*), all the early translations have *filthy lucre*. Modern expressions such as *lots of lovely lucre* show an attempt to rehabilitate the word, but it will be an uphill struggle, because the pejorative associations are very strong. When the word arrived in English (from Latin *lucrum*, 'profit, gain, greed', probably via French) in the fourteenth century, the negative set of associations came with it. We see them when Chaucer opens his *Prioress' Tale*, describing a place in Asia known for *foule usure and lucre of vileynye* ('foul usury and ill-gotten gains'). Both *foul lucre* and *filthy lucre* were early collocations, but the biblical use of the latter guaranteed its primacy.

Today, the phrase is widely used, usually in a somewhat self-conscious way, whenever there's a suggestion of money being used immorally or financial considerations taking place behind the scenes. *Filthy lucre and the UK's relations with Libya* headed a newspaper report in 2009. It provides a nice ironic title for a book on economics (such as the one by Joseph Heath, 2009). Its negative connotations have also been attractive to rebellious youth. When punk rock group the Sex Pistols had a reunion tour in 1996, they called it *Filthy Lucre*.

The negative note is seen again in *Romans* 6:23:

For the wages of sin is death

Here King James is in line with Wycliffe, Geneva, and Douai-Rheims; Tyndale and Bishops go for *reward*. Both words are found today, but it is the earthily working-class *wages* that has captured the popular imagination. People have preferred to keep the older concord, *wages is*, even though *wages* became a plural noun in the seventeenth century.

Writers have played with the expression to the point of fantasy: *The wages of sin is death, but the hours are good.* Often there is a hint of a serious point: *The wages of sin is death, but the profits on sin are fantastic.* And a clear alternative message comes across in examples like these, where *sin* is equated with a bad lifestyle: *the wages of sin is healthcare,... is dementia.* More tongue-in-cheek was this ad for a chocolate bar: *the wages of sin is a dollar.* A bad computer lifestyle is implicated in *the wages of sin is debugging.* And sin is evidently not all it is made out to be, said one writer, after watching an early movie called *Sodom and Gomorrah*: *the wages of sin is tedium.*

Another early movie was called *What Shall it Profit a Man?* (1913), borrowing the opening element of Mark 8:36:

For what shall it profit a man, if he shall gain the whole world, and lose his own soul?

The sentence is echoed in Matthew 16:26 (*For what is a man profited...*). The King James (and Douai-Rheims) use of *gain* has been the preferred usage, as opposed to *win* (in the other early translations), but otherwise the sentence has come down to us as a quotation. Adaptation is uncommon, because it requires people to retain enough of the three-part structure to make the utterance recognizable. An example was a report on the brain damage suffered by boxers. It ran: *What shall it profit a man if he has the perfect body but is mentally deficient?*

The negative pecuniary tone continues in the phrase *thirty pieces of silver* (Matthew 26:15), the recompense Judas received from the authorities for betraying Jesus. Today it is used for anyone who is perceived to have abandoned a principle in return for cash. *Selling cricket's soul for thirty pieces of silver* ran the headline reporting one cricketer who had joined a commercial league.

Not all money expressions have negative connotations. Valuable objects can provide a positive analogy, as is seen in the story about the merchant in Matthew 13:46:

Who, when he had found one pearl of great price, went and sold all that he had, and bought it.

The phrase is in all the early versions, though Bishops has *one precious pearl* and Wycliffe has *margarite*, as before (p. 185).

Pearl meaning 'precious thing' or 'fine example' actually long predates the Bible translations—we find such expressions as *pearl of wisdom* and *pearl of courtesy* in early Middle English. But *pearl of great price* is not recorded before the biblical usage. It started to be used outside the Matthew setting quite soon: a general use of *pearl of price*, meaning 'something of great value', is cited in the *Oxford English Dictionary* as early as 1693.

Surprisingly, it has not proved to be one of the great sources of modern idiomatic adaptation. It tends to retain its literal associations. Anyone called *Pearl* is likely to find the expression used about her at some point in her life. And it will be seen regularly in jewellery advertising. Probably the majority of modern instances remain in the religious domain, with some groups making great use of it. The Church of Jesus Christ of Latter-day Saints, for example, has compiled a collection of its doctrinal materials under the title *The Pearl of Great Price*.

A positive tone also surrounds the usage we find in Mark 12:42 (and also in Luke 21:2):

And there came a certain poor widow, and she threw in two mites, which make a farthing.

Two mites is in all the early translations. A *mite*, in the singular, meaning 'a very small amount', was an everyday word in the sixteenth century. Today it's hardly used at all as a noun, apart from in a few fixed phrases, such as *little mite* (of a child), and, of course, *widow's mite*, as a description of the biblical event (a phrase which doesn't appear in the Bible itself). *Two mites* isn't an especially common idiom today, but it will be heard, usually when someone claims to be making a humble (though nonetheless important) contribution to an ongoing discussion. Other phrases, such as *sixpennyworth* and *two cents worth*, have proved to be more popular.

Treasure is another word which today tends to be restricted to fixed collocations, such as *buried treasure* and *treasure chest*, and the usage in Matthew 6:20:

But lay up for yourselves treasures in heaven

None of the other early translations have this phrasing. It's echoed in Mark 10:21, where the word is in the singular:

thou shalt have treasure in heaven

It's the singular usage which is most often found today. *Store up* often replaced *lay up*, but the focus on *treasure* remains, with many adaptations of the kind *lay up for yourselves treasure in the bank* or... *in the pawnshop*. The spiritual sense of *treasure* is also a frequent allusion. *Lay up for yourselves treasure in Tanzania* began one article, describing the rewards of missionary work.

Something of a balance between positive and negative attitudes to money is reached in Matthew 22:21 (echoed in Mark 12:17, but with *to* instead of *unto*):

Render therefore unto Caesar the things which are Caesar's; and unto God the things that are God's.

It is the King James (and Douai-Rheims) *render* which has become distinctive (Wycliffe has *yield*; Tyndale and the others have *give*), and it is this which is found today, along with the archaic *unto*. *Render unto Caesar* is quite a common headline when someone is writing about the distinction between church and state or, more generally, about conflicting loyalties—for example, it is the name of a movement encouraging clergy to separate civil and religious marriage. The syntactic construction has evidently been thoroughly assimilated, judging by the headline of a *Wall Street Journal* article on taxation issues for the Churches: *What to render unto whom?*

The sentence as a whole provides an easy source for adaptation. The ongoing debate between religion and science over evolution prompted this summary: *Render unto Darwin the things that are Darwin's, and unto God the things that are God's.* An article on tipping etiquette in New York was headed *Time to render unto doormen.* A report on a Texas Senate resolution to limit the ability of the government to seize private property for economic development began: *Render unto Seizer?*

The rhetoric of oppositeness turns up again in Acts 20:35:

It is more blessed to give than to receive.

King James emulates Tyndale and Bishops in its rhythmical reinforcement of the semantic contrast. Geneva and Douai-Rheims reduce the force (to modern ears) by adding an intervening stress: ... *to give, rather than to receive.* The usual modern version, *better to give than to receive*, has had its fair share of playful adaptation. The technical use of *receive* in American football has prompted several variants, such as *better to block than to receive.* And *give* is often opposed to *gift, donate*, and other terms with technical financial import. Avoiding inheritance tax is a favourite: *Better to give than pay estate taxes.*

To end this financial chapter with a positive note, here's a nice example of the effect I described in Chapter 4, where a modern usage leaps out at us after a stylistically fallow stretch of reading. It's in the opening verses of 2 Corinthians 9:

9:1 For as touching the ministering to the saints, it is superfluous for me to write to you:

9:2 For I know the forwardness of your mind, for which I boast of you to them of Macedonia, that Achaia was ready a year ago; and your zeal hath provoked very many.

9:3 Yet have I sent the brethren, lest our boasting of you should be in vain in this behalf; that, as I said, ye may be ready:

9:4 Lest haply if they of Macedonia come with me, and find you unprepared, we (that we say not, ye) should be ashamed in this same confident boasting.

9:5 Therefore I thought it necessary to exhort the brethren, that they would go before unto you, and make up beforehand your bounty, whereof ye had notice before, that the same might be ready, as a matter of bounty, and not as of covetousness.

9:6 But this I say, He which soweth sparingly shall reap also sparingly; and he which soweth bountifully shall reap also bountifully.

9:7 Every man according as he purposeth in his heart, so let him give; not grudgingly, or of necessity: for God loveth a cheerful giver.

It's one of those moments that sends a shiver down a linguistic spine. Most of the early translations have it (though Wycliffe has *a glad giver*), and it's had quite a lot of adaptation. Several have claimed that God loves *a cheerful receiver* too, and a number of other categories of person have been substituted, such as *lender*, *worshipper*, and *loser*. Needless to say, it is not only God who loves a cheerful giver. Fund-raising politicians on the campaign trail do as well. And so (according to some cynical commentators) does the department of Inland Revenue.

Chapter 31
Blessed are the servants

oney turns up again in the context of service, as we read in Matthew 6:24:

> No man can serve two masters: for either he will hate the one, and love the other; or else he will hold to the one, and despise the other. Ye cannot serve God and mammon.

The personification is echoed in Luke 16:13, who precedes it with two other uses of *mammon*, where the meaning seems to be more general: *the mammon of unrighteousness* (16:9) and *the unrighteous mammon* (16:11). King James adds a marginal note here: 'riches.' In the Matthew verse, both Wycliffe and Geneva replace *mammon* by *riches*, but it is *mammon*, used also in Tyndale, Bishops, and Douai-Rheims, that has held the attention over the centuries. Indeed, that translation goes back much further, for *mammon* appears in the Anglo-Saxon Gospels too.

The word was picked up by poets and essayists early on—for example, Langland uses the personification in *Piers Plowman* (Passus 8, line 90): *And with Mammonaes moneie he hath maad hym frendes* ('And with Mammon's money he hath made him friends'). It is widely used today, though alternative expressions exist, such as *you cannot serve God and wealth/money/*

riches/profit. Adaptations are widespread too, and evidently have been for some time. *You cannot serve God and Boss McLaughlin* is found in the *New York Times* in 1893. And modern variants include *You cannot serve God and technology/spam/sports/Darwin.*

But it's the service element which is the dominant theme of the verse. *No man can serve two masters* is in all the translations (except Wycliffe, who has *two lords*) and has also survived into the twenty-first century, notwithstanding repeated feminist criticism of the *no man* element in the 1970s and after. A satisfactory replacement is difficult, however. *No woman can serve two masters* is sometimes encountered, but this is only a half-solution, and *no woman can serve two mistresses*—rare, but it does exist—is even more excluding than the original.

Today, the relevance of the expression is widely acknowledged, especially in contexts where people are being pulled in two directions. Should a company think of its shareholders or its customers? Should a politician think of the party or the people? These are the sorts of contexts in which the expression is likely to appear. And of course, pragmatic solutions are often required. *Serving two masters* headed a piece on military chaplains. Another headline, *The man who served two masters*, was all about a spy.

Another service expression appears in Matthew 25:21:

Well done, thou good and faithful servant

The regular iambic rhythm makes this expression much more appealing to modern ears than the *good servant and faithful* of Wycliffe, Tyndale, and Geneva. Today, *thou* is surprisingly common, though *you* often replaces it. *Servant* is sometimes replaced by a noun of similar thrust, and often pluralized, such as *stewards*, *parishioners, fans,* even *blog-buddies* (a blogger expressing gratitude to those who keep in touch with him)—one of the more incongruous stylistic juxtapositions I encountered in this project. *Thou good and faithful blog-buddies.* You couldn't make it up.

The expression as a whole is often seen, maintaining the spirit of the original context, on Christian tombstones. No religious spirit is intended, by contrast, when it appears, often inscribed, as part of a gift marking the retirement of a long-serving member of an organization. Many would find it something of a cliché, though the intention is doubtless sincere. Not so the ironic farewell paid by one newspaper to a Whitehall retiree, as he took up a senior post in business: *Well done, thou good and civil servant.*

It's the *good and faithful* part which has become the chief element of the idiom. The other words are highly variable. A write-up of an American graduation party began with *Farewell, good and faithful seniors.* A story about an American snake-handling minister was headed *Good and faithful serpents.* An online report praised those committed to writing open-source software: *Well done, you good and faithful developers.* And *well blogged, you good and faithful,* began a message from one blogger to his contacts.

Service is the dominant theme of Matthew 5:3:

Blessed are the poor in spirit: for theirs is the kingdom of heaven.

This, and the following six verses which begin *Blessed are . . . (they that mourn, the meek, they which do hunger and thirst after righteousness, the merciful, the pure in heart, the peacemakers)* are known as the *Beatitudes,* because of their reiterated use of the initial word. All the translations follow this style. They have come down to us as a quotation, with people referring to one or other of them as occasion suggests. But the *Blessed are . . . for . . .* construction has had a more profound linguistic influence, being now used as an accolade for any group that one wishes to praise. The *Economist* provided a splendid example in 2009, following Barack Obama's decision to invite scientists into his administration: *Blessed are the geeks, for they shall inherit the Earth.*

In fact, the full use of the construction is unusual. Far more common is the adaptation of just the first part of the expression, in such headings as *Blessed are the caregivers/sceptics/nobodies/sick/ uncool.* A short, succinct phrasing is normal, but sometimes an exaggerated length is effective: *Blessed are they who turn off their mobile phones in theatres.* Joan Baez used this strategy in the wistful, lilting opening track of her album *Blessed Are...* (1971):

> Blessed are the one way ticket holders
> on a one way street.
> Blessed are the midnight riders
> for in the shadow of God they sleep.

Especially effective are coinages which echo the words in the original. *Peacemakers* has been the most productive, with dozens of adaptations. *Blessed are the cheesemakers/mapmakers/ majority makers/cakemakers/yogurt makers/filmmakers* (especially when Mel Gibson's *The Passion* came out). The cleverest to my mind was a medical article about treatment for heart conditions: *Blessed are the pacemakers.*

A cautionary note about good intentions is introduced in Matthew 26:41:

Watch and pray, that ye enter not into temptation: the spirit indeed is willing, but the flesh is weak.

Mark (14:38) echoes it with *The spirit truly is ready, but the flesh is weak.* Several translations from Tyndale on share this expression with King James (though Wycliffe and Geneva have *ready* instead of *willing*, and Wycliffe also has *sick* instead of *weak*), and it has become so well known that we routinely drop its second element. All we need to say, when some bodily limitation makes us unable to do something we would like to do, is *the spirit is willing*. A world full of infirmities due to age and disease doubtless explains its popularity. It's rather nice to see, then, someone defying the trend. *Not just the spirit is willing*, ran a headline in *The Baltimore Messenger* (2009), reporting a nun still teaching in the city at the age of 80.

There's very little one can do, by way of adaptation, to the first element of the expression. Mediums, spiritualists, and others involved in what is sometimes called 'the psychic industry' have made some use of *the spirits are willing*, as have people involved in parapsychological investigations; and we sometimes find the plural form used by poets, musicians, and other artists. Most wordplay, however, focuses on the second element, as these examples of media usage illustrate:

the spirit is willing, but the details are weak [said of a company report]

the spirit is willing, but the cash is weak [said of a business plan]

the spirit is willing, but the wallet is weak [said by a parent to teenagers]

the spirit is willing, but the Force is weak [review of a *Star Wars* movie]

The Spirit is willing, but the movie is weak [review of a 2008 film *The Spirit*]

Sometimes the word *weak* is replaced:

the spirit is willing, but the flesh needs new weapons [on the war in Afghanistan]

and sometimes the entire phrase goes:

the spirit is willing, but my feet are sore [on not hiking any further]

The cleverest examples are those which retain a phonetic echo of the original:

> the spirit is willing, but the flash is weak [on a photography exhibition]
>
> the spirit is willing, but the flush is weak [on a new design of toilet]
>
> the spirit is willing, but the flèche is wet

I had to look that last one up. *Flèche* (from French 'arrow') in this context is the name of a type of cycle road race. On that particular occasion, it seems it had been raining a lot, but the cyclists carried on.

Chapter 32
Heal thyself

D amaged flesh is a running theme in relation to the healing ministry of Jesus, and some of the associated phrases have entered modern English. Not all have been widely taken up. With a phrase such as *sick of the palsy* (Matthew 8:6, 9:2), the influence has been limited to a few jocular conversational references. *Tomorrow morning you'll get a wire from me announcing that I'm sick of the palsy*, says a malingering character in one of *Punch*'s 'Charivari' columns (1 September 1920). I've heard it used in that way a few times, in contexts which never have anything to do with paralysis.

The healing theme in Matthew 14:36 has been rather more productive:

And besought him that they might only touch the hem of his garment: and as many as touched were made perfectly whole.

It's the 'touching of the hem' that has attracted the attention. The description of the clothing has always had some variation. Wycliffe has *clothing*; Tyndale has *vesture*. *Garment* is the dominant form, but it has a slightly archaic ring about it today, so that the expression is widely adapted. Virtually anything that has a hem has been used as a replacement noun: *jersey, apron, leotard*... The interviewer of an American basketball star was evidently overawed: *You don't know whether to get his autograph or his blessing. Or just touch the hem of his warmup suit.* A fan of Janis Joplin commented dismissively about some other singers: *They aren't fit to touch the hem of her bellbottoms.* A fan of Frank Sinatra enthused: *In sheer productivity, few popular artists could touch the hem of his tuxedo jacket.* This isn't a recent trend. When Amelia Earhart flew the Atlantic in 1928, the report in the *New York Times* said *Miss Earhart was nearly crushed by the anxiety of the crowd of men, women and children to touch the hem of her flying suit.*

These days, the expression has been extended even to things that don't have hems. When Bob Dylan got a Pulitzer prize in 2008, the New York composer David Lang, who was also a prize-winner, commented: *I am not fit to touch the hem of his shoes.* And pop star Bono is once reported to have said that his group U2 was *not fit to touch the hem of the Beatles.* For some people, this might be taking metaphor a little too far.

Acts 9:18 records the way St Paul's blindness left him, at the moment of his conversion:

And immediately there fell from his eyes as it had been scales: and he received sight forthwith, and arose, and was baptized.

The vivid simile appears in all the early translations, and expressions of the type *scales fell from my eyes* (a phrasing used by Wycliffe) soon entered the language to express a general sense of 'suddenly coming to know the truth of a situation'. Here are some modern examples:

The scales fell from my military eyes [a former soldier rethinks his position on the war in Afghanistan]

When did the scales fall from your eyes about UKIP? [a critique of the UK Independence
   Party]
Some scales finally fall from the FB-eyes [on methods used by the FBI]
Disaster strikes as the scales finally fall from American eyes: not all Brits are gentlemen
   [a shocked reaction to the arrival of 'lager lout' behaviour in the US]

The medical expression which has had most impact is found
in Luke 4:23:

Ye will surely say unto me this proverb, Physician, heal thyself

The proverbial phrasing that has come down to us is biblical. All
the translations use it (apart from Wycliffe, who uses the old
word for a doctor, *leech*). The modern idiom has taken it over
directly, though sometimes we find it in the plural (*thyselves*) and
sometimes with the modern pronoun (*yourself*).

Jesus was anticipating a rejection from the people of his own
town: if you can work miracles elsewhere, why not here? With
the modern use of the expression, the challenge is one of incon-
sistency, whether deliberate or otherwise, and it tends to be
found when we encounter someone or some institution not following the behaviour we expect. It is the obvious remark whenever we hear stories of a heart surgeon who needs heart surgery,
or a psychotherapist who needs psychotherapy. The remark is by
no means restricted to medicine, however; for example, it has
headlined a story about a computer security company that suffered a virus attack. We especially hear it used when our reaction
is one of incredulity, such as towards the end of 2008 (when the
financial crisis was at its height) and it was reported that banks
were offering online advice about risk management.

Because anyone can 'heal themselves', the opening vocative
varies. The arrival of medical self-diagnosis online elicited

Patient, heal thyself. The discovery that neurones can be stimulated to aid recovery following a stroke saw a piece headed *Brain, heal thyself.* It need not be a person, or person-related. A project to automatically repair damage to the surface of the international space station led to *Spacecraft, heal thyself.* And a report that the Japanese city that gave its name to the 1997 environmental protocol was itself having clean-air problems was headed *Kyoto, heal thyself.*

The miracles that Jesus performed are called *signs and wonders* in John 4:48:

Except ye see signs and wonders, ye will not believe.

The phrase is also used several times in the Old Testament, and is shared by all the early translations except Wycliffe (who has *tokens and great wonders*). Douai-Rheims has the more modern syntax *unless you see signs and wonders.* Today we find it still being used in relation to spectacular events, such as solar eclipses and UFOs; but most present-day uses are motivated by other senses of the word *sign.* It proved an apt heading for a news article on a village which had an above-average number of deaf people, so that sign language was routinely encountered in the streets. And in its sense of 'identity marker', we find the expression used by companies that provide signage for vehicles or buildings. *Signs and Wonders* is also the title of a 1998 book by Tayma Starr and Edward Hayman about the way lighting and signs express modern USA; the subtitle is *The spectacular marketing of America.* For anyone who has stood marvelling among the animated neon giants of Las Vegas Strip or Times Square, New York, that sounds exactly right.

Chapter 33
Times and seasons

S igns and wonders provide John the Divine (Revelation) with much of its force. It is a book which has given modern English one of its most apocalyptic phrases:

1:8 I am Alpha and Omega, the beginning and the ending

Alpha and omega appears in all the early translations, and evidently made quite an impact on people, for it had entered general usage, in its sense of 'beginning and ending', by the end of the sixteenth century. The Elizabethan poet George Turberville dedicated a book of poems to his lady in 1567, describing her as *Alpha* when he began his book and as *Omega* at the end of it. Over four hundred years later, we find a writer lauding the 1969 Woodstock Festival on its fortieth anniversary with language just as strong. Woodstock, he says, was unique, marking the beginning and end of the counterculture movement: *The Alpha and the Omega of the Aquarian age.* Today we tend to use the phrase (usually with definite articles) more to mean 'the whole story'. When an agricultural writer says *Harvest timing is the Alpha and the Omega*, he means timing is everything.

The phrase is ripe for adaptation, though it isn't easy to do much with the Greek words. Pluralization is one option, seen for example in Thomas Carlyle's *History of Friedrich II of Prussia* (1865, Vol. 19): *this Siege of Dresden is the alpha to whatever omegas there may be.* Another option is to pun on other uses of the Greek word used as a brand name. *Daniel Craig is the Alpha and the Omega* headed one report, referring to the James Bond star who donated his Omega watch for a BBC Children in Need appeal. Rather cheeky was the Macintosh computer geek who wrote on his website: *I am the Apple and the Omega.* Still, these instances show the phrase is alive and well.

Also alive and well, and almost as apocalyptic, is *times and/or seasons*. This is chiefly known from Acts (1:7):

It is not for you to know the times or the seasons, which the Father hath put in his own power.

but it had occurred in this collocation once before, in Daniel (2:21), and would occur again in 1 Thessalonians 5.1:

But of the times and the seasons, brethren, ye have no need that I write unto you.

Wycliffe and Douai-Rheims have *moments* instead of *seasons*, but otherwise the phrase has been quite widely taken up. Today, the version with *and* is far more common than the one with *or*, and an article-less variant is the norm. It's a popular book title, for all kinds of topics. Anything seasonal attracts its use, such as material to do with gardening, travel, or the weather. One holiday brochure is headed *The best times and seasons to fly*. A *Times of Zambia* report in 2007 ran with the headline *Flooding—sudden shift of times and seasons*.

These biblical expressions of time tend to retain their elevated style. Another typical example is in Matthew 24:6:

all these things must come to pass, but the end is not yet.

Come to pass is used frequently, in both Old and New Testaments (see the examples at the beginning of Chapter 4), and is the translation of choice in sixteenth-century versions (not in Wycliffe, who uses such locutions as *behoveth to be done*). Its stylistic stature is confirmed when we see it forming part of the magisterial opening of John the Divine:

The Revelation of Jesus Christ, which God gave unto him, to shew unto his servants things which must shortly come to pass

It retains that stylistic force today, especially when used with an auxiliary verb (*shall come to pass*) and is rarely playfully adapted. It adds gravitas to a situation, and is therefore likely to be found in reference to sad or tragic situations, as in this 2009 headline: *Indonesian earthquake: Padang's worst fears come to pass.*

Also portentous is Matthew 6:34, which has given us two modern expressions:

Take therefore no thought for the morrow: for the morrow shall take thought for the things of itself. Sufficient unto the day is the evil thereof.

Tomorrow will take care of itself is the first. Here we see the greater influence of Tyndale (it's also in Bishops), which has *the morrow shall care for itself. Take thought of, shall be busy for* (Wycliffe), and *be solicitous for* (Douai-Rheims) never caught on. Today it appears in several variant forms (such as *Let tomorrow take care of itself, Tomorrow will look after itself*), and its status is proverbial. We'll find it used in diverse contexts, usually with some advisory sentiment in mind. To investors: concentrate on today's stock-market trends. To football teams: forget about next week's cup match, because it's tonight's league match which counts. *Will tomorrow take care of itself?* is a common question asked in relation to retirement planning schemes and health and fitness regimes.

The other expression, *sufficient unto the day*…has been even more widely taken up. It's easy to sense how the rhythmical bounce of the King James version (shared also by Bishops and Douai-Rheims) made this the popular choice over Wycliffe (*it suffiseth to the day his own malice*), Tyndale (*the day present hath ever enough of his own trouble*), or Geneva (*the day hath enough with his own grief*). The sentiment—dealing with today's problems rather than future worries—has had immense appeal, and the expression is found now in a wide range of variant forms, with *evil(s)* often replaced by *headaches, troubles, problems, hassles, cares, obligations*, and other alternatives. Anything perceived as an evil will do. *Sufficient unto the day are the emails thereof,* wrote one online forum participant, glumly. *Sufficient unto the day are the viruses thereof,* offered another, bitterly. And a different kind of infestation was in the mind of a flour merchant, who thought up the simple yet ingenious *Sufficient unto the day are the weevils thereof.*

The expression has attracted the attention of several well-known authors. Shelley wrote a poetic fragment in 1862 called 'Sufficient unto the day':

> Is not to-day enough?
> Why do I peer
> Into the darkness of the day to come?
> Is not to-morrow even as yesterday?
> And will the day that follows change thy doom?
> Few flowers grow upon thy wintry way;
> And who waits for thee in that cheerless home
> Whence thou hast fled, whither thou must return
> Charged with the load that makes thee faint and mourn?

207

Mark Twain, in a speech in 1879, illustrates the kind of adaptation that the phrase commonly receives:

Sufficient unto the day is one baby. As long as you are in your right mind don't you ever pray for twins. Twins amount to a permanent riot; and there ain't any real difference between triplets and a insurrection.

James Joyce, in *Ulysses*, offers us this variant: *Sufficient for the day is the newspaper thereof.* And Henry James, writing to Donna Isabella (29 July 1892) after arriving in Lausanne to stay with his brother and his family, realizes what he has let himself in for: *sufficient unto the day are the nephews thereof.*

But you don't have to be a famous author to manipulate this expression. The sense has been subverted by people convinced they *do* have to worry about the future, such as the writer who attacked the commercial philosophy of those who believe that *sufficient unto the current business period is the evil thereof.* And for some reason the expression has been used several times by reviewers, especially when damning a production with faint praise. I'm not sure which is the worse review:

Sufficient unto the performance is the evil thereof
Sufficient unto the play is the performance thereof

I think perhaps the second.

Chapter 34
Birth, life, and death

Quotations about birth, life, and death abound in the New Testament. *Let the dead bury their dead* (Luke 9:60), *Why seek ye the living among the dead?* (Luke 24:5), *I am the resurrection, and the life* (John 11:25)—this last particularly well known because of its use in the Christian burial service. But hardly any have become part of the fabric of everyday modern English. There's an exception in Mark 14:21:

woe to that man by whom the Son of man is betrayed! good were it for that man if he had never been born.

I wish I'd never been born is the sad cry of many a lyricist. For the generation that grew up with the pop group Queen, it's an unforgettable line in 'Bohemian Rhapsody'.

Birth, life, and death expressions usually retain a sense of their biblical origins. Echoes of Acts 17:28 are heard whenever we encounter this unusual three-verb sequence:

For in him we live, and move, and have our being

It wouldn't normally be considered stylistically elegant to have a sequence of two *and*s, but the biblical echo is enough to carry it through when we read (in a book on school practices) *the* *systems in which we live and move and have our first legal education.*

A life expression which has achieved some popularity beyond quotation is found in John 14:6:

Jesus saith unto him, I am the way, the truth, and the life

It's rare to find any translation departing from the *way, truth, life* sequence, though the use of a medial *and* is optional. Quite a few writers have replaced *life* by *light*, over the years, but whether the change is deliberate or a misquotation is always difficult to say. Usually, when this phrase is adapted, there's a clear point being made—such as in an article on the crusading mentality of some religions (*the way, the truth, and the sword*), the launch of a Bible software review site (*the way, the truth, and the iLife*), or the official e-zine of the Christian Gamers Guild (*the way, the truth, and the dice*).

It's invariably the last word in the sequence which is adapted. Criticism of a politician has several times used *the way, the truth, and the lie*. A writer, licking his wounds after a particularly savage piece of copy-editing, grumbled about *the way, the truth, and the sub-editor*. And an entry in the *Urban Dictionary* <http://www.urbandictionary.com> for *awesomesauce* ('something that is more awesome than awesome'—I kid you not) at one point went biblical: *Awesomesauce is the way, the truth, and the awesome.*

As for death, the pair of sentences in 1 Corinthians 15:55 have proved to be very productive:

O death, where is thy sting? O grave, where is thy victory?

Tyndale and Bishops have *hell* for *grave*, and Wycliffe has *prick* for *sting*. Douai-Rheims has the curious reversed repetition: *O death, where is thy victory? O death, where is thy sting?*

It is the King James (and Geneva) version which has survived, doubtless reinforced in many modern ears by its use in Handel's *Messiah*. Both elements are widely adapted today, either singly or in combination, by replacing the initial or final nouns, as the following examples illustrate. The vocative *O* is optional. *Death* and *sting* are the words which attract most attention:

Racism: where is thy sting? [on the success of ethnic community work]

O curse of dimensionality, where is thy sting? [a high-tech paper on economic analysis]

Prison, where is thy sting? [on prisoners who reoffend]

Nematode, where is thy sting? [on new products for controlling sting nematodes on golf courses]

O cookie, where is thy victory? [on someone winning a recipe competition]

O death, where is thy definition? [on the question of brain death]

O death, where is thy dignity? [on the 'right to die' debate]

The most unusual application of the *O death*...sentence arose out of a naming coincidence. A report on the 1994 Grammys focused on a well-known pop singer. The headline ran: *Mockery, where is thy Sting?: Gordon Sumner, causing a buzz at the Grammys*. The pun has since been used several times. It evidently proved irresistible in 2007 when Sting's group, Police, had a reunion. One reviewer, it seems, found the occasion uninspiring: *Sting, where is thy sting?*

The most productive birth expression comes from John 3:3:

Except a man be born again, he cannot see the kingdom of God.

All the early translations use the phrase *born again*, except Tyndale, who has *born anew*. The expression had status only as a quotation until the 1960s. Then it became the defining word of the spiritual renewal movement associated especially with evangelical Christianity: *born-again Christians* were those who had been newly converted or who had had their faith revitalized in some way. Within a decade, the expression was being used for any person or group who had taken on a fresh identity or been given a new opportunity. We find *born-again chefs* who have adopted a new television persona; *born-again singers* who have taken up a new singing style; *born-again writers* who have picked up the pen again after years of writer's block; and *born-again students* who go back to university after several years away from full-time education. Gore Vidal is attributed with the statement *I'm a born-again atheist.*

Politicians are especially prone to renewal in this way: in the UK, there have been stories of the *born-again Labour Party*, and people talk about *born-again socialists.* There have been *born-again Tories* and *Liberals* too. In 2003, a *Times* headline read *Blair pours scorn on record of 'born-again' Tory* (referring to Michael Howard). In the USA there have been both *born-again Democrats* and *born-again Republicans.*

Other senses have developed. Locations can now be born again, if they have been renovated or restored in some way, such as Canary Wharf or the East End Olympic site in London. Places that have been ravaged by war or civil strife, such as Beirut, Berlin, and Belfast, are especially likely to attract the adjective. Institutions likewise. *The National Palace Museum is born again* was the headline in the *Taipei Times* in 2007, reporting the end of a three-year period of renovation.

A famous birth-related expression occurs in Luke 2:7:

And she brought forth her firstborn son, and wrapped him in swaddling clothes, and laid him in a manger; because there was no room for them in the inn.

No room at the inn is what has come down to us, later stylists avoiding the phonetic repetition of *in/inn. Inn* is sometimes taken literally, as in this headline reporting the ban on smoking in pubs and restaurants in England: *No room at the inn for smokers*. An ingenious variant appeared in the Scottish *Highland News*, when a bumper tourist invasion filled hotels in one town and forced some visitors to sleep in their cars or travel miles to find accommodation: *No room at the Inn-verness*.

The application of the expression broadened significantly in the twentieth century. *Inn* came to include any place of residence, temporary or permanent. It has been used in relation to articles about bed shortages in hospitals (especially when mothers about to give birth are affected) and about cases where applicants for political asylum have been turned down. It has even referred to a presidential residence. When the news broke that George Bush had declined Barack Obama's request to move into the White House's guest-house just before Christmas 2008, with his Washington inauguration just a few weeks away, the *Independent* headline was *No room at the inn for Obama after Bush snub*. Playful adaptations, of course, can take the word in several directions, as *inn* rhymes with many other words in English. One local council found itself unable to cope with the huge amount of waste accumulated after Christmas. The headline read: *No room at the bin*.

Chapter 35
Countries, kingdoms, Armageddon

We wouldn't expect the names of specific places to have much long-term influence on a language, but a small number have crept through. *Can there any good thing come out of Nazareth?* (John 1:46) is a case in point. Today the expression is usually *Can anything good come out of...*, but the places so described range from whole continents to major cities. *Can anything good come out of Hollywood?* asked one disaffected film critic. The expression does seem to be extending its range. *Can anything good come out of this recession?* was a headline in 2009.

Samaria has achieved modern English renown through its inhabitants—or, to be precise, a particular inhabitant, the *good Samaritan* (Luke 10:33). That phrase doesn't actually appear in the Bible, but it didn't take long for it to arise: it was the title of a book about the parable in 1640. Today it is a favourite name for a caring organization, used for hospitals, care centres, nursing homes, even pet adoption agencies. Anyone who comes to the aid of anyone else can be so labelled, whether in real life or fiction. It's a common T-shirt motif. So is its inverse, for someone who claims to stand around and do nothing: *the bad Samaritan*. (A similar development of meaning happened to *Philistines*, found from Genesis onwards. Being the 'bad guys' of the Old Testament narratives, it's not surprising to find the word being used with negative senses—at first, as early as 1600, to refer to debauched and drunken people, and later to anyone culturally backward or materialistic. The geographical source of the name is obscure, though an ancient philological link with the origins of *Palestine* has been noted, and an ancient people referred to as *Palusata* or *Purusati* is recorded in Egyptian records from around 1200 BC.)

One of the best-known place-names of the New Testament is found in John the Divine (Revelation) 16:16:

And he gathered them together into a place called in the Hebrew tongue Armageddon.

This name, the place of the last battle on Earth, appears in all the translations. In modern English it has developed the sense of 'a final conflict on a grand scale' and thus 'the ultimate disaster'. How long it has had this general sense isn't clear. The earliest *Oxford English Dictionary* citations date only from 1811, though I think it's only a matter of time before earlier instances are found. Today, its fame is mainly due to the popularity of disaster films, notably *Armageddon* (1998). The word has really become a synonym for 'disaster', especially if the crisis is likely to destroy the planet. Hence we find the strapline for *Armageddon Online: your source for disaster news and end of the world scenarios.*

Smaller-scale enterprises also attract the term, sometimes with a touch of hyperbole, as in the annual professional wrestling event called *Armageddon. Financial Armageddon* became almost a cliché in 2008–9. *Software Armageddon* is another common phrase, as viruses and other malware become more sophisticated. And the ecological movement employs the name quite a bit, especially when talking about the impending extinction of a species.

Countries, kingdoms, Armageddon

Frog-killing disease jumps Panama Canal, ran one report in 2008. It was headed *Armageddon for amphibians?*

Kingdom and *country* are rather more fruitful. *My kingdom is not of this world* (John 18:36) is usually encountered just as a quotation, but it goes beyond this when used about a superstar. *Usain Bolt is not of this world*, claimed several articles, following the Jamaican sprinter's athletic achievements in 2009. *A kingdom divided against itself shall not stand* has been even more influential. It appears succinctly in Mark (3:24):

And if a kingdom be divided against itself, that kingdom cannot stand.

King James (along with Geneva and Douai-Rheims) departs here from the Wycliffe/Tyndale/Bishops tradition, which uses *realm* and *endure*. An 'expanded' version appears in Matthew (12:25, echoed in Luke 11:17):

Every kingdom divided against itself is brought to desolation; and every city or house divided against itself shall not stand

Over the years, we find other nouns replacing *kingdom/city/house*, such as *nation*, *people*, and *profession*.

The sentiment has appealed greatly to politicians, whenever factions arise within a political party or government. Probably the most famous use of the expression was by Abraham Lincoln in 1858, just before the secession that led to the American Civil War:

'A house divided against itself cannot stand.' I believe the government cannot endure permanently half slave and half free. I do not expect the Union to be dissolved—I do not expect the house to fall—but I do expect it will cease to be divided.

The same expression has been used in the debate surrounding the ratification of the European Union constitution.

The sentence has had remarkably little playful use, suggesting that it remains in people's minds as a quotation. But I did find one adaptation, in an article about inconsistencies in the treatment of the mythical characters in some video games. If I've got this right, it appears that, in some games, low-scoring creatures are able to outplay high-value rulers—a procedure which the rules ought not to allow. The critic's comment: *Every story divided against itself shall not stand*.

Country has proved influential as a result of Matthew 13:57:

A prophet is not without honour, save in his own country, and in his own house.

The sentiment is expanded a little in Mark (6:4), who adds *and among his own kin*, and it appears in shortened form in Luke (4:24): *No prophet is accepted in his own country*. The modern version typically uses the shorter version, but reflects the variation found here and in the other translations, generally using *honour* (Wycliffe has *worship*), and recognizing both *country* and *house*. If the male pronoun is felt to be biasing, it is sometimes replaced by *her*, or the expression pluralized to *their*.

The meaning has changed. It's no longer only 'prophets' who fail to receive the honour due to them. Anyone whose merit has been ignored or played down in their own country can attract the expression—writers, environmentalists, academics, painters. Famous examples include Dylan Thomas, Arthur Miller, Woody Allen, and Alexander Solzhenitsyn. It may even be a group of people. An article about the Portugal rugby team, apparently little known at home but highly praised abroad, elicited the comment that *if Portugal's players seem to be without much honour in their own country, that is certainly not the case anywhere else*. The expression may even be used with self-reference. It's quite common to hear speakers, whose views are not being accepted by their audience, affirm (referring to themselves) that *A prophet is never heard in his own country.*

Nor does *country* have to be taken literally. The expression can be used if the unrecognized contribution has been to a town or a village, or to an institution such as a university or society. One story reported an American academic who held a viewpoint that his college found unpalatable. The headline read: *A prof without honour in his own country.* The sense perhaps becomes a little strained when the pun involves an inanimate noun. One writer, objecting to the newspaper cartoon caricatures of profit-generating businessmen, argued that without such people an economy would quickly go under. He concluded his piece: *Profit is without honor in its own country.*

Chapter 36
Building houses, mansions, sepulchres

Matthew 16:18 introduces one of the most famous building metaphors of all time:

thou art Peter, and upon this rock I will build my church

The first punning use of *rock* in this way is found in Tyndale's translation, and it has had such iconic status in Christian tradition that it's unusual to find a translation that departs from it (Wycliffe is one of the exceptions, with *stone*). Its modern meaning, covering such notions as 'foundation', 'support', 'shelter', and 'protection', has made it appeal greatly to lyricists. Innumerable popular songs have made use of such lines as *You are my rock* and *Upon this rock*. And the 'foundation' sense has brought a wide range of uses, as soon as someone has established a basis for a project. *Upon this rock I will build my survey*, wrote one researcher. In 2006, Oprah Winfrey was a guest on Rachael Ray's new cookery talk show. The unimpressed *Time* critic began his piece with a biblical pastiche: *And Oprah spake, 'Blessed are you, for you are Rachael, and upon this rock I will build my television empire.'*

The adaptations chiefly focus on *rock*. All keep the spirit of the original expression, stressing the notion of a turning-point:

> Upon this man I will build my life [a romance website]
> Upon this Web I will build my stories [a new website]
> Upon this Flock I will build my world [a new browser]
> Upon this spirit I will build my jazz [review of a jazz CD]

The prize for innovation, however, has to go to a report on the Blingdom of God website. Forty volunteers spent 18 months building a figure of Jesus composed of 30,000 Lego pieces. The headline? *Upon this Lego brick I will build my church.*

A little earlier, Matthew reports another building metaphor. In 7:24 we hear of a wise man who *built his house upon a rock*, and two verses later of a foolish man who *built his house upon the sand*. The contrast has appealed to all ages and statuses, from tiny tots to presidents. Countless numbers of children have learned about it in nursery school or Sunday school by performing the action song *The wise man built his house upon a rock* (*And the rain came tumbling down*). Barack Obama used it in a major speech in April 2009:

We cannot rebuild this economy on the same pile of sand. We must build our house upon a rock. We must lay a new foundation for growth and prosperity.

Another house metaphor appears in John 14:2:

In my Father's house are many mansions.

Doubtless it was the alliteration and internal rhyme of *many mansions*, used by both Tyndale and Douai-Rheims, that gave this phrase popular appeal. Wycliffe has *dwellings*, and Bishops/ Geneva have *dwelling places*, neither of which have the same ring. An example of the way the sense generalized can be found in one of Charles Lamb's *Elia* essays (1823), 'The Old and the New Schoolmaster':

Not that I affect ignorance—but my head has not many mansions, nor spacious; and I have been obliged to fill it with such cabinet curiosities as it can hold without aching.

In the twentieth century, its place in popular intuition was assured (at least for a while) when it became an Elvis Presley ballad. But it was always a popular idiom among academics, politicians, and others who routinely deal with different points of view. *There are many mansions on the political right*, began one report. And the heading *Two houses, many mansions* has been used several times with reference to a parliamentary system which has two houses but many policy divisions. More literally, the phrase appeals to those working in real estate and housing associations. The sudden availability of houses for sale during a recession led to *In a falling house market there are many mansions*. The comment would have made people nod in agreement in 2009. In fact that particular headline was written in 1993. Some biblical adaptations, it seems, are cyclical.

One of the most distinctive biblical phrases appears in Matthew 23:27:

Woe unto you, scribes and Pharisees, hypocrites! for ye are like unto whited sepulchres, which indeed appear beautiful outward, but are within full of dead men's bones, and of all uncleanness.

This is very much a King James expression (though it appears also in Douai-Rheims). Wycliffe has the similar *sepulchres whited*, but Tyndale has *painted tombs*, Geneva *whited tombs*, and Bishops *painted sepulchres*. The metaphor is based on the practice of painting the stone covering a tomb with whitewash, so that Jews would be sure to notice it and not defile themselves by touching it. Today, the phrase has the same connotations of hypocrisy, referring to people who are not what they purport to be. It can apply to companies or even their products, as when one critic of a new computer chip called it a *whited sepulchre*, because it didn't perform as the makers said it should. Neither word is common outside this expression today. People talk about things being *whitened*, not *whited* (cf. *fatted*, p. 184), and *sepulchres* are only likely to be seen on tourist routes or in horror films. I've found no playful adaptation of the phrase worth mentioning.

Houses have keys, and so it seems do bottomless pits, according to John the Divine (Revelation) 9:1:

> And the fifth angel sounded, and I saw a star fall from heaven unto the earth: and to him was given the key of the bottomless pit.

Wycliffe has *pit of deepness*, but it is *bottomless pit*, used several times by John, which has captured the popular imagination. Today it is primarily applied to financial situations. Harassed parents reject their offspring's continual requests for money with *I'm not a bottomless pit!* Harassed mortgage advisors describe the process of people getting deeper into debt as *falling into a bottomless pit. Fannie Mae: a bottomless pit for U.S. taxpayers,* warned one financial website in 2009.

But it isn't only expenditure that is described in this way. The metaphor is also there for people who have voracious appetites (*Your stomach is a bottomless pit!*), or who can't stop eating for whatever reason. People with a binge-eating disorder often say *My stomach feels like a bottomless pit.* And the expression has been extended to abstract notions, with people talking about *a bottomless pit of confusion* or *stupidity* when they feel a difficult situation has got out of control.

One further example from Matthew continues the housing theme, in 21:13:

It is written, My house shall be called the house of prayer; but ye have made it a den of thieves.

The same phrase *den of thieves* is found in Mark 11:17 and Luke 19:46, and in all the early translations. It probably came into everyday English during the seventeenth century, but citations are lacking. Certainly by the time Daniel Defoe wrote *Robinson Crusoe* (1719), the phrase was in general use: Crusoe reflects at one point that the inhabitants of the island might have turned pirates *and so made the island a den of thieves* (Volume 2, Chapter 8). Today the meaning has broadened: it no longer means only people who steal, but any kind of villain, and it has been used in that way for many a title of a book, game, or television episode. People who write online viruses have been called *a virtual den of thieves*. The phrase has received very little adaptation in its phrasing—*den of robbers* is quite common, and (in the twentieth century) *den of iniquity*, but little else.

I had thought that Matthew 7:7 would complete my housing theme, given that it mentions knocking on doors:

Ask, and it shall be given you; seek, and ye shall find; knock, and it shall be opened unto you

It is a rhetorically striking sequence, repeated in Luke (11:9), and appearing in all the early translations, so we might have expected all three elements to be influential. However, only the *seek* element has proved productive.

Perhaps it is the information age which has fuelled the modern use of the expression. We find it beckoning us towards any kind of search initiative, such as looking in an online retail directory, a library catalogue, a holiday travel brochure, or a 'yellow pages' type of database. The *Daily Telegraph* in 2001 had the headline *Seek and ye shall find a wife on the internet*—about the increase in vicars using online dating agencies. And indeed, it is the internet which has promoted the expression as a virtual slogan, with search engines preaching *e-seek and you shall find*. Now that the wiki movement has taken it up, its linguistic future seems assured: *Seek and you shall find (and the search will be refined!)* says wikiseek.com.

The auxiliary verb tends to be *you will*, these days, but a surprising number of people stay with *ye shall*, both in speech and writing. Several verbs have replaced the one which begins the expression: the invitation is often to *speak/ask/search/surf/click/ google and ye shall find*. And even more adaptation has taken place at the end, as this small selection of examples illustrates:

seek and ye shall be sent the hyperlink [giving access to a site]

seek and ye shall be found [on privacy issues online]

seek and ye shall be confused [because stores offer us too much choice]

seek and ye shall fine [on librarians keeping tabs on their books-unreturned file]

A prize, I think, must go to the heading of a blog about the search for Osama bin Laden: *seek and ye shall seek*.

Chapter 37
Millstones, crosses, yokes, pricks

There are some words which are always mentioned whenever people talk about 'words from the Bible'. *Stumbling-block* is one, appearing several times in the Old and New Testaments (initially in Leviticus 19:14), and first used by Tyndale (Wycliffe has *hurting*). *Shibboleth*, we have seen (p. 74), is another. These are unusual. Modern English has been influenced far more by biblical phrases than by individual words.

The point can be illustrated from the theme of burdens. A word like *millstone* is of little linguistic interest as long as we think of it only as one of the heavy stones which millers traditionally used to grind their corn. But when it is used as in Matthew 18:6 (and Mark 9:42) it becomes memorable:

But whoso shall offend one of these little ones which believe in me, it were better for him that a millstone were hanged about his neck, and that he were drowned in the depth of the sea.

The literal meaning of *millstone* is ancient; the word is found in some Anglo-Saxon glossaries. The biblical sense is plainly literal too, and the vivid locution is found in all translations, with only minor variations. The first figurative usage of *a millstone (a)round someone's neck*, meaning 'a heavy or inescapable burden

225

or responsibility', is not recorded in the *Oxford English Dictionary* until the late eighteenth century. It turns up regularly in literature thereafter. Charles Dickens has Mr Wickfield remark about Uriah Heep: *You see the millstone that he is about my neck* (in *David Copperfield*, Chapter 39). It is often shortened to simply *millstone*.

The popularity of the phrase continues today. A politician is often criticized as being *a millstone around his (or her) party's neck*. A footballer who hasn't behaved himself is described as *a millstone around the neck of his club*. An expensive local government building venture can become *a millstone around the neck of the Council*. Barack Obama, during his 2009 African visit, described the conflicts in the region as *a millstone around Africa's neck*. After such instances, it comes as a bit of a relief to see *neck* used literally. A report on men's fashions began: *The tie: a millstone around our necks?*

It isn't always a neck. *Extra pounds can be a millstone around a career*, said one report about a perceived problem of weight among female executives. Another talked about the war in Vietnam being *a millstone around Nixon's presidency*. Be careful about the software you buy, said another, for it can be *a millstone around your cyberneck*.

Yoke is another everyday rural term which has become memorable on account of its biblical collocation. It appears in Matthew 11:30:

For my yoke is easy, and my burden is light.

The early translations are broadly similar, though Wycliffe has *my yoke is soft and my charge light*, and Douai-Rheims has *my yoke is sweet*. The expression has proved remarkably resistant to adaptation. It is hardly ever used outside its original religious context, and playful adaptations are very rare. One of these exceptions appeared on a New Age site: *my yoga is easy, and my burden is light.*

Burden by itself is another inconsequential word, in use since Anglo-Saxon times. In Galatians 6:5, though, it appears in a phrase which has had some influence:

For every man shall bear his own burden.

There's nothing biblical about the collocation of *bear* and *burden* as such, which is used several times in both Old and New Testaments. That too can be found in Old English. But *bearing one's own burden* has a different ring to it. The phrasing is in Tyndale and several other early versions, and was already in general use before King James. Bishop Lancelot Andrewes used it in his Christmas Day sermon in 1606: *meet it is every one should bear his own burden.* It became a favourite expression among novelists, as this small sample illustrates:

Rosine! bear your own burden. Be brave (Charlotte Brontë, *Villette*, Chapter 28)

Ah me! you must bear your own burden, fashion your own faith (William Thackeray, *Pendennis*, Chapter 35)

I have borne my own burden in silence (Walter Scott, *The Abbott*, Chapter 5)

Perhaps as a consequence of that, the expression sounds somewhat literary today, and is common only in writing on serious topics. For example, a business report recommended the investigation of *companies who do not bear their own burden of health care for their workers*; and an article on cyclists breaking the law (by going through red lights) commented: *Cyclists do bear their own burden.* At the same time, journalists find it difficult to resist making the obvious pun. I've lost count of the number of times I've seen headlines such as *Teen mothers bear their own burden.*

227

A whole cluster of biblical references focus on the notion of someone *having a cross to bear*. Matthew (10:38, 16:24) and Mark (8:34) talk about a man *taking* or *taking up* his cross, and all the translations have similar phrasing. Luke, however, has *bear* (14:27):

And whosoever doth not bear his cross, and come after me, cannot be my disciple.

Perhaps because of the way *bearing a cross* is used in all four Gospels (Matthew 27:32, Mark 15:21, Luke 23:26, John 19:17) in relation to Jesus's crucifixion, it is this verb which is most often used today. The phrase continues to have a Christian content for many people, and the notion of 'accepting a trial with Christian patience' remains strong in their minds. But for others, the allusion to a physical cross has been lost, and the Christian element is irrelevant; for them, the sense is simply 'a burden of responsibility that has to be coped with alone'. *We all have our cross to bear* is said by believers and nonbelievers alike.

The phrase turns up in some unusual contexts. It's a theme of several pop songs, for example, such as this one by Billy Joel:

We all have our cross to bear.
We all walk in darkness sometimes.
Though I know it don't seem fair,
We all have our cross to bear.

In 2009, several papers alluded to the *cross* (aka Bill) that Hillary Clinton was having to bear in her role as secretary of state. Another news report was headed *Air-conditioning: our cross to bear* (because of the impact it has on our environment). And when, in 2007, the firm Johnson & Johnson sued the American Red Cross over the right to use the red-cross emblem, more than one journal seized upon the pun: *Whose red cross to bear?*

The notion of a burden has an unusual lexical expression in Acts 9:5:

it is hard for thee to kick against the pricks.

This expression, heard by Paul at the moment of his conversion, is currently having a confusing time. The origin of the expression lies in the notion of a prick or goad used for driving cattle. If the animal kicked out against the prick, it would be used again, and harder. The early translations generally use *prick*, in either singular or plural; Douai-Rheims uses *goad*. The modern meaning has evolved into 'argue or fight against those in authority' or 'struggle against fate', especially in such a way that one ends up hurting oneself. The verb by itself, *kick against*, meaning 'object strongly to', emerged in English at about the same time, and was probably influenced by the other expression.

The uncertainty over the modern use of *kick against the pricks* stems from the other meanings of the noun. The 'penis' sense has been in English since the sixteenth century, so a *double entendre* must often have been lurking in the wings, though, one imagines, rarely surfacing in genteel speech or writing. In the less genteel atmosphere of the twenty-first century, there has been no such reluctance, and *prick* developed an additional sense: 'a really stupid, contemptible, or annoying person'. As a result, it is now virtually impossible to use the expression without the secondary meaning coming to mind, so that many people avoid it. On the other hand, some writers make capital out of it. This extract from a 2006 *Guardian* report on a football coach illustrates the kind of thing that happens. The headline was *Katanec looks to kick against the pricks with Macedonia.*

Millstones, crosses, yokes, pricks

As epitaphs go, most people would probably hope for something rather better than 'you're a prick of a coach and you were a prick of a player.' Srecko Katanec certainly deserves better but he accepts that unless he does something remarkable with the Former Yugoslav Republic of Macedonia, he is stuck with it.

When people try to use the expression without additional nuance, it's generally in relation to the constraints imposed by tradition or authority, especially political authority. In 2004, Charles Wheeler wrote an article for the *Guardian* entitled *We have to kick against the pricks*, arguing that Britain had to lose its reluctance to question its special relationship with the USA. An interview with Noam Chomsky in a *Times* periodical in 1999 was headed: *A lifetime kicking against the pricks*.

The potential sexual nuances haven't stopped the adaptation of the expression. Indeed, we encounter it in a highly diverse range of situations:

Kicking against the prejudice [on a woman football player]

Kicking against the iX [on a plan to form a pan-European stock-exchange, iX]

Kicking against the prickles [on a weed-clearing day in Australia]

It's good to kick against the prigs [on religious practice being interpreted too narrowly]

They're kicking against the bricks [on a dance company that used a tower of bricks as a prop for their performance]

Here, it seems, the original expression is being recalled without the modern 'nudge nudge' causing any interference.

Chapter 38
Sowing seeds

T hings that grow are a rich source of religious metaphor. The New Testament has a great deal to say about vines, crops, fruit, and seed, and the whole process of harvesting. Most of the references have come down to us as quotations, such as John 15:5 *I am the vine, ye are the branches* or Matthew 6:28 *Consider the lilies of the field, how they grow*. Admittedly, some lines have become famous outside their original context, but this is because they have been adopted as titles of literary works, such as Christina Rosetti's poem *Consider the lilies of the field* (1853) or William Edmund Barrett's book *Lilies of the Field* (1962). The latter became especially well-known when it was turned into an award-winning film the following year. It got Sidney Poitier an Oscar.

Matthew 9:37 *The harvest truly is plenteous, but the labourers are few* has had rather more influence. It is echoed in Luke (10:2), but with *great* replacing *plenteous*. Modern versions add a certain amount of variation, such as *plentiful* for *plenteous* and *workers* for *labourers* (though it should be noted that Wycliffe has *there is much ripe corn but few work men*). It's a much-quoted saying, made applicable to many situations. Thomas Carlyle, for example, uses it in a letter to Matthew Allen (7 June 1820):

After all, however, I think, if it pay, you do well to write on politics. The harvest truly is great but the labourers are few.

However, the expression has received little modern adaptation. Among the few allusions I found was one in an article on shortages in agricultural equipment (*the harvest is great but the combines are few*) and another about agricultural rates of pay (*the harvest is great but the labourers are grumbling*). For the most part, it remains steadfastly a quotation.

Fruits has proved more influential. This is a reference to Matthew 7:20:

Wherefore by their fruits ye shall know them.

There is an echo in Luke 6:44: *For every tree is known by his own fruit.* Virtually the same phrasing is found in all the early translations. Today, we find the same sentiment—'knowing who someone really is by the way they behave'—expressed through a wide variety of nouns: *fruits* or *fruit* is often replaced by *deeds, acts, methods*, and other nouns of performance. What is interesting is to see the individual slants placed upon the expression by different groups. Visiting someone's house for the first time? *By their books you shall know them.* Politicians at election time? *By their campaign gear you shall know them.* A project on regional accents and dialects? *By their speech you shall know them.* An article discussing the National Geographic Society's amazing genographic project on the patterns of human migration led with *By their genes you shall know them.* And which world would *By their logos you shall know them* belong to? Or *By their lights you shall know them?* Advertising and car design respectively.

Undoubtedly the two most productive growth idioms have come from sowing seeds. The first is in Matthew 13:4:

And when he sowed, some seeds fell by the way side, and the fowls came and devoured them up

The phrasing is echoed in Mark (4:4) and Luke (8:5), and appears in all the translations, with minor variants (Tyndale and Bishops have *wayes side*, Wycliffe has *besides the way*). The idiom has worn well, despite *wayside* becoming less used as an independent word. *Roadside* often replaces it. The modern meaning—'fail to stay the course', 'drop out'—is so general that the expression has been applied in all kinds of situations. People, places, objects, processes, activities—virtually anything can *fall by the wayside*, as these examples illustrate:

Climate bill may fall by the wayside

Green issues falling by the wayside

Potential Newcastle owners fall by the wayside [a football event]

Bloggers will fall by the wayside [as people stop reading them]

Don't let customer service fall by the wayside

Have your hobbies fallen by the wayside?

The tweets that fell by the wayside [by ending up in the wrong place]

Tennis, of course, allows the perfect piece of wordplay:

Top seeds fall by the wayside

The same wide range of uses is found in the associated expression of seeds falling *on stony ground* (Mark 4:5), the phrasing that has been preferred at the expense of *upon stony places* (Matthew 13:5). The words are used in relation to many kinds of argument or appeal where the response has been negative. A software company issued an upgrade which was widely felt not to solve a problem: *security updates fall on stony ground*. President Bush travelled around the Middle East calling for more democracy: *Fragile seeds that fall on stony ground* was the headline in the *Times*. Another headline reported that a request for extra funding to meet an aid shortfall had proved unsuccessful: *UNICEF appeals fall on stony ground*. And the literal sense must not be forgotten. An article about farming in crisis was headed simply: *Seeds falling on stony ground*.

We've already seen (in Chapter 21) the influence of sowing and reaping, and the theme recurs in Galatians 6:7:

Be not deceived; God is not mocked: for whatsoever a man soweth, that shall he also reap.

This expression appears in all the translations, and has come down to us as the proverbial *as you sew, so shall you reap*—with varying pronouns and conjunctions (*whatever a man sows...*, *as we sow...*). It's a highly productive expression, presumably because there's no limit to the number of situations where someone needs to be warned about the consequences of an action. And it has attracted an enormous variety of adaptations.

The agricultural basis of the expression has made it appeal to all who work on the land. It has headed articles giving advice about organic food and green living in general, as well as a warning to farmers about the importance of using only certified seed for planting. A piece on planting at the right time motivated *As you sow, so shall you ripen*. One on garlic-growing in Scotland resulted in *As you sow, so shall you reek*. Another on planting soya began *As we soy, so shall we reap*. A rather glum article on gardening led to *As you sow, so shall you weed*. And an even sadder piece was headed *As you sow, so shall you weep*. It was about floods wiping out a harvest in Bangladesh. That is, unfortunately, a common headline.

Virtually anything can be sown and reaped. We see the headline above such diverse articles as stock-market investments, examination preparations, car engine maintenance, and personal exercise. Either end of the expression can be adapted, but it is the opening clause which is most often varied, as these newspaper reports illustrate:

As you tow, so shall you reap [a breakdown van is caught going through a red light]

As you spin, so shall you reap [the consequences of political manipulation]

As you spend, so shall you reap [the importance of saving]

As you show, so shall you reap [new designs on the fashion catwalk]

As you vote, so shall you reap [in many a political commentary]

New adaptations are common. The latest (at the time of writing) draws netizens' attention to the importance of maintaining their social networking connectivity: *As you tweet, so shall you reap.*

Chapter 39
Salt and wine

Re+eferences to food and drink abound in the New Testament, but hardly any have influenced the formation of a general-purpose idiom in modern English. Most of the metaphors remain firmly grounded in their original religious setting. For example, *I am the bread of life* (John 6:35) has been the naming motivation for hundreds of missionary and pastoral projects, but little beyond that, other than its adoption as the name of various bakery stores. This is a striking contrast with the way *manna* has come to be used (Chapter 10).

A similar treatment has been afforded to *five loaves and two fishes* (in the parable recounted in Mark 6:41 and elsewhere). All the references I have found are either references to the parable or to mission-related activities, such as the name of charitable organizations providing food for the hungry. They rarely adapt the expression—one joyful exception being a book on missionary work in Ukraine called *Five Loaves and Two Bowls of Borscht*. And the same is found when we look at other quotations involving food, such as Matthew 15:27: *yet the dogs eat of the crumbs which fall from their masters' table*. The vast majority of modern uses maintain the religious connection. For example, there is a charity whose aim is to place collection boxes in restaurants, to alleviate world hunger: it is called *Crumbs from the Table*. Just occasionally we encounter a non-religious use, such as a gossip column called *Crumbs from the table*.

Two expressions make up a little for the lack of food-related idiom. The first is in Matthew 5:13:

Ye are the salt of the earth

This is Jesus, in the 'Sermon on the Mount', talking to the crowds. The earliest reference in English is in one of the Anglo-Saxon Gospels (Lindisfarne), and it appears in all the translations. It eventually became an everyday phrase, as illustrated by Chaucer's use in his *Summoner's Tale* (line 2196). 'You be the salt of the earth, and the savour', says the lord to the friar.

The application of the phrase has varied somewhat over the centuries. In the Middle Ages, according to some writers, the salt was to be found in the universities; for others, it was the aristocracy; for others, the army. Even as late as the nineteenth century, there remained an upper-class ring to the phrase: the *Oxford English Dictionary* has a quotation from the *Literary Gazette* of 1842: 'To dine like queens, kings, princes, potentates, and the other "salt of the earth".' The sense then moved in the opposite direction, as we hear in the opening lines of the Rolling Stones song *Salt of the Earth* (1968):

Let's drink to the hard working people
Let's drink to the lowly of birth
Raise your glass to the good and the evil
Let's drink to the salt of the earth.

Today, it refers more to personality than to class. Anyone who by their behaviour demonstrates trustworthiness, reliability, honesty, or kindness might be described as *the salt of the earth*.

Not surprisingly, then, the expression has come to be adopted as a company name by firms wanting to suggest that their service is reliable, down-to-earth, and customer friendly. If their products are for everyday use (such as clothing), so much the better; and even more so if they contain natural ingredients, such as deodorants, skin care, and bath salts. Restaurants like the name, as do organic food stores. And of course the phrase appeals whenever someone writes a piece about salt in its literal sense, such as in relation to desalination plants or ice management on roads.

The other nourishment idiom is drink-related. It is in Matthew 9:17:

Neither do men put new wine into old bottles: else the bottles break, and the wine runneth out, and the bottles perish: but they put new wine into new bottles, and both are preserved.

You'd think people could hardly fail to remember this piece of imagery, for it is echoed virtually word for word in Mark (2:22) and Luke (5:37), yet it has come down to us surrounded in confusion. Which is it? Do we say *new wine in/into old bottles* or *old wine in/into new bottles*? It turns out that we say both, and in a mixed-up sort of way, according to search-engine counts. *Old in new* is twice as common as *new in old*; but *new into old* is ten times as common as *old into new*. Both orders are found quite early on—certainly in the 1700s. It suggests that, when the translations first appeared, ordinary people didn't fully understood what was going on. Perhaps if the translators had used *wineskins* (as some later versions did), the sense would have been clearer, for it is the flexibility of new wineskins that allows new wine to ferment without bursting the skins. Biblical commentators vary in their elucidation of the verse, though the thrust of the point seems clear enough: it's no good trying to take up a new way of thinking if people are firmly stuck in their old ways.

The influence of King James (along with Wycliffe and Douai-Rheims) seems to have been decisive, for today the expression is predominantly *bottles*, with the *vessels* of Tyndale, Bishops, and Geneva hardly ever encountered. But the meaning has changed. Anyone who talks about *old wine in new bottles* nowadays is referring to any attempt to pass something old off as new. It's an alternative to *there's nothing new under the sun* (p. 102). Whether it's a new political policy, a new car model, a development in medical treatment, or a new staging of an opera, if the enterprise fails to convince people that it is original, it will attract the charge of *old wine in new bottles*.

Or, ironically, *new wine in old bottles*. This is the remarkable thing that's happened to this phrase: the meaning stays the same even when the words have been reversed. The emphasis is different, of course: now it is the supposed novelty of the enterprise that has been obscured by the older frame of reference. But the rhetorical effect is the same. There's no real difference of meaning, these days, between these two reactions:

A: Have you seen the new production of the Ring?
B (dismissively): Yes…old wine in new bottles.
C (dismissively): Yes…new wine in old bottles.

And the same kind of reversal can be seen even when people play with the expression, replacing *bottles* with such containers as *glasses*, *barrels*, *flasks*, and *jars*.

When people pun on the phrase, they usually take the *old in new* form. Thus we find *old fridges in new bottles*, *old scams in new bottles*, and *old brands in new bottles*. Rather clever was a criticism of a serial complainer: *Old whine in new bottles*.

Even cleverer was an artistic commission to redraw illustrations for George Orwell's *Animal Farm,* described as *Old swine in new bottles.* Cleverest of all, to my mind, because of the ingenious dissociation between spelling and pronunciation, was the heading of an article on new museum developments in Vienna (German *Wien,* pronounced 'veen'): *Old Wien in new bottles.*

Chapter 40
The law, judges, thieves, swords

One of the most productive biblical expressions in modern English occurs in Romans 2:14:

> For when the Gentiles, which have not the law, do by nature the things contained in the law, these, having not the law, are a law unto themselves.

Wycliffe and Douai-Rheims have *to* instead of *unto*, but otherwise all the early translations agree: *a law unto themselves*. Today, the expression has generalized, with *law* in either singular or plural and all reflexive pronouns available—*myself, yourself*, etc. It is used of anyone who has achieved something special, who has an idiosyncratic or controversial way of life, or who acts regardless of accepted laws or conventions. In former times, the expression would only have had negative connotations, but in an age which prizes the individual and the rebel we find usages which are positive as well as pejorative. The following are just a few of the thousands of celebrities who have attracted the description, sometimes even adjectivally (*her law-unto-herself behaviour*): Johnny Cash, Nicole Kidman, Cliff Richard, the Pope, Madonna, Michael Mansfield QC, Colonel Ghaddafi, Rupert Murdoch, Amy Winehouse, Jonathan Ross.

We interpret the expression depending on our view of the person's achievement or behaviour. *He's a law unto himself* can be said in a highly appreciative tone or a roundly dismissive one. And in print we have to look at the context before knowing which one the writer intends. Wordplay usually suggests a positive attitude. A judge called his autobiography *A Law unto Myself*. An article on filmstar Jude Law's rise to fame was headed *A law unto himself*.

With groups, the tone is usually negative. We regularly read that, in such-and-such a country, *the police force has become a law unto itself*. Militias and pirates are *laws unto themselves*. The negative tone even survives a pun: an article on the failings of a social care department began *Lore unto themselves*.

The same pun can turn up in several different contexts. A travel article about tourism began: *Ireland: a lore unto themselves*. (The usage gains piquancy when we realize that Irish English uses the reflexive pronoun differently—*Is himself coming this evening?*—from other regional dialects.) One of the cleverest puns I found was also in a travel brochure inviting people to appreciate the special character of a not-so-well-known but easily confused tributary of the River Loire in France: *a Loir unto itself*.

The word *law* seems to attract puns, for some reason. An article about a croquet club was headed *A lawn unto themselves*. And the same headline was used, even more appositely, when the Inner Temple in London decided to host its first flower show in nearly a century. In 2002, Bill Gates opened a Microsoft software development centre in southern India, and one report began: *A Bangalore unto himself*. When champion motorcyclist Jorge Lorenzo changed his lifestyle for the better, the headline read: *Jorge Lorenzo no longer a flaw unto himself*.

The underlying construction has also taken on a life of its own: 'X (VERB) a Y unto PRONOUN', as these examples illustrate:

Dog people are a breed unto themselves

Quentin Tarantino: a genre unto himself

How Bush became a government unto himself

Facebook: an Internet unto itself

Wal-Mart: a nation unto itself

Russia: a continent unto itself

Few other biblical expressions match that one for productivity.

The law is no respecter of persons. This axiom, long recognized in legal practice, derives from Acts 10:34:

God is no respecter of persons.

There is an echo of Deuteronomy (16:19): *thou shalt not respect persons.* This is a case where the King James version has no competition from other early translations. Douai-Rheims comes closest, with *not a respecter,* but the other versions are very different: Bishops has *no regard of;* Wycliffe and Geneva have *no acceptor of;* and Tyndale has *not partial.*

The expression has been taken to heart in an age when equality is a dominant theme. *God is no respecter of* has been completed by *geography, class, race, colour, gender,* and several other potentially discriminating nouns. At the other end of the sentence, *God* is often replaced. *AIDS, bulimia, depression, fear, drugs, natural disasters,* and *baldness* are among the phenomena that have been said to be *no respecter of persons.* Quite often, both sentence beginning and ending are replaced: *debt is no respecter of class; drug abuse is no respecter of age; global terrorism is no respecter of human values.*

The opening words of John 7:24 have also proved popular in the climate of an age where being judgemental is frowned upon:

Judge not according to the appearance, but judge righteous judgment.

Judge not is the watchword. For many people, the expression recalls Bob Marley's first single in 1961:

> Judge not
> Before you judge yourself.
> Judge not
> If you're not ready for judgement.

For others, it is a book of essays by André Gide. For yet others it is an early silent film (1914). Its popularity seems confirmed by its arrival on T-shirts: *judge not, lest ye be smacked in the mouth* reads one frontal statement. At the same time, there is suspicion of the sentiment. An article in 2005 was headed *How 'Judge not' is destroying America—the great American open-mindedness mantra.*

The law judges thieves and murderers, among others. Thieves have their moment of linguistic glory in 1 Thessalonians 5:2:

For yourselves know perfectly that the day of the Lord so cometh as a thief in the night.

All the early translations have the vivid expression *a thief in the night*, and it has been used frequently ever since, sometimes with plural *thieves*. Many books and films have it as a title, the subject matter being remarkably various. The expression has been used of a disease which arrives suddenly, or one which creeps up on us (such as Alzheimer's). It has described the moment of falling in love. And it has been used to express departures: a critic of a government's environmental policies wrote *green ideas that vanished like a thief in the night.*

Violence is directly addressed in Matthew 26:52, at the point where Peter has tried to defend Jesus with his sword:

all they that take the sword shall perish with the sword.

There is an echo in John the Divine (Revelation) 13:10: *he that killeth with the sword must be killed with the sword.* The early translations have similar phrasing, *take...perish*, though Tyndale has *lay hand on...perish*. It's somewhat surprising, then, that the expression which is most often used today as a source of adaptation reflects the sentiment but not the vocabulary: *those who live by the sword, die by the sword.*

Sword, of course, is usually replaced by a modern weapon: *by the gun, the bomb, pistol, machete*, and so on. But a surprising number of examples occur which go well beyond the semantic field of weapons. Any of us could complete the following statement: *those who live by the rules...* And in place of *rules* we can find *tabloids, polls, spin, hype, Net, blog, Facebook*, and many more. If you rely on Facebook for your social life, the writer of this last example was saying, don't be surprised if it lets you down. On the other hand, another writer believed in the resurrective (or at least rejuvenative) powers of social networking, and reversed the polarity: *those who die by Twitter, live by Twitter.* Nor is it essential to maintain the repetition. *Those who live by the Net, die by the spam,* wrote one disenchanted netizen.

Chapter 41
Love and charity

The words of Leviticus (19:18) resonate throughout the New Testament: *Thou shalt love thy neighbour as thyself.* We find it in Matthew (5:43, 19:19, 22:39), Mark (12:31), and Paul (Romans 13:9, Galatians 5:14). The various translations present it with hardly any variation. It is, in effect, a version of the 'golden rule': 'Do unto others as you would have them do unto you.' However, that precise formulation is in no Bible translation of the time. Luke (6:31) comes closest to it with *And as ye would that men should do to you, do ye also to them likewise.* It is to the catechism that we owe the *do unto* formulation. The *Catechism* or *Christian Doctrine* of Laurence Vaux in 1567 has the phrasing *Do unto others as we would be done to ourselves.*

Being a golden rule, it applies in all kinds of circumstances, and is adapted accordingly. The things that thou shouldst love as thyself are many and various. Pets are especially cited: *love thy doggy as thyself.* Humans too: *love thy fellow driver as thyself.* Objects: *love thy potty as thyself* (this from a parent engaged in toilet training her child). Processes: *love thy spam filter as thyself.* One of the 'ten commandments' on a website about cancer survival reads:

Thou shalt love thy chemotherapy, thy radiation, thy monoclonal antibodies, thy vaccines, and thy other treatments even as thyself, for they are thy friends and champions.

The expression is often shortened to *Love thy neighbour/neighbor*, and is found thus in many titles of films, books, and cartoons. In the UK it named a popular television sitcom in the 1970s. In the full form, *love* is sometimes replaced. We find *know* and *trust thy neighbour as thyself*, for example, and even *build thy neighbour as thyself*, referring to the architectural suitability of a building project in a particular area. Reports of trouble, such as yobbish behaviour on the streets, have generated *fear thy neighbour*. Some racial sites twist the expression completely: *hate thy neighbour*.

Love and *charity* alternate in the translations, as in 1 Peter 4:8:

for charity shall cover the multitude of sins.

Wycliffe and Douai-Rheims also have *charity*, but the other early translations have *love*. Both became widely used, and were sometimes theologically contentious, but it is *charity* which forms the modern proverbial expression. There was uncertainty over how to use *multitude* during the sixteenth century: should it be *the multitude*, *a multitude*, or neither (as in *we saw great multitude of people*)? By 1600, *a* was coming in and *the* was going out, so the King James version is a somewhat conservative usage. (Only Douai-Rheims uses *a*.)

Today, the expression is widely adapted in non-religious settings, always in an ironic or jocular way. *Profitability covers a multitude of sins*, says an economics journal. *Art* does (in a debate about 'what is art?'). *A fresh coat of paint* does (in house selling). So does *cosmetics*. The literati have favoured the expression.

Mark Twain turned it into *Martyrdom covers a multitude of sins*. Oscar Wilde reversed it: arguing that the people who do most harm are the people who try to do most good, he opined *Charity creates a multitude of sins* (in 'The soul of man under socialism'). O Henry summarizes the views of anyone who is remorseful about having made huge profits out of 'skinning' the common labouring man: *Charity covers a multitude of skins* (in *The Gentle Grafter*, Chapter 4).

The meaning of *charity* has weakened somewhat over the centuries, so that it now includes such notions as benevolence and fair-mindedness. It has sometimes even acquired negative connotations, as in the phrase *cold as charity*, especially heard in the eighteenth and nineteenth centuries, referring to the unfeeling way that some public charities were administered. The proverbial expression *charity begins at home* is often used in a self-serving context. Today, *charity shops*, *Charity Commissioners*, and other such phrases have added an institutionalized tone to the word. Notwithstanding St Paul's reiterated use in 1 Corinthians 13 (ending with *And now abideth faith, hope, charity, these three; but the greatest of these is charity*), anyone these days wanting to emphasize the emotional force originally carried by this word would do better to use *love*.

The point is well illustrated in John 15:13, where the use of *charity* would denude the sentence of its poignancy:

Greater love hath no man than this, that a man lay down his life for his friends.

This formulation has carried the day. The first part competed with Douai-Rheims (*Greater love than this no man hath*), Tyndale and Geneva (*Greater love than this hath no man*), and Wycliffe (*No man hath more love than this*). The second part competed with Wycliffe (*put* for *lay down*) and Tyndale/Geneva (*bestow* for *lay down*). There is still some stylistic variation today, but *Greater love hath no man than this* is the favourite expression, often summarized as *No greater love.*

The summary form has achieved fame through its association with war memorial monuments and remembrances. The opening lines of Wilfred Owen's poem, *Greater love* (1917) express a feeling that, a century later, is still annually acknowledged.

> Red lips are not so red
> As the stained stones kissed by the English dead.
> Kindness of wooed and wooer
> Seems shame to their love pure.
> O Love, your eyes lose lure
> When I behold eyes blinded in my stead!

The expression has been institutionalized in this context in the USA, where *No Greater Love* is a charity dedicated to the planning of remembrance events.

The power of the statement has given it a much broader appeal. It has been used repeatedly for examples of selflessness that go above the ordinary. *No Greater Love* has provided the title of several books, such as one by Mother Teresa and others (1997). It has named several films, such as one in 2009 about an order of Carmelite nuns. And it has provided a stimulus for innumerable romantic song lyrics, though the notion of self-sacrifice is usually absent.

It might be thought that the theme of personal sacrifice is so powerful that the expression would be sacrosanct. However, the first part of the expression, usually abbreviated to *Greater love*... (with the rest left to the imagination) is widely used in contexts where the nature of the sacrifice is relatively trivial, though considered not to be so by the doer. The tone is invariably jocular or ironic, as is evident when the expression appears in its full form. One instance out of thousands on the internet is *Greater love hath no woman than the one who makes her husband hot chocolate while he plays poker on the internet.* Wordplay is common. *Greater love hath no fan* said a boastful enthusiast for *Star Wars.*

It would seem that a favourite expression of St Paul was *brotherly love.* It turns up in Romans (12:10), 1 Thessalonians (4:9) and Hebrews (13:1). Wycliffe and Douai-Rheims go for *charity of brotherhood,* but the other early translations all use *brotherly love.* It has generated a whole family of adverbs. Today we will find references to *sisterly love, cousinly love, motherly love, fatherly love,* even *daughterly* and *auntly love.* The phonetic awkwardness of *unclely love* makes it very rare, and I've still to find an instance of *sonly love.* As for *brotherly love* itself, the most famous (albeit hidden) instance of its modern usage is in the etymology of the city of Philadelphia.

Two modern expressions are strongly associated with love, even though they don't actually contain the word. The first is unique, in that it has developed into a modern expletive, heard especially in the UK, Ireland, and Australia as a strong exclamation of surprise, disbelief, or dismay: *Jesus wept* (John 11:35). Why this particular utterance should have become so used isn't clear. Exclamations and oaths using the name of Jesus are recorded from the fourteenth century, but *Jesus wept!* isn't recorded until the twentieth. Something about its succinctness must have appealed (this is the shortest verse in the New Testament). I've found hints of its use in London music-hall. *Jesus wept* is on the gravestone of eccentric music-hall comedian T. E. Dunville.

The other expression occurs at the end of the story of the Good Samaritan (Luke 10:37): *Go, and do thou likewise.* It was probably the iambic rhythm, once again, which made this the preferred usage over *in like manner* (used by Geneva and Douai-Rheims), but that effect seems less salient today, for a version without the *thou* is also widespread. The expression still has its application to individual performance today: someone writing a piece about 'doing the right thing' headed it *I went and did likewise*. But, more often, it is used to capture the dynamism within a social movement as it is on the point of expanding. *Go thou and do likewise* headed an account of the spread of the nursing profession in the USA. A pedagogical note enters into some of the adaptations: *look, learn, and do likewise* was on one instructional site. Completely unexpected was the ingenuity of the travel firm advertising holidays in India: *Goa and do likewise*.

Chapter 42
Peace, patience, wrath, whore

C harity (King James: love) is the first fruit of the Holy Spirit (Galatians 5:22–3), and several of the other fruits such as joy, peace, and patience (King James: long suffering) have also sourced or popularized an expression.

Joyfulness lies behind *Be of good cheer*, used a number of times in the New Testament (such as Matthew 9:2, John 16:33). The early translations vary the noun: Geneva has *comfort*, Douai-Rheims has *heart*. This isn't a biblical innovation, as the expression is recorded in English in the 1400s, and was probably already an everyday expression when the first translators were working. The role of the Bible, in such a case, has been to keep the expression alive when otherwise it might have died out, replaced by more modern expressions (such as *cheer up*).

Today its archaic tone tends to keep it restricted to special occasions, especially as a written Christmas greeting. It's often used in a mock-heroic way: one August headline announced *Merry men (and women) of mirth, be of good cheer! Football season is finally here!* The occasional pun is found. *Be of good cheer* headed a column about how to be a successful cheerleader.

I've never encountered it in speech, apart from in one of Charles Schulz's *Peanuts* cartoons. Linus and Charlie Brown, both warmly clad, are walking through a snowstorm. They see Snoopy shivering. 'Snoopy looks kind of cold, doesn't he?' says Charlie Brown. 'I'll say he does', says Linus, 'Maybe we'd better go over, and comfort him.' They talk to the dog. 'Be of good cheer, Snoopy', says Linus. 'Yes, be of good cheer', says Charlie Brown. They walk off, leaving Snoopy still shivering. A question mark appears above his head.

Peace, for many churchgoers, brings to mind the passage in Philippians 4:7, because they know it as part of the blessing which ends a service:

And the peace of God, which passeth all understanding, shall keep your hearts and minds through Christ Jesus.

There's occasional variation in the early translations—Wycliffe has *passeth all wit*; Douai-Rheims has *surpasseth*—but these don't affect our modern awareness of the sentence's grammatical structure. It's the *passeth all understanding* part which has held the attention. A ferocious critique of a government decision had the headline *the idiocy which surpasseth all understanding*. A history of the West of England Cocker Spaniel Club contained a reflection on a poor policy decision in 1995 when *the Club became subject to a rota system which passeth all understanding*. The expression even became a music-hall joke, which still gets a laugh when trotted out from time to time (though it depends on the way you tell 'em): *the piece of cod which passeth all understanding*.

In John the Divine (Revelation) 14:12 we hear about *the patience of the saints*. It appears in this form in all the early translations, and entered English in both plural and singular forms—the latter being the norm today. We say *it's enough to try the patience of a saint* when we find ourselves in an especially frustrating or unbearable situation. Older versions of the idiom existed, but they are rarely heard nowadays. Nelly comments about Catherine that *It was enough to try the temper of a saint, such unbearable, wicked rages!* (Emily Brontë, *Wuthering Heights*, Chapter 11).

Saints are not the only ones, these days, whose patience is tried. The expression ends with various categories of person— *the patience of a monk/a nun/a priest/a Zen Buddhist/Job.* Not only persons: *a tortoise* and *a snail* are just two of the animals that are ascribed this virtue.

Writers have a field day with the expression if a proper name contains the word *saint*. *Villa slide tests the patience of a saint* went one football headline—the point being that Villa had just lost to Southampton (aka the *Saints*) 0–1, but Southampton's winning goal came just before the final whistle blew. *O'Donnell has the patience of a saint* was another football headline—the saint this time being the Scottish team St Mirren, to which the player was returning after a long absence from injury. A book on the history of St Helens rugby team is called *The Patience of a Saint.* Quite a few teams in sport belong to a place with a *Saint* in the name, so the biblical expression has been used almost to the point of cliché. It's refreshing, then, to find a non-sporting context. *Pups try the patience of a saint* went the headline. A Saint Bernard dog had given birth to a rare litter of nine puppies.

Mildness, another fruit of the Holy Spirit, underlies the recommendation of St Paul in Ephesians 4:26:

let not the sun go down upon your wrath

It's in all the early translations, with Douai-Rheims using *anger* instead of *wrath*, and today both words are used. Most people adopt modern syntax: *Don't let the sun go down on your wrath/anger*. The usual focus is on the everyday relationship between individuals, as can be seen in the adaptations, such as *Don't let the sun go down on the washing-up*. But the advice is available for any kind of setting, domestic or otherwise. It has made an ideal motto for a sundial.

Romans 12:19 provides us with another take on angry retribution:

Vengeance is mine; I will repay, saith the Lord.

In modern English, the utterance has been collapsed into *Vengeance is mine, saith the Lord* (some follow Douai-Rheims, which has *revenge*). When it isn't being used as a quotation, it's usually adapted by replacing the final word. A review of Peter Shaffer's play *The gift of the gorgon* in 1994 began with *Vengeance is mine, saith the playwright*. A proposal in one of the US jurisdictions to prevent people without law degrees from representing others in court was headed *Vengeance is mine, saith the court*. The pronoun can change, though it usually stays first person. *Vengeance is ours, saith the Jews* introduced a review of the 2009 film *Inglourious Basterds*. And a glut of films all about grim vigilantes roaming the world in search of revenge prompted *Vengeance is mine, saith Hollywood*.

The chastity motif surfaces in several quotations, but few have stimulated widespread use. *Unto the pure all things are pure* (Titus 1:15) has sparked the parallel *To the impure all things are impure*, but there are actually hardly any other adjectives which fit the syntactic pattern 'to the X all things are X'. Longfellow provides a nice exception, writing in the *North American Review* in July 1837: *As to the pure mind all things are pure, so to the poetic mind all things are poetical*. Apart from this, the expression, out of its religious context, tends to be used as a riposte whenever someone reads a double meaning into an utterance that the speaker didn't intend. Its word order and rhythm are unique to King James; Tyndale, Bishops, and Geneva have *unto the pure are all things pure*; Wycliffe and Douai-Rheims have *clean* for *pure*.

Finally, the *great whore* of Babylon, introduced in St John the Divine (Revelation) 17:1 has also survived outside its biblical setting. It's sometimes used as a term of abuse by one religious group against another, but it's by no means restricted to religion. In the political domain, the American peace and justice activist Father Bill O'Donnell gave it some publicity on one occasion when he was defending himself in court: *your honor, you are just a pimp for the great whore of the Pentagon.* And it's even been used in linguistics. English, the word-borrower par excellence, has been described (in a *Telegraph* book review in 2008) as the *great whore of all languages*.

Certainly, nothing is sacrosanct, where loan words and phrases are concerned, as we have seen throughout this book.

Epilogue

I am now in a position to answer the questions I asked myself in the Prologue to this book. How extensive has biblical influence been in shaping the character of modern English? Just how many expressions of biblical origin are part of present-day idiom? And how many of these show the specific influence of the King James translation? I had better say 'try to answer', for the issues turn out to be quite complicated.

The range of illustrative subject matter introduced in the book is powerful evidence of a substantial stylistic influence. Some might have expected this influence to be restricted to the more elevated styles of English. This is indeed the case with quotations, which are likely to be used only in contexts where their inclusion is appropriate to the religious (specifically Christian or Jewish) subject matter. But the items discussed in this book are not quotations: they are everyday expressions used by speakers and writers of modern English, most of whom will have no religious motivation for their use. Thus we find a full stylistic range from the most formal (*come to pass*) and reverent (*blessed are ...*) to the most colloquial (*unclean, unclean*) and taboo (*Jesus wept*). Moreover, the idioms are to be found in all contexts in which language is used, as can be seen from a quick glance down the general index, which runs from *ABC television* to *zoology*, taking in on the way such varied domains as basketball, comic strips, dentistry, engineering, pornography, and social networking. The people implicated cover all walks of life: Shakespeare and Sinatra, Byron and Beckham, Osama and Obama. The sources range from the *News of the World* to *Newsweek*, from *Henry IV* to *The Hitch-hiker's Guide to the Galaxy*. The most popular domains are politics, economics, football, advertising, and the titles of books, films, pop songs, and works of art.

This remarkable stylistic and playful diversity stems from a surprisingly small number of instances. In the Appendix, I've classified all the expressions discussed in this book: there are only 257 of them. I recognize that a different analyst, reading through the Bible looking for modern English expressions, could arrive at a different total, for not everyone will share my intuitions about what counts as an idiom (and thus to be included) as opposed to a quotation (and thus to be excluded); but the totals will not differ greatly.

I say 'only 257', because this puts in perspective the sometimes wild claims made about the role of the Bible in the history of the English language, where people talk of 'thousands' of influential expressions. Even 'hundreds' is somewhat misleading. At the same time, 257 is notable. No other single source has provided the language with so many idiomatic expressions. Shakespeare is the nearest, but the number of idioms we can confidently attribute to him (such as *to the manner born*) is under a hundred. His influence on the language's lexicon—the number of words he coined that have remained in English—is far greater than the Bible, as is clear from the listing made for *The Shakespeare Miscellany* (David and Ben Crystal, Penguin, 2005). He was a linguistic innovator, working in a genre which motivated lexical novelty, whereas Bible translators, as we have seen (p. 7), were linguistically conservative, constrained by their subject matter and their theological tradition. However, when it comes to idioms, the Bible reigns definitely supreme.

But which bible? As I have repeatedly suggested, the 'authorized' status of the King James Bible makes it likely that it had a role to play in the popularization of most of the 257 cases. But when we examine the question of origination, the answer is very different. In only 18 cases is a modern idiom found in King James in its exact form (see Category I in the Appendix: example, *a thorn in the flesh*). In 37 cases there is no exact King James antecedent (Category VII: example, *fly in the ointment*), and we have to argue that some additional (and usually unknown) process made the link with the modern usage. In 7 cases (Category VIII: example, *the way of all flesh*), the link might have come via a different translation (usually Douai-Rheims).

That leaves 196 cases where another translation has the same form as the King James expression, or the expression was already in the English language before the age of bibles. Geneva has the most parallels (160), closely followed by Bishops (149) and Douai-Rheims (135); then we find Tyndale (86) and Wycliffe (40). Other bibles, not examined in this book, might of course add to these figures. In 16 cases (shown by *), the expressions appear in Coverdale's Psalter as used for the Book of Common Prayer (example: *deep waters*). It is impossible to establish the relative influence of the translations when an expression is shared; but I think it's reasonable to make the general claim that the fewer translations using the same expression, the more likely we can attribute the influence to King James. I have therefore classified the 196 cases as follows.

Category II: one other translation uses the same expression as King James (example: *be fruitful and multiply*). Total: 27.

Category III: two other translations use the same expression as King James (example: *land of Nod*). Total: 39.

Epilogue

Category IV: three other translations use the same expression as King James (example: *pillar of salt*). Total: 47.

Category V: four other translations use the same expression as King James (example: *my brother's keeper*). Total: 50.

Category VI: all five other translations use the same expression as King James (example: *apple of his eye*). Total: 27.

Category IX: none of the five translations use the same expression as King James, but Coverdale's Psalter does (example: *deep waters*). Total: 3 (a further 13 cases are also found in Coverdale, as mentioned above).

Category X: none of the five translations use the same expression as King James, but the usage is known from Old or Middle English (example: *give up the ghost*). Total: 2 (a further 25 cases of early influence are shown by + in the Appendix).

How we evaluate the quantitative influence of King James, therefore, will depend on how we rate these shared instances. If we exclude them all, we have only 18 (Category I). If we include indirect processes (Category VII), we have 55. If we include one other translation equivalent (Category II), we have 82. And so on. If we include everything, we have 257. Your choice.

It should also be noted that the distribution of influential idioms throughout the Bible is uneven. Most books of the New Testament (23 out of 27) yield at least one expression, but fewer than half (19 out of 39) of the books of the Old Testament do; and I have found only one instance in the 14 books of the Apocrypha (see Appendix 2). Of the expressions listed in Appendix 1, just over half (143) are from the New Testament, the majority (99) coming from the four Gospels, with Matthew pre-eminent. Over half the Old Testament references (51) are in just three books: Exodus, Genesis, and Ecclesiastes.

But a quantitative account is only a small part of this story. Of far greater interest is what the use of biblical expressions tells us about the character of written and spoken English. A recurrent theme of this book is the way language users adapt these expressions to make a rhetorical point or to convey a clever or humorous effect, especially through the use of puns (see the range at *a law unto himself*). While some expressions are resistant to adaptation (*my yoke is easy*), others offer language users a remarkable number of opportunities for language play (*a coat of many colours*). The phonetic properties of the various idioms have also been identified as an important factor motivating their continuing use, especially iambic rhythms (*from strength to strength*), alliteration (*many mansions*), assonance (*from the cradle to the grave*), euphony (*still small voice*), monosyllabicity (*you know not what you do*), and rhyme (the variations on *signs of the times*). We also encounter a wide range of traditional rhetorical features when biblical idioms are adopted and adapted. They include bathos (*thou shalt not covet thy neighbor's wifi*), chiasmus (*the last shall be first, and the first last*), hyperbole (*financial Armageddon*), irony (*how are the mighty risen*), mock-heroism (*be horribly afraid*), oxymoron (*whisper from the housetops*), personification (*wandering star*), and satire (*casting pearls before parliament*). The short length of most biblical idioms has been a notable feature, the occasional longer item requiring some special treatment, such as syntactic parallelism (*tell it not…, publish it not…*). I've also noted the occasional overlap with proverbial expressions (*physician, heal thyself*).

So, was Alan Thomas right, when I quoted him in the first line of my Prologue? 'No book has had greater influence on the English language.' If this claim is interpreted with reference to the number of innovative idiomatic expressions in a single canonical work of literature, I think we have to say yes. And if we interpret it with reference to the extent to which these idioms have permeated genres of modern spoken or written English, again I think we have to say yes. But if we are referring to other properties of language, we have to say either no (e.g. for innovative lexicon) or unproven because little explored (e.g. for innovative grammar). In particular, the thorny question of stylistic influence, which so impressed Coleridge and Macaulay, also remains to be answered, for idiom is only one of many elements of style.

We must immediately curb our enthusiasm, therefore, by reflecting on the facts summarized in this Epilogue. Very few idiomatic expressions unquestionably originate in the language of the King James Bible. An entire biblical era, of over a century, lies behind them. There can be little doubt that this 'authorized' translation did more than any other to fix these expressions in the mind of the English-speaking public. But the myriad contributions of Wycliffe, Tyndale, and many others also need to be remembered, especially in an anniversary year. Their linguistic fingerprints are to be found in the pages of the King James Bible. They are an essential element in the story of how the English language was 'begat'.

Appendix 1
Expressions discussed in this book
(total: 257)

* also in Coverdale's Psalter (psalm number shown in parentheses)
+ found in Old or early Middle English
n/a not applicable
The order of entries within categories follows the conventional biblical sequence of books.
[ ] enclose entries which are minor variants

	Wycliffe	Tyndale	Geneva	Bishops	Douai-Rheims	King James
I Expressions apparently unique to the KJB (Total: 18)						
east of Eden (Genesis 4.16)	n	n	n	n	n	y

W at the east coast of Eden
T on the east side of Eden
G toward the Eastside of Eden
B eastward from Eden
D at the east side of Eden

know for a certainty (Joshua 23.13)	n	n/a	n	n	n	y

W wit ye right now
G know ye for certain
B be ye sure
D know ye for a certainty

how are the mighty fallen (2 Samuel 1.19)	n	n/a	n	n	n	y

W   how fell strong men
G B how are the mighty overthrown
D   how are the valiant fallen

Appendix 1: Expressions discussed in this book

	Wycliffe	Tyndale	Geneva	Bishops	Douai-Rheims	King James
a still small voice (1 Kings 19.12)	n	n/a	n	n	n	y

   W the issuing of thin wind
   G a still and soft voice
   B a small still voice
   D a whistling of a gentle air

	Wycliffe	Tyndale	Geneva	Bishops	Douai-Rheims	King James
the root of the matter (Job 19.28)	n	n/a	n	n	n	y

   W   find we the root of a word against him
   G B there was a deep matter in me
   D   let us find occasion of word against him

	Wycliffe	Tyndale	Geneva	Bishops	Douai-Rheims	King James
to every thing there is a season (Ecclesiastes 3.1)	n	n/a	n	n	n	y

   W all things have time
   G to all things there is an appointed time
   B every thing hath a time
   D all things have their season

	Wycliffe	Tyndale	Geneva	Bishops	Douai-Rheims	King James
much study is a weariness of the flesh (Ecclesiastes 12.12)	n	n/a	n	n	n	y

   W oft thinking is torment of flesh
   G much reading is a weariness of the flesh
   B to much study wearieth the body
   D much study is an affliction of the flesh

	Wycliffe	Tyndale	Geneva	Bishops	Douai-Rheims	King James
beat their swords into plowshares (Isaiah 2.4)	n	n/a	n	n	n	y

   W   well together their swords into shares

			Wycliffe	Tyndale	Geneva	Bishops	Douai-Rheims	King James
G B	break their swords also into mattocks							
D	turn their swords into ploughshares							
	set thine [your] house in order (Isaiah 38.1)		n	n/a	n	n	n	y
W	command to thine house							
G	put thine house in an order							
B	put thine household in an order							
D	give charge concerning thy house							
	be horribly afraid (Jeremiah 2.12)		n	n/a	n	n	n	y
W	be ye desolate greatly							
G	be afraid and utterly confounded							
B	be afraid and abashed							
D	be very desolate							
	lay up for yourselves treasures in heaven (Matthew 6.20)		n	n	n	n	n	y
W	gather to you treasures in heaven							
T	gather ye treasure together in heaven							
G	lay up treasures for yourselves in heaven							
B	lay up for you, treasures in heaven							
D	lay up to yourselves treasures in heaven							
	get thee behind me (Luke 4.8)		n/a	n	n	n	n/a	y
T G B	hence from me							
	suffer little children (Luke 18.16)		n	n	n	n	n	y
W	suffer the children							

	Wycliffe	Tyndale	Geneva	Bishops	Douai-Rheims	King James
T B D suffer children						
G suffer the babes						
no small stir (Acts 12.18, 19.23)	n	n	n	n	n	y
W not little troubling, a great troubling						
T B no little ado						
G no small trouble						
D no small disturbance (19.23)						
turned the world upside down (Acts 17.6)	n	n	n	n	n	y
W move the world						
T B trouble the world						
G subverted the state of the world						
D set the city in an uproar						
a thorn in the flesh (2 Corinthians 12.7)	n	n	n	n	n	y
W the prick of my flesh						
T unquietness of the flesh						
G a prick in the flesh						
B a prick to the flesh						
D a sting of my flesh						
unto the pure all things are pure (Titus 1.15)	n	n	n	n	n	y
W all things are clean to clean men						
T B G unto the pure are all things pure						
D all things are clean to the clean						
let us now praise famous men (Sirach 44.1)	n/a	n/a	n/a	n/a	n	y
D let us now praise men of renown						

	Wycliffe	Tyndale	Geneva	Bishops	Douai-Rheims	King James
II King James usage shared with one other translation (Total: 27)						
be fruitful and multiply (Genesis 1.22, 28)	n	n	n	y	n	y

W wax ye, and be ye multiplied; increase ye, and be ye multiplied
T grow and multiply
G bring forth fruit and multiply
D increase and multiply

	Wycliffe	Tyndale	Geneva	Bishops	Douai-Rheims	King James
there were giants in the earth in those days (Genesis 6.4)	n	n	y	n	n	y

W giants were on earth in those days
T there were tyrants in the world in those days
B there were giants in those days in the earth
D giants were upon the earth in those days

	Wycliffe	Tyndale	Geneva	Bishops	Douai-Rheims	King James
rain bread from heaven...manna (Exodus 16.4,15) *(78)	n	n	n	y	n	y

W rain to you loaves from heaven...man hu
T rain bread from heaven...bread
C rained down manna...bread from heaven
G bread to rain from heaven...manna
[**D** rain bread from heaven...manhu!]

	Wycliffe	Tyndale	Geneva	Bishops	Douai-Rheims	King James
tables of stone (Exodus 31.18)	n	n	n	y	n	y

W stone tables of witnessing
T tables of witness; which were of stone

Appendix 1: Expressions discussed in this book

	Wycliffe	Tyndale	Geneva	Bishops	Douai-Rheims	King James
G tablets of stone **D** stone tables of testimony						
unclean, unclean (Leviticus 13.45)	n	n	n	y	n	y
W defouled and vile **T** and shall be called unclean **G** I am unclean, I am unclean **D** that he is defiled and unclean						
love thy neighbour as thyself (Leviticus 19.18)	n	n	y	n	n	y
W D love thy friend as thyself **T B** ...even as thyself						
white as snow (Numbers 12.10)	n	n	n	n	y	y
W white with leprosy as snow **T B** as it were snow **G** like snow						
shibboleth [in this spelling] (Judges 12.6)	n	n/a	y	n	n	y
W sebolech **B** schibboleth **D** scibboleth						
whips...scorpions (1 Kings 12.11)	n	n/a	n	n	y	y
W scourges...scorpions **G B** rods...scourges						
tell it not...publish it not... (2 Samuel 1.20)	n	n/a	n	n	y	y
W nill ye tell...neither tell ye... **G B** nor publish it...						
miserable comforters (Job 16.2)	n	n/a	y	n	n	y
W heavy comforters						

Appendix 1: Expressions discussed in this book

	Wycliffe	Tyndale	Geneva	Bishops	Douai-Rheims	King James
B miserable givers of comfort **D** troublesome comforters						
the skin of my teeth (Job 19.20)	n	n/a	y	n	n	y
W D lips are left about my teeth **B** the skin about my teeth						
out of the mouth of babes and sucklings (Psalms 8.2, Matthew 21.16)	n	n	y	n	n	y
W (Psalms)...of young children **C B** (Psalms)...of very babes and sucklings* **D** (Psalms)...of infants and of sucklings **W** (Matthew) of the mouth of young children, and of sucking children **T** (Matthew) of the mouth of babes and sucklings **G** (Matthew) by the mouth of babes and sucklings						
from strength to strength (Psalms 84.7)*	n	n/a	y	n	n	y
W shall quicken us **B** from a stout courage to a stout courage **D** from virtue to virtue						
woe is me (Psalms 120.5)* +	n	n/a	n	n	y	y
W alas to me **G** woe is to me **B** woe be unto me						
cast thy bread upon the waters (Ecclesiastes 11.1)	n	n/a	y	n	n	y
W send thy bread on waters passing forth						

269

Appendix 1: Expressions discussed in this book

	Wycliffe	Tyndale	Geneva	Bishops	Douai-Rheims	King James
B lay thy bread upon wet faces **D** cast thy bread upon the running waters						
of making many books there is no end (Ecclesiastes 12.12)	n	n/a	n	n	y	y
W none end is to make many books **G** there is none end in making many books **B** to make many books, it is an endless work						
reap the whirlwind (Hosea 8.7)	n	n/a	y	n	n	y
W reap whirlwind **B D** reap a whirlwind						
sufficient unto the day is the evil thereof (Matthew 6.34)	n	n	n	n	y	y
W it sufficeth to the day his own malice **T** the day present hath ever enough of his own trouble **G** the day hath enough with his own grief **B** sufficient for the day is the evil thereof						
what... God hath joined together, let not man put asunder (Matthew 19.6)	n	n	n	n	y	y
W a man depart not that thing that God hath joined **T G B** Let not man...put asunder, that which God hath coupled together						

270

	Wycliffe	Tyndale	Geneva	Bishops	Douai-Rheims	King James
many are called, but few are chosen (Matthew 22.14)	n	n	n	n	y	y
render…unto Caesar the things which are Caesar's (Matthew 22.21)	n	n	n	n	y	y
whited sepulchres (Matthew 23.27)	n	n	n	n	y	y
the way, the truth, and the life (John 14.6)	n	y	n	n	n	y
kick against the pricks (Acts 9.5)	n	n	n	y	n	y

many are called, but few are chosen (Matthew 22.14)

W many be cleped but few be chosen
T many are called and few be chosen
G many are called but few chosen
B many be called but few are chosen

render…unto Caesar the things which are Caesar's (Matthew 22.21)

W yield ye to the emperor the things that are the emperors
T give…to Caesar that which is Caesar's
G give…to Caesar the things which are Caesars
B give…unto Caesar the things which are Caesars

whited sepulchres (Matthew 23.27)

W sepulchres whited
T painted tombs
G whited tombs
B painted sepulchres

the way, the truth, and the life (John 14.6)

W   I am way, truth, and life
G B D the way, and the truth, and the life

kick against the pricks (Acts 9.5)

W T kick against the prick
G   kick against pricks
D   kick against the goad

Appendix 1: Expressions discussed in this book

	Wycliffe	Tyndale	Geneva	Bishops	Douai-Rheims	King James
see through a glass darkly (1 Corinthians 13.12)	n	n	n	n	y	y
grave, where is thy victory (1 Corinthians 15.55)	n	n	y	n	n	y
lesser light (Genesis 1.16)	n	n	y	n	y	y
in our image (Genesis 1.26) +	n	n	y	y	n	y
dust thou art (Genesis 3.19)	n	n	n	y	y	y
land of Nod (Genesis 4.16)	n	n	y	y	n	y
I am that I am (Exodus 3.14)	n	n	y	y	n	y

see through a glass darkly (1 Corinthians 13.12)

W   by a mirror in darkness
T B   in a glass, even in a dark speaking
D   through a glass in a dark manner

grave, where is thy victory (1 Corinthians 15.55)

W D   death, where is thy victory
T B   hell, where is thy victory

III King James usage shared with two other translations (Total: 39)

lesser light (Genesis 1.16)

W T B   less light

in our image (Genesis 1.26) +

W D   to our image
T   in our likeness

dust thou art (Genesis 3.19)

W G   thou art dust
T   earth thou art

land of Nod (Genesis 4.16)

W   fleeing about in earth
T   the land Nod
D   as a fugitive on the earth

I am that I am (Exodus 3.14)

W   I am that am

	Wycliffe	Tyndale	Geneva	Bishops	Douai-Rheims	King James
T I will be what I will be **D** I am who am						
ten commandments (Exodus 34.28)	n	n	y	y	n	y
W ten words of the bond of peace **T** ten verses **D** ten words of the covenant						
what hath God wrought (Numbers 23.23)	n	n	y	y	n	y
W what the Lord hath wrought **T D** what God hath wrought						
heap mischiefs upon (Deuteronomy 32.23) +	n	y	n	y	n	y
W gather evils **G** send plagues **D** heap evils						
I am the least in my father's house (Judges 6.15)	n	n/a	y	n	y	y
W I am the least in the house of my father **B** I am little in my father's house						
a man after his own heart (1 Samuel 13.14)	n	n/a	y	y	n	y
W a man to himself after his heart **D** a man according to his own heart						
God forbid (1 Samuel 14.45) +	n	n/a	y	y	n	y
W this is unleaveful **D** this must not be						

Appendix 1: Expressions discussed in this book

	Wycliffe	Tyndale	Geneva	Bishops	Douai-Rheims	King James
blood shall be upon thine own head (1 Kings 2.37) +	n	n/a	y	y	n	y
W on thine head						
D thy own head						
take root (2 Kings 19.30) +	n	n/a	y	n	y	y
W send root						
B take rooting						
rod of iron (Psalms 2.9)*	n	n/a	n	y	y	y
W iron yerde						
G scepter of iron						
no new thing under the sun (Ecclesiastes 1.9)	n	n/a	n	y	y	y
W D nothing under the sun is new						
two are better than one (Ecclesiastes 4.9)	n	n/a	y	y	n	y
W it is better, that twain be together than one						
D It is better…that two should be together, than one						
the race is not to the swift (Ecclesiastes 9.11)	n	n/a	y	n	y	y
W running is not of swift men						
B in running it helpeth not to be swift						
unto us a child is born (Isaiah 9.6)	n	n/a	y	y	n	y
W a little child is born to us						
D a child is born to us						

	Wycliffe	Tyndale	Geneva	Bishops	Douai-Rheims	King James
eye to eye (Isaiah 52.8)	n	n/a	y	n	y	y
W see with eye to eye B see plainly						
holier than thou (Isaiah 65.5)	n	n/a	y	y	n	y
W D thou art unclean						
the leopard [change] his spots (Jeremiah 13.23)	n	n/a	y	n	y	y
W a pard may change his diversities B and the cat of the mountain her spots						
den of lions (Daniel 6.12)	n	n/a	y	y	n	y
W lake of lions D den of the lions						
bread alone (Matthew 4.4, Luke 4.4)	n (M) y (L)	n	n	n	y	y
W not only in bread (Matthew) T G B bread only						
sick of the palsy (Matthew 8.6)	n	n	n	y	y	y
W sick on the palsy T G sick at home of the palsy						
be of good cheer (Matthew 9.2)	n	y	n	y	n	y
W have thou trist G be of good comfort D be of good heart						
new wine into old bottles (Matthew 9.17)	y	n	n	n	y	y
T G B new wine into old vessels						

Appendix 1: Expressions discussed in this book

	Wycliffe	Tyndale	Geneva	Bishops	Douai-Rheims	King James
fell by the way side (Matthew 13.4)	n	n	y	n	y	y
W fell besides the way **T B** fell by the ways side						
pearl of great price (Matthew 13.46)	n	n	y	n	y	y
W precious margarite **T B** precious pearl						
upon this rock I will build my church (Matthew 16.18)	n	n	y	n	y	y

W   on this stone I shall build
      my church
T B upon this rock I will build
      my congregation						

the last shall be first (Matthew 20.16)	n	y	y	n	n	y
W B the last shall be the first **D** shall the last be first						
my words shall not pass away (Matthew 24.35)	n	n	y	y	n	y
T my words shall abide **W D** my words shall not pass						
thou good and faithful servant (Matthew 25.21)	n	n	n	y	y	y
W T G good servant and faithful **[D** good and faithful servant]						
a kingdom…divided against itself… *cannot stand* (Mark 3.24)	n	n	y	n	y	y

W T B if a realm be divided against
         itself, that realm cannot
         endure [W departed]						

	Wycliffe	Tyndale	Geneva	Bishops	Douai-Rheims	King James
eat, drink and be merry (Luke 12.19)	n	y	n	y	n	y
W eat, drink, and make feast						
G eat, drink, and take thy pastime						
D eat, drink, make good cheer						
fatted calf (Luke 15.23)	n	y	n	n	y	y
W G B fat calf						
they know not what they do (Luke 23.34)	n	n	y	n	y	y
W T B they wot not what they do						
many mansions (John 14.2)	n	y	n	n	y	y
W many dwellings						
G B many dwelling places						
what I have written, I have written (John 19.22)	n	n	y	n	y	y
W that that I have written						
T B what I have written, that have I written						
live, and move, and have our being (Acts 17.28)	n	n	y	y	n	y
W live, and move, and be						
T live move and have our being						
D live, and move, and are						

IV King James usage shared with three other translations (Total: 47)

let there be light (Genesis 1.3)	n	y	y	y	n	y
W light be made						
D be light made						

	Wycliffe	Tyndale	Geneva	Bishops	Douai-Rheims	King James
begat (Genesis 5.6)	n	y	y	y	n	y
W gendred						
D begot						
a pillar of salt (Genesis 19.26)	n	y	y	y	n	y
W an image of salt						
D a statue of salt						
harden his heart (Exodus 4.21) *(95) +	n	y	y	n	y	y
W make hard his heart						
B hold his heart						
still as a stone (Exodus 15.16) +	n	y	y	y	n	y
W **D** unmoveable as a stone						
thou shalt not bear false witness (Exodus 20.16)	n	n	y	y	y	y
W thou shalt not speak false witnessing						
T thou shalt bear no false witness						
scapegoat (Leviticus 16.8)	n	y	y	y	n	y
W the goat that shall be sent out						
D emissary goat						
fell flat on his face (Numbers 22.31)	n	y	y	y	n	y
W lowly in to earth						
D flat on the ground						
dreamer of dreams (Deuteronomy 13.1) +	n	y	y	y	n	y
W to have seen a dream						
D dreamed a dream						

	Wycliffe	Tyndale	Geneva	Bishops	Douai-Rheims	King James
thy servant heareth (1 Samuel 3.9) **B** thy servant heareth thee	y	n/a	y	n	y	y
God save the king (1 Samuel 10.24) + **W** live the king	n	n/a	y	y	y	y
put the words in her mouth (2 Samuel 14.3) **G** taught her what she should say	y	n/a	n	y	y	y
laughed thee to scorn (2 Kings 19.21) *(e.g. 22.7) + **W** and scorned thee	n	n/a	y	y	y	y
lick the dust (Psalms 72.9) * **W** her tongue passed in earth	n	n/a	y	y	y	y
two-edged sword (Proverbs 5.4, Hebrews 4.12) *(149) **W** (Proverbs) sword carving on each side **W** (Hebrews) twain edged sword	n	n/a	y	y	y	y
vanity of vanities (Ecclesiastes 1.2) **B** most vain vanity	y	n/a	y	n	y	y
a time to… (Ecclesiastes 3.1) **W** time of…	n	n/a	y	y	y	y
let thy words be few (Ecclesiastes 5.2) **W** thy words be few	n	n/a	y	y	y	y
drop of a bucket (Isaiah 40.15) **B** a drop of a bucket full	y	n/a	y	n	y	y

Appendix 1: Expressions discussed in this book

	Wycliffe	Tyndale	Geneva	Bishops	Douai-Rheims	King James
you cannot serve God and mammon (Matthew 6.24) +	n	n	y	y	y	y
W G you cannot serve God and riches						
sheep's clothing (Matthew 7.15) +	n	y	y	y	n	y
W clothings of sheep						
D the clothing of sheep						
built his house upon the sand (Matthew 7.24)	n	n	y	y	y	y
W built his house upon gravel						
T built his house upon sands						
my yoke is easy, and my burden (is) *light* (Matthew 11.30)	n	y	y	y	n	y
W my yoke is soft, and my charge light						
B my yoke is sweet and my burden light						
touch the hem of his garment (Matthew 14.36)	n	n	y	y	y	y
W the hem of his clothing						
T the hem of his vesture						
the greatest in the kingdom (Matthew 18.1)	n	y	y	y	n	y
W D greater in the kingdom						
go through the eye of a needle (Matthew 19.24)	n	y	y	y	n	y
W pass through a needle's eye						
D pass through the eye of a needle						

	Wycliffe	Tyndale	Geneva	Bishops	Douai-Rheims	King James
the spirit indeed is willing, but the flesh is weak (Matthew 26.41)	n	y	n	y	y	y

W the spirit is ready, but the flesh is sick
G the spirit indeed is ready, but the flesh is weak
[D the spirit indeed is willing, but the flesh weak]

the sabbath was made for man, and not man for the sabbath (Mark 2.27)	n	n	y	y	y	y

W the sabbath is made for man, and not a man for the sabbath
T the sabbath day...the sabbath day

if [one] had never been born (Mark 14.21)	n	y	y	y	n	y

W if thilke man had not to be born
D if that man had not been born

no room for them in the inn (Luke 2.7)	n	n	y	y	y	y

W no place to him in no chamber
T no room for them within the inn

go, and do thou likewise (Luke 10.37)	n	y	y	y	n	y

W go thou, and do thou on like manner
D go, and do thou in like manner

riotous living (Luke 15.13)	n	y	y	y	n	y

W living lecherously
D living riotously

	Wycliffe	Tyndale	Geneva	Bishops	Douai-Rheims	King James
and the word was made flesh (John 1.14)	n	y	y	y	n	y
W the word was made man						
B the same word became flesh						
a shining light (John 5.35)	n	y	n	y	y	y
W lantern burning and shining						
G shining candle						
the times or the seasons (Acts 1.7)	n	y	y	y	n	y
W D times or moments						
led as a sheep to the slaughter (Acts 8.32)	n	n	y	y	y	y
W as a sheep he was led to slaying						
T led as a sheep to be slain						
to give than to receive (Acts 20.35)	y	y	n	y	n	y
G D to give, rather than to receive						
a law unto themselves (Romans 2.14)	n	y	y	y	n	y
W law to themself						
D a law to themselves						
wages of sin is death (Romans 6.23)	y	n	y	n	y	y
W B reward of sin is death						
vengeance is mine…saith the Lord (Romans 12.19)	n	y	y	y	n	y
W to me vengeance, and I shall yield						
D revenge is…						
the powers that be (Romans 13.1)	n	y	y	y	n	y
W those things that be						
D those that are						

Appendix 1: Expressions discussed in this book

	Wycliffe	Tyndale	Geneva	Bishops	Douai-Rheims	King James
let not the sun go down upon/on your wrath (Ephesians 4.26)	n	y	y	y	n	y
W the sun fall not down on your wrath						
D …upon your anger						
all things to all men (1 Corinthians 9.22)	n	n	y	y	y	y
W to all men I am made all things						
T I fashioned my self to all men						
suffer fools gladly (2 Corinthians 11.19)	n	y	y	y	n	y
W suffer gladly unwise men						
D gladly suffer the foolish						
vile body (Philippians 3.21)	n	y	y	y	n	y
W body of our meekness						
D body of our lowness						
money is the root of all evil (1 Timothy 6.10)	n	n	y	y	y	y
W the root of all evil is covetousness						
T covetousness is the root of all evil						
[D money is the root of all evils]						
passeth all understanding (Philippians 4.7)	n	y	y	y	n	y
W passeth all wit						
D surpasseth all understanding						

V King James usage shared with four other translations (Total: 50)

my brother's keeper (Genesis 4.9)	n	y	y	y	y	y
W whether I am the keeper of my brother						
a coat of many colours (Genesis 37.3)	y	y	y	y	n	y
D a coat of divers colours						

Appendix 1: Expressions discussed in this book

	Wycliffe	Tyndale	Geneva	Bishops	Douai-Rheims	King James
lion's whelp (Genesis 49.9) + *(17)	n	y	y	y	y	y
W a whelp of lion						
let my people go (Exodus 5.1)	n	y	y	y	y	y
W deliver thou my people						
fleshpots (Exodus 16.3)	n	y	y	y	y	y
W pots of flesh						
house of bondage (Exodus 20.2)	n	y	y	y	y	y
W house of servage						
graven image (Exodus 20.4)	y	y	y	y	n	y
D graven thing						
take the name of the Lord thy God in vain (Exodus 20.7) *(139)	n	y	y	y	y	y
W take in vain the name of thy Lord God						
firstfruits (Exodus 23.16)	n	y	y	y	y	y
W first things						
stiff-necked (Exodus 32.9)	n	y	y	y	y	y
W hard nol						
a stumbling block (Leviticus 19.14)	n	y	y	y	y	y
W a hurting						
light a candle, and put it under a bushel (Matthew 5.15)	n	y	y	y	y	y
W tendeth not a lantern, and put it under a bushel						

	Wycliffe	Tyndale	Geneva	Bishops	Douai-Rheims	King James
eye for an eye (Matthew 5.38) **W** eye for eye	n	y	y	y	y	y
turn to him the other [cheek] (Matthew 5.39) **W** show to him also the other	n	y	y	y	y	y
left hand know what thy right hand doeth (Matthew 6.3) **W** know not thy left hand what thy right hand doeth	n	y	y	y	y	y
the blind lead the blind (Matthew 15.14) **W** a blind man lead a blind man	n	y	y	y	y	y
the signs of the times (Matthew 16.3) **W** the tokens of times	n	y	y	y	y	y
my name is legion (Mark 5.9) **W** a legion is my name	n	y	y	y	y	y
shake off the dust from / under your feet (Mark 6.11) **W** shake away the powder from your feet [**T G B** dust that is under your feet]	n	y	y	y	y	y
coals of fire on his head (Romans 12.20) + **W** coals on his head [**D** coals of fire upon his head]	n	y	y	y	y	y

Appendix 1: Expressions discussed in this book

	Wycliffe	Tyndale	Geneva	Bishops	Douai-Rheims	King James
eye hath not seen (1 Corinthians 2.9) **W** eye see not	n	y	y	y	y	y
fallen from grace (Galatians 5.4) **W** fallen away from grace	n	y	y	y	y	y
fight the good fight (1 Timothy 6.12) **W** strive thou a good strife	n	y	y	y	y	y
wandering stars (Jude 1.13) **W** erring stars	n	y	y	y	y	y
no man can serve two masters (Matthew 6.24) **W** no man can serve two lords	n	y	y	y	y	y
pearls before swine (Matthew 7.6) **W** margaritis before swine	n	y	y	y	y	y
seek, and ye/you shall find (Matthew 7.7) **W** seek ye, and ye shall find	n	y	y	y	y	y
by their fruits ye/you shall know *them* (Matthew 7.20) **W** of their fruits ye shall know them	n	y	y	y	y	y
the lost sheep (Matthew 10.6) **W** the sheep…that have perished	n	y	y	y	y	y

	Wycliffe	Tyndale	Geneva	Bishops	Douai-Rheims	King James
a prophet is not without honour, save in his own country (Matthew 13.57)	n	y	y	y	y	y
W a prophet is not without worship, save in his own country						
crumbs which fall from … table (Matthew 15.27)	n	y	y	y	y	y
W crumbs, that fall down from the board						
where two or three are gathered together (Matthew 18.20)	n	y	y	y	y	y
W where twain or three are gathered [D where there are two gathered together]						
all these things must come to pass (Matthew 24.6)	n	y	y	y	y	y
W it behoveth these things to be done						
thirty pieces of silver (Matthew 26.15)	n	y	y	y	y	y
W thirty pans of silver						
fell on/upon stony ground (Mark 4.5)	n	y	y	y	y	y
W fell down on stony places						
what shall it profit a man (Mark 8.36)	n	y	y	y	y	y
W what profiteth it to a man						
physician, heal thyself (Luke 4.23)	n	y	y	y	y	y
W leech, heal thy self						

Appendix 1: Expressions discussed in this book

	Wycliffe	Tyndale	Geneva	Bishops	Douai-Rheims	King James
the harvest…is great, but the labourers are few (Luke 10.2)	n	y	y	y	y	y
W there is much ripe corn, and few work men						
born again (John 3.3)	y	n	y	y	y	y
T born anew						
signs and wonders (John 4.48)	n	y	y	y	y	y
W tokens and great wonders						
judge not (John 7.24)	n	y	y	y	y	y
W nil ye deem						
greater love (John 15.13)	n	y	y	y	y	y
W more love						
behold the man (John 19.5) +	n	y	y	y	y	y
W Lo! the man						
death, where is thy sting (1 Corinthians 15.55)	n	y	y	y	y	y
W Death, where is thy prick						
bear his own burden (Galatians 6.5) +	n	y	y	y	y	y
W bear his own charge						
God loves a cheerful giver (2 Corinthians 9.7)	n	y	y	y	y	y
W a glad giver						
filthy lucre (1 Timothy 3.8)	n	y	y	y	y	y
W foul winning						

	Wycliffe	Tyndale	Geneva	Bishops	Douai-Rheims	King James
bottomless pit (John the Divine 9.1) W pit of deepness	n	y	y	y	y	y
that old serpent (John the Divine 12.9) W the great old serpent	n	y	y	y	y	y
great whore (John the Divine 17.1) D great harlot	y	y	y	y	n	y

VI King James usage shared by all other translations (Total: 27)

	Wycliffe	Tyndale	Geneva	Bishops	Douai-Rheims	King James
forty days and forty nights (Genesis 7.4)	y	y	y	y	y	y
Babel (Genesis 11.9)	y	y	y	y	y	y
milk and honey (Exodus 3.8)	y	y	y	y	y	y
thou shalt not (varying verses in Exodus 20) *(16,91)	y	y	y	y	y	y
honour thy father and thy mother (Exodus 20.12)	y	y	y	y	y	y
covet (Exodus 20.17)	y	y	y	y	y	y
apple of his eye (Deuteronomy 32.10) + C the apple of an eye	y	y	y	y	y	y
blessed are the… (Matthew 5.3)	y	y	y	y	y	y
salt of the earth (Matthew 5.13)	y	y	y	y	y	y

Appendix 1: Expressions discussed in this book

	Wycliffe	Tyndale	Geneva	Bishops	Douai-Rheims	King James
o ye of little faith (Matthew 6.30) [W you of little faith]	y	y	y	y	y	y
mote... in thine own eye (Matthew 7.3)	y	y	y	y	y	y
he that is not with me is against me (Matthew 12.30)	y	y	y	y	y	y
flesh and blood (Matthew 16.17)	y	y	y	y	y	y
a millstone... about his neck (Matthew 18.6) +	y	y	y	y	y	y
den of thieves (Matthew 21.13)	y	y	y	y	y	y
washed his hands (Matthew 27.24)	y	y	y	y	y	y
two mites (Mark 12.42)	y	y	y	y	y	y
hair of your head (Luke 21.18)	y	y	y	y	y	y
in the beginning was the word (John 1.1)	y	y	y	y	y	y
Jesus wept (John 11.35)	y	y	y	y	y	y
my kingdom is not of this world (John 18.36)	y	y	y	y	y	y
in the twinkling of an eye (1 Corinthians 15.52) *(30) +	y	y	y	y	y	y
itching + ears (2 Timothy 4.3)	y	y	y	y	y	y

	Wycliffe	Tyndale	Geneva	Bishops	Douai-Rheims	King James
a thief in the night (1 Thessalonians 5.2)	y	y	y	y	y	y
the patience of Job (James 5.11)	y	y	y	y	y	y
Alpha and Omega (John the Divine 1.8)	y	y	y	y	y	y
Armageddon (John the Divine 16.16)	y	y	y	y	y	y

VII Modern usage is indirect, not occurring in this exact form in any of the translations (Total: 37)

	Wycliffe	Tyndale	Geneva	Bishops	Douai-Rheims	King James
Adam and Eve (Genesis 2.19, 3.20)	n	n	n	n	n	n
two by two (Genesis 7.9)	n	n	n	n	n	n

W   by twain and by twain
T   by couples
G B D K two and two

	Wycliffe	Tyndale	Geneva	Bishops	Douai-Rheims	King James
burning bush (Exodus 3.2)	n	n	n	n	n	n

W   bush burned
T G B K burned with fire
D   bush was on fire

	Wycliffe	Tyndale	Geneva	Bishops	Douai-Rheims	King James
girded loins (Exodus 12.11)	n	n	n	n	n	n

W D   gird your reins
T G B K loins girded

	Wycliffe	Tyndale	Geneva	Bishops	Douai-Rheims	King James
golden calf (Exodus 32.4)	n	n	n	n	n	n

W   yotun calf
T B   calf of molten metal
G D K molten calf

	Wycliffe	Tyndale	Geneva	Bishops	Douai-Rheims	King James
David and Goliath (1 Samuel 17.4)	n	n/a	n	n	n	n

Appendix 1: Expressions discussed in this book

	Wycliffe	Tyndale	Geneva	Bishops	Douai-Rheims	King James
from the cradle to the grave (Job 10.19)	n	n/a	n	n	n	n

W   from the womb to
the sepulchre
G B D K from the womb to
the grave

	Wycliffe	Tyndale	Geneva	Bishops	Douai-Rheims	King James
old as the hills (Job 15.7)	n	n/a	n	n	n	n

W   art formed before all
little hills
G B D K wast thou made before
the hills?

	Wycliffe	Tyndale	Geneva	Bishops	Douai-Rheims	King James
a rod for one's own back (Proverbs 10.13) +	n	n/a	n	n	n	n

W a yerd in the back of him
G a rod shall be for the back of him
B the rod belongeth to the back
D a rod on the back of him
K a rod is for the back of him

	Wycliffe	Tyndale	Geneva	Bishops	Douai-Rheims	King James
pride goes before a fall (Proverbs 16.18) +	n	n/a	n	n	n	n

W pride goeth before sorrow;
and the spirit shall be enhanced
before falling
G B pride goeth before destruction,
and an high mind before a fall
D pride goeth before destruction,
and the spirit is lifted up before
a fall
K pride goeth before destruction,
and an haughty spirit before a fall

	Wycliffe	Tyndale	Geneva	Bishops	Douai-Rheims	King James
you can't take it with you (Ecclesiastes 5.15)	n	n/a	n	n	n	n

W he shall take away with him no
thing of his travail

			Wycliffe	Tyndale	Geneva	Bishops	Douai-Rheims	King James
D		he shall take nothing away with him of his labour						
K	**B**	he…shall take nothing of his labour						
G		he…shall bear away nothing of his labour						
		fly in the ointment (Ecclesiastes 10.1)	n	n/a	n	n	n	n
W		flies that die, lessen the sweetness of ointment						
G		dead flies cause to stink, and putrefy the ointment						
B		a dead fly doth corrupt sweet ointment						
D		dying flies spoil the sweetness of the ointment						
K		dead flies cause the ointment…to send forth a stinking savour						
		no peace for the wicked (Isaiah 48.22, 57.21)	n	n/a	n	n	n	n
W		(48, 57) peace is not to wicked men						
G	**K**	(48) there is no peace…unto the wicked						
G	**K**	(57) there is no peace…to the wicked						
B		(48) as for the ungodly, they have no peace						
B		(57) the wicked have no peace						
D		(48, 57) there is no peace to the wicked						
		eating one's words (Jeremiah 15.16)	n	n/a	n	n	n	n
W		thy words are found, and I eat them						

Appendix 1: Expressions discussed in this book

		Wycliffe	Tyndale	Geneva	Bishops	Douai-Rheims	King James

G thy words were found by me, and I did eat them
B when I had found thy words I did eat them up
D K thy words were found, and I did eat them

		Wycliffe	Tyndale	Geneva	Bishops	Douai-Rheims	King James
set one's teeth on edge (Jeremiah 31.29)		n	n/a	n	n	n	n

W the teeth of sons were astonied
G his teeth shall be set on edge
B K the childrens teeth are set on edge
D the teeth of the children are set on edge

		Wycliffe	Tyndale	Geneva	Bishops	Douai-Rheims	King James
wheels within wheels (Ezekiel 10.10)		n	n/a	n	n	n	n

W D K as if a wheel had been/were/be in the midst of a wheel
G as if one wheel had been in another wheel
B as if one wheel had been in another

		Wycliffe	Tyndale	Geneva	Bishops	Douai-Rheims	King James
fuel to the fire (Ezekiel 21.32) +		n	n/a	n	n	n	n

W meat to fire
G in the fire to be devoured
B feed the fire
D fuel for the fire

		Wycliffe	Tyndale	Geneva	Bishops	Douai-Rheims	King James
feet of clay (Daniel 2.33)		n	n/a	n	n	n	n

W some was of earth
G feet were part of iron, and part of clay
B feet that were of iron and clay
D feet that were of iron and of clay
K feet part of iron and part of clay

	Wycliffe	Tyndale	Geneva	Bishops	Douai-Rheims	King James
the writing is on the wall (Daniel 5.5)	n	n/a	n	n	n	n

W	writing…in the plain part of the wall
G K	wrote…upon the plaster of the wall
B	writing…upon the plaster of the wall
D	writing…upon the surface of the wall

	Wycliffe	Tyndale	Geneva	Bishops	Douai-Rheims	King James
root and branch (Malachi 4.1)	n	n/a	n	n	n	n

W	root and buriownyng
G B D K	root nor branch

	Wycliffe	Tyndale	Geneva	Bishops	Douai-Rheims	King James
baptism of fire (Matthew 3.11)	n	n	n	n	n	n

W D	he shall baptize you in…fire
T B K	he shall baptize you…with fire
G	he will baptize you…with fire

	Wycliffe	Tyndale	Geneva	Bishops	Douai-Rheims	King James
jot or tittle (Matthew 5.18)	n	n	n	n	n	n

T G B D K	one jot or one tittle
W	one letter or one tittle

	Wycliffe	Tyndale	Geneva	Bishops	Douai-Rheims	King James
go the second mile (Matthew 5.41)	n	n	n	n	n	n

W	thousand paces, go with him other twain
T G B K	mile, go with him twain
D	mile, go with him other two

	Wycliffe	Tyndale	Geneva	Bishops	Douai-Rheims	King James
tomorrow will take care of itself (Matthew 6.34)	n	n	n	n	n	n

W	the morrow shall be busy to himself

Appendix 1: Expressions discussed in this book

	Wycliffe	Tyndale	Geneva	Bishops	Douai-Rheims	King James
T let the morrow care for itself						
G B the morrow shall care for itself						
D the morrow will be solicitous for itself						
K the morrow shall take thought for the things of itself						
weeping and wailing and gnashing of teeth (Matthew 8.12, 13.42, 13.50, 22.13)	n	n	n	n	n	n
W (8.12, 13.50, 22.13) weeping and grinding						
W (22.13) weeping and biting together of teeth						
T B G D K (8.12, 13.42, 22.13) weeping and gnashing (also D 13.42, 50)						
T G B K (13.42, 50) wailing and gnashing						
from the housetops (Matthew 10.27)	n	n	n	n	n	n
W on houses						
T on the house tops						
G B on the houses						
D K upon the housetops						
faith can move mountains (Matthew 21.21)	n	n	n	n	n	n
W say to this hill, take						
T G say unto this mountain, take thyself away						
B K say unto this mountain, be thou removed						
D say to this mountain, take up						

	Wycliffe	Tyndale	Geneva	Bishops	Douai-Rheims	King James
live by the sword, die by the sword (Matthew 26.52)	n	n	n	n	n	n

W	take sword shall perish by sword
T	lay hand on the sword shall perish with the sword
G B D K	take the sword shall perish with the sword

	Wycliffe	Tyndale	Geneva	Bishops	Douai-Rheims	King James
a voice crying in the wilderness (e.g. Luke 3.4)	n	n	n	n	n	n

W	the voice of a crier in desert
T B	the voice of a crier in wilderness
G	the voice of him that crieth in the wilderness
D	a voice of one crying in the wilderness
K	the voice of one crying in the wilderness

	Wycliffe	Tyndale	Geneva	Bishops	Douai-Rheims	King James
do unto others (Luke 6.31)	n	n	n	n	n	n
good Samaritan (Luke 10.33)	n	n	n	n	n	n
cross to bear (Luke 14.27)	n	n	n	n	n	n

W G	beareth not his cross
T	bear not his cross
B K	bear his cross
D	carry his cross

	Wycliffe	Tyndale	Geneva	Bishops	Douai-Rheims	King James
can anything good come out of Nazareth? (John 1.46)	n	n	n	n	n	n

W	of Nazareth may some good thing be?

	Wycliffe	Tyndale	Geneva	Bishops	Douai-Rheims	King James
T G B K can there any good thing come out of Nazareth? **D** can any thing of good come from Nazareth?						
speak in tongues (Acts 2.4)	n	n	n	n	n	n
W speak divers languages **T G B K** speak with other tongues **D** speak with divers tongues						
as you sow, so shall you reap (Galatians 6.7)	n	n	n	n	n	n
W those things that a man soweth, those things he shall reap **T** whatsoever a man soweth, that shall he reap **G B K** whatsoever a man soweth, that shall he also reap **D** what things a man shall sow, those also shall he reap						
old wives' tales (1 Timothy 4.7)	n	n	n	n	n	n
T G B D K old wives' fables **W** old womens fables						
the patience of a saint (John the Divine 14.12)	n	n	n	n	n	n
W T G the patience of saints **B D K** the patience of the saints						

VIII Not in King James but in one of the other translations (Total: 7)

	Wycliffe	Tyndale	Geneva	Bishops	Douai-Rheims	King James
the way of all flesh (1 Kings 2.2)	n	n/a	n	n	y	n
W the way of all earth **G B K** the way of all the earth						

	Wycliffe	Tyndale	Geneva	Bishops	Douai-Rheims	King James
spare the rod (Proverbs 13.24) +	n	n/a	n	y	y	n

W spareth the yerde
K G spareth his rod

let [one's] light shine (Matthew 5.16)	n	n	n	n	y	n

W so shine your light
T G B K let your light so shine

divide/separate the sheep from the goats (Matthew 25.32)	n	y	y	y	y	n

W departeth sheep from kids
K divideth his sheep from
the goats

cast the first stone (John 8.7)	n	y	y	y	n	n

W D K first cast a stone

scales fell from his eyes (Acts 9.18)	y	n	n	n	n	n

T G there fell from his eyes as
it had been scales
B K there fell from his eyes as
if it had been scales
D there fell from his eyes as
it were scales

charity covers a multitude of sins (1 Peter 4.8) [D covereth]	n	n	n	n	y	n

W charity covereth the multitude
of sins
T love covereth the multitude
of sins
G B love shall cover the multitude
of sins
K charity shall cover the
multitude of sins

299

Appendix 1: Expressions discussed in this book

	Wycliffe	Tyndale	Geneva	Bishops	Douai-Rheims	King James
IX Expressions in KJB which are in none of the other translations but which do occur in Coverdale's Psalter (Total: 3)						
fire and brimstone (Genesis 19.24) *(11)	n	n	n	n	n	y
W T G B D brimstone and fire						
deep waters (Psalms 69.2)*	n	n/a	n	n	n	y
W slime of the depth						
G B deep mire						
D mire of the deep						
at their wit's end (Psalms 107.27)* +	n	n/a	n	n	n	y
W all the wisdom of them was devoured						
G all their cunning is gone						
B their wisdom faileth them						
D all their wisdom was swallowed up						
X Expressions in KJB that are in none of the other translations but which do have a history in Old/Middle English (Total: 2)						
let us play the men etc (2 Samuel 10.12) +	n	n/a	n	n	n	y
W fight we						
G B let us be valiant						
D let us fight						
give up the ghost (Job 3.11) +	n	n/a	n	n	n	y
W B D perish						
G die						

Appendix 2
Number of references made to Old and New Testament sources

New Testament	Number of references
Matthew	60
Luke	16
John	15
Acts	9
Mark	8
1 Corinthians	6
John the Divine	6
Romans	5
1 Timothy	4
2 Corinthians	3
Galatians	3
Philippians	2
Ephesians	1
Hebrews	1
James	1
1 Peter	1
1 Thessalonians	1
2 Timothy	1
Titus	1
TOTAL NT	144

Old Testament	Number of references
Exodus	21
Genesis	18
Ecclesiastes	12
Isaiah	7
Psalms	7
Job	6
1 Kings	5

Appendix 2: Old and New Testament sources

Leviticus	4
Jeremiah	4
Proverbs	4
1 Samuel	4
2 Samuel	4
Daniel	3
Deuteronomy	3
Ezekiel	2
Judges	2
2 Kings	2
Numbers	3
Hosea	1
Joshua	1
Jude	1
Malachi	1
TOTAL OT	116

Apocrypha	Number of references
Sirach	1
TOTAL OT + NT	260[1]

[1] The total is 260 because there are three instances where more than one source for an idiom is listed in Appendix 1.

Index of expressions

The alphabetical arrangement of this index is word-by-word. Initial grammatical words, such as indefinite and definite articles, have been ignored, unless they are essential to the identity of the phrase.

Index of expressions

Index of expressions

Index of expressions

Index of Bible translations

Index of Books of the Bible

Index of Books of the Bible

General index

The alphabetical arrangement of this index is letter-by-letter.

General index

General index

General index

General index

General index

General index